BLOOD OATH

The heroic story of a gangster

turned government agent

who brought down

one of America's

most powerful mob families

GEORGE FRESOLONE
AND ROBERT J. WAGMAN

Simon & Schuster

NEW YORK LONDON TORONTO SYDNEY TOKYO SINGAPORE

SIMON & SCHUSTER
Rockefeller Center
1230 Avenue of the Americas
New York, New York 10020

Designed by Paulette Orlando

Manufactured in the United States of America

1   3   5   7   9   10   8   6   4   2

Library of Congress Cataloging-in-Publication Data
Fresolone, George, date
Blood oath : the heroic story of a gangster turned government agent
who brought down one of America's most powerful mob families /
George Fresolone and Robert J. Wagman.
p.   cm.
1. Mafia—New Jersey—Case studies.   2. Organized crime—
New Jersey—Case studies.   3. Organized crime investigation—
New Jersey—Case studies.   I. Wagman, Robert J.   II. Title.
HV6452.N22M344   1994
364.1'06'09749—dc20   94-20356
CIP
ISBN: 0-671-77905-2

All photographs courtesy of the New Jersey State Police

TO ANN,

TO THE KIDS,

AND OF COURSE

TO PATTY

AS PATTY OFTEN SAID:

If you have friends and know them well,

Then your secrets you do not tell;

For if your friends become your foes,

Then your secrets the world will know.

CONTENTS

THE CAST OF CHARACTERS

THE BRUNO-SCARFO FAMILY

"Patty Specs" Martirano (left) and "Tony Buck" Piccolo ("Cousin Anthony") discussing the future of the family outside of Gino's restaurant in Manhattan.

Attanasio, Anthony ("Slicker" or "Duke")

Loanshark and bookmaker who was around Patty Martirano and became a made member of the family in June 1986.

Bruno, Angelo

The boss of the Philadelphia organized crime family that took his name. Called "the Docile Don" because his management style tried to avoid confrontation. Murdered March 21, 1980.

Caponigro, Anthony ("Tony Bananas")

Angelo Bruno's consigliere and the most powerful member of the family in northern New Jersey in the 1960s and 1970s. Murdered in the Bronx, N.Y., on April 18, 1980, in retaliation for the killing of Angelo Bruno without Commission approval.

c. 1940s

Caramandi, Nick ("Nicky the Crow")

> Philadelphia member of the family who flipped and became a federal witness. His testimony put Nicky Scarfo Sr. in jail for the first time.

Centorino, Vincent ("Beepsie")

> A big-time loanshark and a millionaire from fencing stolen gold and jewels. Became a made member July 29, 1990.

Cifelli, Nicholas ("Turk" or "the Bird")

> Bookmaker, gambler, and long-time associate of the family going back to the days of Tony Bananas. Despite his long association with the family, he was not straightened out until the July 1990 ceremony.

Idone, Santo

> Old-line member of the family who was around Angelo Bruno.

Leonetti, Philip ("Crazy Phil")

> Nicky Scarfo's nephew and his long-time second-in-command and closest confidant. A killer who carried out almost a dozen hits for Nicky, he bought his way out of a long prison term by becoming a federal witness.

Licata, Joseph ("Scoops")

> Bookmaker and loanshark who was an associate of Patty Martirano's and close to George Fresolone from the earliest days. He became a made member in June 1986, and when Patty fled to Italy in 1988 was made acting captain in charge of the family in northern Jersey.

Martirano, Pasquale ("Patty Specs")

George Fresolone's closest friend and mentor in organized crime. As a young man he was close to Tony Bananas and in 1984 was made captain and head of the Bruno-Scarfo family in northern New Jersey. In May 1990, he was elevated to underboss. He died from cancer on August 9, 1990.

Merlino, Joseph ("Skinny Joey")

Chuckie Merlino's son, believed to have been behind the failed hit on Nicky Scarfo Jr. in an attempted payback for his father's murder on Nicky Scarfo Sr.'s orders. More recently became the leader of the "young turk" faction of the family and the rival to new boss John Stanfa. A central figure in the Philadelphia mob war that broke out in 1993.

Merlino, Salvatore ("Chuckie")

Long-time member of Nicky Scarfo's Atlantic City "crew," later killed by Nicky's order when he saw Merlino as a possible rival.

Napoli, Ralph ("Blackie")

Captain of the northern crew until Nicky Scarfo Sr. demoted him and elevated "Patty Specs" in October 1984.

Oliveri, Nicholas ("Nicky O")

A gambler who had been around Patty since he was a young man. Became a made member on July 29, 1990.

Piccolo, Anthony ("Tony Buck" or "Cousin Anthony")

Old-time member of the family from Philadelphia who acted as Nicky Scarfo Sr.'s consigliere until Nicky went to federal prison in June 1987. He then became acting family boss until 1991, when John Stanfa was made permanent boss and he resumed his role as consigliere.

Praino, John ("Johnny Phones")

New York City bookmaker who was a close friend of Patty's and in whose house Patty lived when he returned to New York for cancer treatment. Became a made member July 29, 1990.

Ricciardi, Mickey ("The Walker")

Long-time member of Blackie Napoli's crew.

Scarfo, Nicodemo ("Little Nicky")

Violent head of the family's operations in Atlantic City, where he had been banished by Angelo Bruno. Became head of the family in April 1981, after the death of Phil Testa. Currently serving a life sentence in the Marion, Illinois, federal prison.

Scarfo, Nicky Jr. ("The Kid")

Son of Nicky Sr., who at the time of his arrest in 1990 was not yet a made member of the family but who acted as a conduit to transfer messages and orders from his father in prison to the family in Philadelphia and New Jersey.

Sodano, Joseph ("The Nodder")

Powerful made member of the family who was a big-time bookmaker operating in New York City, with close ties to high-level members of other crime families. Became a made member in January 1981.

Sparacio, Salvatore ("Shotzie")

Old-time member of Angelo Bruno's crew, who lived in southern New Jersey, near Philadelphia.

Stanfa, John

A Sicilian who, by happenstance, was Angelo Bruno's driver the night he was killed in 1980. After keeping a low profile for most of the 1980s, was made permanent head of the family in 1991. Started a major shooting war in Philadelphia in 1992–93, and is now under multiple federal indictments including several for ordering mob hits.

Testa, Phil

Old-guard member of the Bruno family and Angelo Bruno's underboss, who became boss after Bruno was killed. He himself was killed a year later.

Testa, Salvatore

Phil Testa's son, who was seen as a rival by Nicky Scarfo after Scarfo was made boss. Scarfo ordered him killed.

ASSOCIATES OF THE BRUNO-SCARFO FAMILY

Cifelli, Alan

A Bruno-Scarfo associate who became an employee of Grayhound Electronics and was in charge of collecting money.

Dente, Anthony

Big-time bookmaker and major drug trafficker.

Fasano, Daniel

A partner in Giordano Waste Haulers.

Giordano, Patrick ("Patty the Coo")

Principal partner in Giordano Waste Haulers, who was also around Patty in other family activities.

Hingos, Don

Former police officer and gambler who became a bookmaker and George Fresolone's partner in a bookmaking operation.

Manno, Donald

> Camden lawyer for Cousin Anthony Piccolo, who used Manno's offices to conduct family business.

Mavilla, John

> A member of the Newark Zoning Board who pleaded guilty to "Official Misconduct" for accepting an "illegal gratuity" to obtain a zoning variance for Giordano Waste Haulers.

McFillin, Phil

> Long-time family associate in Philadelphia who could not become a made member because he was Irish. Close to both Nicky Scarfo and Cousin Anthony Piccolo.

Notti, Greg

> High school gym teacher and gambler who was around Patty. A blackjack expert.

Parisi, John

> Nicky Scarfo's nephew, who, while not a direct member of the family, helped both Nicky and Nicky Jr.

Petaccio, Brian

> Carmen Ricci's son-in-law and a principal in Grayhound Electronics.

Pillari, Dominic

> A general contractor who ran the Just Development Company and was close to several members of the family.

Ricci, Carmen

> Principal stockholder in Grayhound Electronics, CEO of the company, and effectively the partner of Nicky Sr. in the video game business.

Salimbene, Michael
> Construction firm owner who had been around Patty and was the subject of a shakedown by John Riggi.

Simone, Robert
> Top Philadelphia criminal lawyer who represented Nicky Sr. Convicted in 1993 on federal conspiracy charges.

Steo, Dennis
> Former family associate who is serving a life term in Rahway state prison in New Jersey, where he is a trustee who runs the Society for the Handicapped.

Stewart, Frederick
> A close associate of Anthony Dente's and active with him in the drug business and bookmaking.

Wilson, Eugene ("Little Gene")
> Dente's chief lieutenant in both the bookmaking and drug trafficking businesses. Also a major fence of stolen property.

The Gambino-Gotti Family

Bisaccia, Robert ("Bobby Cabert")

> Made member of the Gambino family elevated to captain in May 1990. Partner in monte games.

Casiere, Joseph ("Joe Rackets")
> Bobby Cabert's driver and another partner in the monte games.

DeVino, Anthony ("Babe")

Gambino family associate and gambler who was also involved in the monte games as a partner.

Luciano, Charles ("Blackie")

Made member of the Gambino family who was a partner with Bruno-Scarfo members in the original Bronx-Manhattan monte game.

THE DECAVALCANTE FAMILY

D'Amico, Jack

New boss of the DeCavalcante family and a close friend of John Gotti's. He became boss when John Riggi went to jail.

DeCavalcante, Simone ("Sam the Plumber")

Founder of the family, and a plumber by trade.

Riggi, John ("The Eagle")

Longtime boss of the DeCavalcante family and head business agent of Local 394, International Brotherhood of Laborers and Hod Carriers.

THE LUCCHESE FAMILY

Franks, Steve

Family associate who ran the day-to-day bookmaking operations.

Perna, Michael

Boss of the family's operations in New Jersey.

Perna, Ralph
>
> Associate who was Michael's brother and the comptroller of the bookmaking operations.

Ricciardi, Tommy
>
> Made family member who was a big-time loanshark and gambler, active in the video gambling machine business. Now a protected federal witness.

Spagnola, Robert ("Bobby Spags")
>
> Associate who operated as the "bank" in the bookmaking and gambling operations.

THE COLOMBO FAMILY

Prosperi, Dominick ("Don Doode")
>
> Colombo family associate who ran the baccarat game in 1989.

Randazzo, James ("Jimmy Ran")
>
> Made member who represented the Colombo family's interests in the monte and baccarat games in 1989–90.

THE GENOVESE FAMILY

Catrambone, Ronald ("Fat Ronnie")
>
> Associate who as a bookmaker and a partner in the monte games ran the game and was the bank.

DeNoia, Philip ("Philly")
>
> Associate who was a bookmaker and a partner in the monte games.

Manna, Bobby
>
> Genovese family consigliere and a power on the Commission.

Quelli, James, Jr.

> High school principal and gambler who was around the Genovese family. Killed when he held out on bribes.

Zarra, Joseph ("Joe Z")

> A made member who became partner in what was to become the biggest monte game ever.

NEW JERSEY STATE POLICE/ATTORNEY GENERAL'S OFFICE

Billy Newsome (left) and Ed Quirk of Operation Broadsword in Las Vegas.
Their mission: the destruction of the Bruno-Scarfo family

Bozza, Michael

> Deputy Director of Criminal Justice for the State of New Jersey.

Brody, David

> Supervising Deputy State Attorney General, second-in-command of the Organized Crime Bureau and the Attorney General's representative to Operation Broadsword.

Buckley, Charles

> Assistant Attorney General in charge of the prosecution of the main cases growing out of Operation Broadsword.

Crescenz, Charley, Sergeant
> Number-three man in Operation Broadsword in charge of logistics from August 1989 to June 1990.

Del Tufo, Robert
> New Jersey State Attorney General.

Dintino, Justin, Colonel
> Superintendent of the New Jersey State Police

Drummond, Alan, Sergeant
> State police Organized Crime Bureau officer in charge of tape transcriptions.

Gaugler, Bobby, Captain
> Commander of New Jersey State Police Organized Crime Bureau.

Lardiere, Barry, Lieutenant
> Organized Crime Bureau officer in charge of Operation Broadsword.

Newsome, Billy, Sergeant
> Detective in the state police's Organized Crime Bureau who was the day-to-day number two man in Operation Broadsword.

Quirk, Edward, Sergeant
> Detective in the state police Intelligence Bureau who recruited George Fresolone, became his case officer, and who was the day-to-day operational head of Operation Broadsword.

Tezza, Lindy, Major
> Head of the Criminal Investigation Section of the New Jersey State Police, who negotiated the agreement with George Fresolone.

PROLOGUE

STRAIGHTENED OUT

It was July 29, 1990, and it was hot that afternoon in John Praino's living room in the Bronx. There were five of us sitting on chairs in a semicircle waiting to be straightened out—to be formally accepted as a "made" member of our organized crime family. My name is, or more technically was, George Fresolone. I was in the center chair and would be the first to go. Actually, the primary purpose of the ceremony about to take place was to straighten me out. Even though at thirty-seven I was the youngest guy in the room, this was, for me, long overdue. The other four guys had been added later as an afterthought.

Next to me was "Johnny Phones," as we called him—John Praino —whose bayside home we were in. John, forty-seven, was a high-stakes New York–based bookmaker who years earlier had come to our family for protection from the five New York Mafia families. If you called central casting and asked them to send you a Vegas bookmaker type, chances are they would have sent John. With his $75 haircut, expensive sports clothes, patent-leather shoes, gold chains, diamond watch, and ever-present five-dollar cigar, he looked every inch the part. His home reflected his taste. It was small, because there was just John and his wife, but the furnishings were expensive. The house was on Long Island Sound, and in back, tied to a dock, was his pride and joy, a new cabin cruiser, *Lucky Guy,* that he took out whenever the weather allowed. For John, being straightened out was not going to be any big deal. All he wanted from life was to be left alone to book his bets. But we had talked him into accepting the honor.

Next to John was Nicholas "Turk" Cifelli, thin but powerfully built and muscular, a man at the peak of health who certainly did not look his sixty-eight years. Turk had been a loyal associate of our family for almost forty years. For reasons I didn't understand, he had never been straightened out, although he had been around for so long that everybody outside the family just assumed he was a made member long ago. On my other side was Vincent "Beeps" Centorino, who was in his late fifties—an absolute bear of a man who was about six feet two and weighed at least 300 pounds, the product of good living and never missing a meal. Beepsie was one of the wealthiest wiseguys I have ever known. A multimillionaire, he had made his money years ago as a master fence of stolen gold and jewels, and he had invested it wisely. Now he was a loanshark with hundreds of thousands on the street. Finally, seated next to him was "Nicky O," Nicholas Oliveri, forty-two, one of my closest friends in the mob. Even taller than Beeps, Nicky O was almost as heavy, probably 260 or so. But while Beeps's weight was from good living, Nicky O was solid and in great shape. He was good-looking and smooth, and, like me, was a bookmaker and a loanshark.

Running the ceremony was our acting don, Anthony Piccolo. In his early seventies, "Tony Buck," as he was known on the street, looked like a retired banker. Thin and gray, he was always impeccably dressed, usually in a conservative business suit, as he was this day. He was known to us in the family as "Cousin Anthony" because he was Nicodemo Scarfo's cousin. Nicky—actually Nicky Sr., because his son, Nicky Jr., was also active in the family—was the boss of the organization, the Bruno-Scarfo organized crime family. But Cousin Anthony was the acting boss while Nicky enjoyed an extended—and perhaps permanent—all-expenses-paid holiday at the Marion Federal Penitentiary in southern Illinois.

Seated next to Cousin Anthony was my closest friend on earth, Pasquale "Patty Specs" Martirano, our underboss, the number two man in our family. Actually, we were all there that hot Sunday afternoon because of Patty. He no longer looked like the Patty I had known all my life. He had always been robust and full of energy; now, he was thin and stooped, and his skin was almost yellow because he was in the final stages of liver cancer. Everyone in the room, especially Patty, knew he would be dead soon. He had told Cousin Anthony that he wanted to see me straightened out before he died. Actually, I should have been straightened out years before, but first the family had put a kind of moratorium on making new guys, and then when they started making guys again, I had been in jail. Then by the time I got out, Nicky had been busted and was about to go on trial. Then he went to jail, and the family had not held any more ceremonies. But Patty had asked Cousin Anthony to complete my ceremony while he was still here to participate. And when Anthony had said yes, he decided to include the other four. We were here at John's house because that's where Patty had been hiding, and he had grown much too weak to travel anywhere else.

It was because of Patty that I had become a member of the mob. He eventually became my boss and my closest friend, and he was both the best man at my wedding and the godfather of my first child. Far and away, Patty was the most honorable man I ever met in the mob. To many of us close to him he was known as "Doc" or "the Doctor" because he was always waxing philosophical. He often spoke of the old days in the mob when honor and respect meant more than the dollar, and he believed deeply in loyalty. If he was loyal to you, he expected loyalty in return. If he was your friend, he expected friendship in return. I guess that is why he was disappointed so often.

Over the years many things have changed in the Mafia. One thing that hasn't changed is the way each family is set up and how new members gain admittance. Each family is headed by a boss, the "don," and usually one but sometimes more underbosses, a "consigliere" who acts as an advisor, and some captains or "capos" who have under them groups of "soldiers" called crews. All of these soldiers, these wiseguys, have been formally initiated (also called "made" or "straightened out") into the family. Then below them is a larger number of "connected" guys, each involved in the crews' criminal activities but not yet experienced enough or trusted enough to be granted full membership. It is the dream of every connected guy to someday be straightened out. Truthfully, it had been mine. But now that it was coming, it had a very hollow feeling.

Just as the organization of Mafia families remained little changed from the 1920s when they had first fled Sicily and Mussolini's forces to bring their form of organized crime to the United States, the initiation ceremony changed little over the years. You have to be a white male of pure Italian ancestry. You have to be sponsored by another made member (in my case, I was being sponsored by Patty), who not only vouches for you but who becomes responsible for you and what you do in the future. If you screw up, he screws up. If you do something serious enough, it could cost your sponsor his life. Therefore, the responsibility of sponsoring a new member was not taken lightly. No one was straightened out until he had been watched and tested for a long time. In the old days this meant you had to "make your bones"—to kill someone on orders of the family. This showed your loyalty and your commitment. But these days, you could make your bones by earning enough money and by your willingness to share your bounty with those above you. Killing may have been a desired trait in the old days; today, the only important thing was money. If you have shown you can earn enough, the family doesn't care if you have ever seen a gun.

Usually in initiations where more than one guy is being made, each is done separately. But on this Sunday we had two problems. Patty was so weak that we had to hold the ceremony at John's house because he could not be moved. Then we had to complete it while John's wife, Norma, was out shopping. So to get it done in the hour or so that we had, we shortened it a bit and did as much as we could as a group. As is traditional, the boss started the ceremony with a kind of a pep talk.

"You know why you're here," Tony Buck began. "If you have any reservations, any concerns, or if you don't want to be here, just say it and no hard feelings, we'll understand. But if you stay here, you become part of us, then you have to do the right thing. Here it's no bullshit, plain English. This is a family, you stay with the family. This is the man right here. He's your family, I'm your family. We help each other. It's got to be with the family. No outsiders. Anybody approaches you—it's another place, it's another family—you report to your man, whoever's in charge. Don't let nobody try to bullshit you. . . . This is our family, and that's the way it stays."

Patty echoed this by saying, "The family's supposed to be first. It's as simple as that. Before everybody else, *everybody,* even your own family. It's not nice to say, but your own mother, father, sister, brother."

"If you can't make it, God forbid you get sick, got troubles, stuff like that," Tony Buck said next, "we all throw ourselves in that mess, we help each other out. That's the way it's got to be, it's got to stay within our family."

Patty, who had been brought up in the old ways, then reminded us of the old tradition. He had placed a knife and a gun in a paper bag, which he had on a table next to him. He held the bag up and said, "You're supposed to live by the gun and die by the gun, live by the knife and die by the knife."

"This is a thing of honor," Tony Buck continued. "This is not a thing of business. A lot of people misunderstand that. This is honor. You've got to be an honorable person."

Nothing could have been further from the truth, of course. It might have been different in the old days, but I had found very little honor in organized crime. It was every man for himself, every man trying to earn top dollar, doing whatever he had to do and not caring who he hurt.

I went first. "Give me your trigger finger, George," Patty said.

I extended my right hand, and Patty took my index finger and cut the tip until it bled. Then he wiped the finger with a piece of toilet tissue. In the old-fashioned ceremonies they used a torn-up picture of a saint to wipe up the blood, but today we were making do. Then Patty placed the bloody tissue into my cupped hands and lit it with a match. As the paper burned in my hands, I repeated after Anthony, "May I burn in hell if I betray my friends in the family."

It was a solemn oath, and I considered it seriously. But by this time it was clear to me that after growing up in the mob and spending my entire life as a soldier in the Bruno-Scarfo family, the only real friend I had in the family was Patty. I knew that I had never and would never rat on him. The others—who cared? I would give them the same kind of loyalty they had given Patty and me. In fact, it was because of the way these guys had treated Patty and me and our families, at times when we really needed their help and they were too greedy and selfish to give it, that I had vowed that someday I would bring them down. I had been doing just that every day over the past year. Then I would be out of there, far away from this so-called family and my life in the mob. And I would leave behind enough evidence against these guys—and a lot of other people with dirty hands—to put them all away for a very long time.

When I look back on that Sunday, one of the things that sticks in my mind was how hot it was in that house. John had money, big money, but he was too cheap to buy whole-house air-conditioning. All the house had was dinky window units, and I was sweating in part because the lone window unit in the living room couldn't compensate for the crowd and for the July heat. But a lot of the sweat was being caused by the weight of the two recording devices I had hidden on my body, including a very uncomfortable one secreted in my crotch. And in addition to their weight, I was afraid that the radio transmitter on my belt or the recorder in my crotch wouldn't work right, and all this risk would be for nothing. I was burdened with the sure knowledge that if I slipped up and was found out, if somehow the tape recorder in the special pouch fell out, I likely would never be allowed to leave the house alive.

Detective Sergeant Edward Quirk, the New Jersey State Police Intelligence Division investigator I had been working with for the last two years, hadn't been sure we could get away with being the first ever to record an initiation ceremony. He thought the risks were too great. But on more than three hundred occasions over the past thirteen months I had worn a transmission device into meetings with members of my own organized crime family, members of other families, crooked public officials, corrupt union officers, and dirty businessmen. I had gone from model mobster to government agent, and now I was the first undercover agent, state or federal, to attempt bugging a Mafia initiation ceremony. More to the point, I was recording my own straightening out, as I was becoming a fully made member of the Bruno-Scarfo family. On countless occasions over the past year I had lived with the fear that if I was discovered, the penalty would be a very quick death. I had told myself and Ed that this time would be no different. I was ready and I wanted to do it; in fact, I had insisted that we do it. In the end the prospect of being the first law enforcement officer to ever set out and succeed in recording a Mafia initiation won Ed over.

Even though I had told myself this day was really no different from the previous 365 days or more, I knew that was not true. There was something else I had to worry about that afternoon: Ed and I had reason to believe that my dual role might have been leaked, that somehow the family had found out I was working as a police agent.

For over three years the state police had known they had a mole in their midst. Three years ago, when I was still a loyal wiseguy, the state cops had bugged a car we drove a great deal. Within a matter of days after the bug was planted, word came back to us through a guy in another family who had a source high up in the cops, he said, that someplace we were hanging around was being bugged. At first we thought it was a club or bar, but by a process of elimination we figured out it had to be the car. We swept the car and found the bug. The mole had been correct.

More recently the mole had been right again. The mole wasn't ours but was someone connected to the Lucchese family. And earlier that week a Lucchese guy came up to me to say they had learned that "someone close to Patty Specs" had turned rat and was now working for the state. I acted completely shocked and thanked the guy profusely. I told no one in our crew, obviously, because I was the guy. But I told Ed immediately, and we went into overdrive trying to locate the source of these leaks. We thought we had to shut him —or her—down before the mole learned my name, the result of which would undoubtedly be my quick demise.

What happened next was a kind of a good-news, bad-news scenario. About two days before the ceremony Ed told me they were pretty sure they had identified the leak; it was some guy working not for the state police but for the Attorney General's Office. The further good news was that they had shut the guy down, and he would leak no more. The bad news was that it appeared this guy had been able to learn my identity, but the state police investigators were reasonably sure they had gotten to him before he was able to pass the information along.

I must admit "reasonably sure" still left me awful nervous, and it clearly left Ed visibly worried, too. This initiation ceremony had been put together very quickly because of Patty's failing condition. But Ed was suspicious that it might actually be a sham, that it was being used to unmask me. That's why the area around John's house looked like a police convention. Down the street was a nice, almost-new white Mercedes Benz. In it was Ed and a female officer, acting like a romantic couple looking at the Sound and enjoying the sun and a few beers. Ed's partner, Billy Newsome, was in an Eldorado a few hundred feet in the other direction. There were several vans within a few hundred yards; these contained the recording and sur-veillance equipment. Because we were in New York, and the New Jersey cops were out of their jurisdiction, there were numerous New York State Police guys around. There was a NYPD boat a few hun-dred yards offshore, ready to rocket to the dock at John's back door. And although I didn't know this until later, there was a fully armed SWAT team ready to take the house down within a matter of seconds if it appeared from my radio transmission that there was trouble.

Sitting in John Praino's house that Sunday, scared to death I might not get out alive, I guess I had reason to sweat. But so far, so good. I took the oath, and then Patty said, "Now go around and kiss everybody." I did, and my part of the ceremony was over. "Good luck," some of them said. "Congratulations" or "Welcome," said some of the others. Everyone smiled. I tried but couldn't. My lifelong dream had been accomplished. I was finally a made member of the Bruno-Scarfo family. I should have been elated, but under the cir-cumstances all I could feel was empty.

1

DOWN NECK

I was born, as they say, "Down Neck"—that is, in the Down Neck section of Newark, New Jersey— in 1953. In those days Newark was a city that still worked, a patch-work of many good neighborhoods; and Down Neck was one of them. The area was "iron-bound," cut off on all sides from the rest of New-ark by railroad tracks. It was a traffic bottleneck, and thus the name Down Neck. It was a very traditional, churchgoing, blue-collar working-class neighborhood made up mostly of second- and third-generation Italian and Portuguese families. The crime rate was low, and family values were important. It was a great place to raise kids, or if you were a kid, a great neighborhood to grow up in.

Like working-class neighborhoods everywhere in the 1950s and 1960s, Down Neck was crowded with taverns, and the number one recreational activity after drinking was gambling. That's where my father came in. He had been a gambler all his life, and by the time I was born, he had become a successful bookie and was also running a thriving numbers operation. A player picked a three-digit number he thought would hit; if it did, he got back five hundred to one. You could play anywhere from a quarter to a hundred dollars, and the winning combination was based on some widely published number that changed every day, like the last three digits in the number of stocks sold on the New York Stock Exchange or the last three digits of the daily handle at a local racetrack. If you won, you could win big. But the real winners were the guys who ran the operation.

Back in the old neighborhood, making book and running a numbers operation was considered a very reputable business, and my father was looked up to in the community. Like most kids I grew up wanting to be like my dad, and when I got to be old enough, eight or nine, I was proud that I could finally help him. Kids in my neighborhood delivered the papers, and a couple of my friends had paper routes. I had a route, too, but it was a route with a difference. I would come home from school and get into my collection pants—the ones that Mom had sewn a big zippered pocket into the inside front. Then I would jump on my bike and go around the neighborhood collecting the day's "packages" from Dad's numbers writers. Each package contained the numbers that had been written so far that day as well as receipts from the previous day—after the numbers writer had paid off his winners and kept his cut of the action. I would put the packages into the hidden zippered pocket and bring them home to Dad. Doing this every day, I got to meet practically everybody in the neighborhood; and it also paid me a better allowance than any of the kids I knew with paper routes.

My dad was not a member of the mob, but he was connected. You didn't run a book or a numbers operation in those days—or today, for that matter—without "being with someone," that is, without the permission, protection, and paying off of some family guy. So while my dad himself was not really a wiseguy, he was around many who were; and every week he reached deep into his pocket to make the payoffs necessary to stay in business. These guys liked my father, and they liked me. And they were looked up to in the neighborhood, especially by the kids, because they had big cars, good clothes, pretty women, and a lot of money. Like me, many boys growing up dreamed of one day getting straightened out and becoming a real wiseguy. In Down Neck, that meant becoming a part of Angelo Bruno's family.

The Bruno family was part of the Mafia, and eventually I would become quite an expert on how the Mafia was organized on the East Coast and how the Bruno family fit in. It all started back when Mussolini and his Blackshirt fascists came to power in the early 1920s, and one of *il duce*'s first major campaigns was to eradicate from Sicily its "mafioso," who he claimed were holding the island in a backward feudal state. When the killing started, a great many fled and came to the United States where they settled in New York City, Chicago, Philadelphia, and the other urban centers with immigrants who had also come from Sicily. These new immigrants brought with them their customs from the old country, including their propensity to form clans or "families," and by the middle of the 1920s, five such families had emerged in New York City.

The largest and most powerful of these families—it had no name because in those days they really didn't give themselves names, and the media had not yet learned of their existence—was located in Manhattan and Brooklyn. It was headed by Joe Masseria and numbered among its younger members Charles "Lucky" Luciano, Frank Costello, and Joe Adonis. Its close ally was the family headed by Al Manfredi—who had shortened his last name to Mineo—which had among its members Albert Anastasia. Also in the same territory was what was called the Castellammarese clan, named after the area in western Sicily that most of its members came from. It was headed by Colo Schiro and Salvatore Maranzano, and it had branches in Buffalo and Detroit run by Stefano Magaddino and Gaspar Milazzo, two important members of the family who relocated after a run-in with New York City police. The Bronx was controlled by the fourth family, headed by Tom Reina; and Staten Island and a part of Brooklyn provided the base of the fifth family, headed by Joe Profaci.

During Prohibition these families began to flourish as bootleggers. They also ran illegal gambling houses and wildly popular lotteries. Through a combination of luck and violence, Masseria—known as "Joe the Boss"—became the most powerful of the family heads. He and his family dominated three of the other four families. He did not dominate or control the Castellammareses, with whom he coexisted in a very uneasy fashion.

In the 1920s one of Masseria's top lieutenants, Frankie Yale, selected a very ambitious young Neapolitan named Al Capone to go to Chicago to establish a Masseria outpost. There Capone clashed with an established Sicilian, Joe Aiello, who was very close to Gaspar Milazzo, the Castellammarese in Detroit. The clash grew into a feud, and Masseria was drawn into it. Masseria reportedly promised Capone he could become the father of his own family, tied to Masseria's in New York, if he subdued Aiello. But this proved difficult, partly because of Aiello's alliance with Milazzo in Detroit and, through him, the rest of the Castellammareses. In short order Masseria's anger turned against the Castellammarese, and on January 10, 1930, he had Milazzo killed in Detroit as he emerged from shopping at a fish market.

The result was predictable: An all-out war erupted in New York between Masseria's family and the Castellammareses. Because he was experienced in such things back in Sicily, newly arrived Salvatore Maranzano became head of the Castellammareses, and he named as his chief lieutenant young Joe Bonanno. The war went on for a year and left bodies strewn all over New York. Top members of both families were killed, with Masseria himself only narrowly escaping an ambush set by Bonanno and his friend Joe Valachi. Both sides eventually began to grow weary of the violence, and word was sent to Maranzano that Masseria's new second-in-command, Charles Luciano—known as Charlie Lucky—was ready to talk a deal. A meeting was arranged where Luciano and his close friend Vito Genovese were told by Maranzano that they knew what had to happen in order for the war to end, with a slice of the spoils going to Charlie Lucky. Luciano said he understood, and a couple of weeks later he took Masseria to dinner at the Villa Tammaro restaurant in Coney Island. After dinner, Luciano excused himself to go to the bathroom, and as soon as he left the table, four men rushed in and shot Masseria to death. The four were Vito Genovese, Albert Anastasia, Joe Adonis, and Bugsy Siegel. The war was over.

After that there was a kind of natural realignment of the five New York families. A much weakened version of the Masseria family was headed by Luciano, with Vito Genovese as his second; the Reina family was headed by Gaetano Gagliano, with Tommy Lucchese as his second; the Mineo family was headed by Frank Scalise; Joe Profaci, who had stayed neutral in the war, was allowed to remain at the head of his family; and Maranzano emerged as the first among equals, the so-called boss of bosses, as the head of the Castellammareses.

Not only did Maranzano dominate the five New York families, but he was able to impose order among the families in other cities. First, he reached a quick accommodation with Al Capone in Chicago whereby Capone could have Chicago in exchange for recognizing Maranzano as the top boss in the United States. Family leaders in other cities quickly fell in line.

But this new power structure did not hold together for long. Maranzano and Luciano clashed almost at once over who would control New York's garment district. Fearing that Maranzano was about to have him killed, Luciano struck first. In September 1931, less than four months after the Castellammarese war ended, Luciano had Maranzano killed. Joe Bonanno was immediately chosen the new boss of the Castellammareses, and he quickly reached an understanding with Luciano and agreed not to seek vengeance for Maranzano. One other leadership change occurred. Scalise was very close to Maranzano, and with Luciano now the boss of bosses, he had to go. He was replaced by Vincent Mangano.

The five New York families have remained essentially the same since then, with leadership changes occurring mainly through natural deaths and retirements, although in a few well-known situations those retirements were rather involuntary and permanent. Luciano himself met a violent death and was replaced by Frank Costello, who in turn was replaced by Vito Genovese in 1955. Mangano was replaced by Albert Anastasia, who in turn was succeeded by Carlo Gambino. Gagliano remained in power until 1953 when Tommy Lucchese took over. Profaci had the longest reign before succumbing to cancer. He was succeeded by Joe Magliocco, who died of a heart attack in less than a year and was succeeded by Joe Colombo. Joe Bonanno remained the head of his family. It was in the 1960s that the media became aware of and began to write about the structure of organized crime in the New York area. They named each family after the man who was heading it at that time; thus the five New York families became known as Colombo, Gambino, Bonanno, Genovese, and Lucchese.

But there was and is a sixth family, and it is extremely important because in the New York area it is the main link between organized crime and the building trades unions. The DeCavalcante family— named after its longtime head Simone Rizzo "Sam the Plumber" DeCavalcante—operates from its base in New Jersey. Sam, who got his nickname because he was ostensibly a plumbing contractor, specialized in the building trades and construction unions. For years he controlled every major construction job in northern and central Jersey. He controlled the unions, and he was paid off by virtually every contractor who wanted to do any business in the area. Sam shared his take with the New York families, and if a member of any of the families wanted to place someone in a union construction trades job, Sam saw to it that it happened. In exchange, Sam was allowed to establish and operate his own family, as long as he operated generally within his own narrow labor union area. The family has thrived and still exists today under its current head, John Riggi.

The same wave of immigration that brought the Castellammareses to New York also brought numerous Sicilians to Philadelphia. Among those settling there were Salvatore Sabella, a convicted murderer who escaped and came to the United States as a stowaway, and an infant by the name of Angelo Annaloro, who came with his parents and grew up to be known as Angelo Bruno.

Sabella became the head of a loosely allied group of Sicilian racketeers operating in Philadelphia. In 1927 he was involved in a gunfight in which two people were killed. He was acquitted of murder, but the police learned in the course of the trial that he was an illegal immigrant, and he was deported to Sicily. John Avena took over as head of the group and transformed what had been a loose alliance of individuals under Sabella into a more traditionally structured Mafia family. After his leadership of the Philadelphia organization was affirmed by Stefano Maranzano at the national convention held after the Castellammarese war, he quickly expanded his control of gambling and other illegal activities in Philadelphia before he was shot down on a street corner in August 1936. He was succeeded by Giuseppe Dovi, also known as Joseph Bruno (no relation to Angelo), who remained as the head of the family for a decade, during which he expanded the family's activities into other parts of Pennsylvania and into southern New Jersey. After he died of a heart attack, he was replaced by Joseph Idda, who might be termed the reluctant don because he did not really want to be a leader. While Idda was in charge, the real power in the family belonged to Marco Reginelli, Idda's underboss who lived in Camden, New Jersey. He spread the influence of the family far north into New Jersey, and it was he who at least indirectly controlled Down Neck at about the time I was born and my father's bookmaking and numbers operations were expanding.

When Reginelli died in 1956, the family went through several years of confusion. Idda replaced Reginelli as underboss with Dominick Olivetto, who was then dispatched to Apalachin in upper New York State to represent the family at the famous and ill-fated national Commission meeting that was raided by police. This event called attention to the Philadelphia family and put both Idda and Olivetto into the spotlight. They became targets of the Feds, and state and local police. That was all too much for Idda, and he "screwed"—fled—back to Sicily. Olivetto, meanwhile, had so many law enforcement problems that the last thing in the world he wanted was to take over as boss. He simply refused to accept the position.

There was no obvious heir apparent. Below Olivetto there were two almost equally powerful captains, Antonio Dominick Pollina and Angelo Bruno. Clearly it was not going to be an easy choice. Idda had wanted Pollina as his successor, and as an interim solution, the Commission, the committee of family heads, named Pollina acting boss while things were allowed to sort themselves out. Had he been patient about it, Pollina would probably have been named permanent boss; or had he simply reached out to Angelo and named him underboss with a major share, an accommodation between the two could have been worked out. But Pollina was a hothead, and he was ambitious. As far as he was concerned, the only thing that stood between him and immortality was Angelo Bruno. So he resolved to eliminate the problem by whacking Angelo. Lucky for him the guy who picked up the contract was a fellow Sicilian, Ignazio Denaro, who went to Bruno and warned him.

Angelo moved quickly. Because Pollina had been elevated by the Commission on only a temporary basis, Angelo knew the only way that Pollina could legitimately have put a contract out on him was with the Commission's permission. If Pollina had received that permission, Angelo knew his only option was to go into retirement in some distant place. But if Pollina had not gotten permission, and Angelo had to believe that was the case, then Pollina had overstepped badly. So Angelo went to New York to meet with his close friend and fellow-Sicilian Carlo Gambino.

Gambino pledged his protection to Angelo. As Angelo had surmised, Pollina was acting without Commission sanction. Gambino swayed the Commission to Bruno's side, and in return Gambino received a pledge of loyalty from Bruno. Angelo was named permanent boss, the family became known as the Bruno family, and everyone prospered for almost twenty years. Bruno showed what kind of guy he was and raised more than a few eyebrows by not only allowing Pollina to simply step down but also permitting him to continue living in Philadelphia and remain active in family affairs.

In the newspapers, on television, and in the movies, the various mob families have usually been portrayed in conflict. But that is not the way it is. Mob wars, at least over the past twenty or thirty years, have almost always been conflicts within families—power struggles over control, one faction feuding with another, or a new boss doing some necessary house cleaning. Since the advent of the Commission, which is made up of the heads of the five New York families, it has become an unusual event when a member of one family kills a member of another. Organized crime has become very much a cooperative effort. Members from one family work with members of another, so everyone makes money. In northern Jersey, for example, things were laid out pretty carefully. The Genoveses ran the Port of Newark. The Luccheses had lucrative operations in the "bedroom" counties of Bergen, Essex, Morris, Passaic, and Union. The DeCavalcantes had the unions, the building trades, the contractors, and the construction sites. The Gambinos were heavily into both drugs and gambling. The Colombos had a major share of the loan-sharking. And the Philadelphia-based Bruno family controlled much of Newark, and especially Down Neck. So when I was a kid, it was Bruno guys who offered my father protection, it was Bruno guys he paid off, and it was a Bruno guy that I grew up wishing to be.

Why did I want to be a wiseguy? It was really simple: In that kind of working-class world, everyone else broke their backs at some job they hated, trying to make a buck. But the wiseguys just hung around, and the money seemed to roll downhill into their pockets. And they were respected. Next to the parish priests, they were the most respected guys in the neighborhood.

There was another reason. My father died when I was eleven, and my mom had to go to work to help support my two brothers and me. We received a little money each month from some of my dad's former associates who had taken over his bookmaking operation. But things were still tight, and each of us kids was expected to try to bring some money into the house to help out. By the time I finished high school, I was helping out more than a little.

East Side High was okay. I ended up having a lot of fun, and I got a good education, although it was not exactly the kind of education I think the school board had in mind. As far as academics were concerned, my freshman and sophomore years were very easy. My grades were okay, and I did odd jobs after school. Then I started to hang around Pasquale "Patty Specs" Martirano and some of the guys who worked for him.

He had been a friend of my father's, and I had always seen him around. I guess after my dad died I just naturally gravitated toward Patty, who was still only in his thirties. He was already a made guy in the Bruno family and as such was an important man in the neighborhood. Patty was short, stocky, and powerfully built. Even in those days he was already mostly bald, and he wore glasses. He was not a suit-and-tie kind of guy; he wore suits only on special occasions. But he was always in designer slacks and sweaters and three-hundred-dollar shoes.

When I first started hanging with him, he had just finished building a house, and it was the talk of the town: a six-bedroom, four-bath house with an attached three-car garage, a circular driveway, and a patio on top of the garage that could be reached via a circular stairway from the dining room. The word around the neighborhood was that he had done his share of dirty work in the past and would still do it if it was necessary. But he was also a quiet guy who almost never raised his voice. And of all the guys I ever met in the mob, Patty was among the very smartest.

I took after my father in that I liked to gamble, and it was during high school that I learned I was pretty good at it. How dedicated a gambler was I? Like every high school we had a senior yearbook, and we all listed under our pictures what we wanted to be when we grew up. There were all the usual things listed: doctor, lawyer, and even priest in a couple of cases. But under George Fresolone it said simply "bookmaker." As far as I was concerned, there was not a more honorable profession.

I also learned a thing or two about what it meant to be connected. The principal of East Side High was James Quelli, Jr., a real good guy who was tight with the Genoveses. He later got himself whacked after he was put in charge of a multimillion-dollar school renovation and started holding out on kickbacks to the mob-controlled firms he had signed up to do the work. Quelli's two closest pals were gym teachers Frank Poloso and Greg Notti. They hung out together, went to the track together, and played cards together. They thought of themselves as big-time gamblers—Poloso was a horse player and Notti a card player—and I used to run bets to the track for Poloso. He would be stuck at school, so I would leave early to go to the track and bet horses for him. For a guy who spent so much time at it, Poloso had to be the worst handicapper I have ever seen. In two years of running bets for him, I don't ever remember him cashing a big ticket. In my senior year he got so pissed off at my bringing him back losing tickets that he flunked me in gym. Just his little joke, he said.

I owe a very big debt to Greg Notti. He taught me how to play cards, especially how to count cards in blackjack. I guess in my lifetime I have won close to a million dollars using the skills he taught me. No one can ever say I didn't learn a skill in high school.

By my senior year I had started to date Patty's daughter, which he permitted, and I also started doing odd jobs for him and even driving him around. There is almost an unwritten law in the mob that made guys, important guys, never drive themselves; someone always drives them, and he is not so much a chauffeur as a valued assistant and confidant. It's a job new guys on their way up were given. So when I started driving Patty, it was noticed in the neighborhood, and it began to look as if I was going to be with Patty later. It greatly added to my stature.

That year I also began to run around with a group of guys who were a couple of years older than I was. The big mob hangout in Down Neck was the 3-11 Club, which was owned by Anthony Caponigro, called "Tony Bananas," a made Bruno member who was the most powerful mob guy in northern Jersey; although not yet the family consigliere, he acted like it. The 3-11 was located at the intersection of Chestnut and Adams streets, and was actually run by Patty. There were several other clubs in the vicinity, and that area was where all the action was. I found an empty loft on Adams, near the corner, and a bunch of us rented it. We used it as a clubhouse and hung out there. We also started holding a poker game on Friday and Saturday nights that a lot of young guys came to.

It began as a kind of kids' game, with dollar bets and raises, but it quickly escalated. A number of players were also drug dealers, and they would come to the game with $3,000 to $5,000 in their pockets. Dollar bets quickly became hundred-dollar bets. Word got around, and one day at school Quelli came up to me and said that he, Poloso, and Notti wanted to play. There was no way I could say no, so that Friday the three of them showed up, and from then on they became regulars.

Pretty soon they started to win and win big. After about the third session in a row where one of them walked away with the most money—and we're talking about several thousand—I knew it couldn't be just a winning streak or blind luck or even skill. So I started to watch closely. It didn't take long to see that the three of them were cheating big-time—dealing from the bottom of the deck, dealing seconds, working tandem scams. You name it, they were doing it. I confronted Quelli, which put him in a tight spot. I was more than just a kid. He knew I was hanging with Patty, and the last thing he wanted to do was offend Patty. He couldn't just dismiss me, and he didn't want to stop playing in the game because the dumb guys we were playing with were providing him with a nice weekly income. So he made one of those proverbial offers I couldn't refuse: He would cut me in for a full share of the money he was taking off my friends each weekend. From that point on, some nights I would be the big winner, some nights Quelli or Poloso or Notti would be. Then we would split the take four ways, and I would give a part of mine to Patty because that's the way it was done.

Some nights we would shoot craps instead of playing poker. Greg Notti, bless him, showed me how to cheat at dice and roll numbers or sevens almost at will. It got to the point that I was bringing home to my mother $500 a weekend and still had a pocketful of cash to hang around with. I was eighteen when I graduated high school in 1972. I gave college a couple of brief thoughts, but I was already making a pretty good living from cards and dice, and had become the most significant source of income for my mother and brothers. So I dismissed the thought of any further education. It was time to get on with my life. It was time to become a wiseguy.

I did get a nine-to-five job after I graduated, but it was a big mistake. Patty got me the job at People's Express Trucking, down at the Port of Newark, unloading ships and loading trucks. The way things worked at the Port was that the Genoveses ran the place, but the Bruno family had a guy in the union office. He couldn't get you one of the real good "no-show" jobs, where all you did was come by once a week and pick up your check (and then kick back half to the Genoveses). But if you actually wanted to work—and at the time I thought that's what I wanted to do as long as the money was good— our guy could get you a very good paying situation, and all you had to do was give him a small kickback.

I lasted about eight months on that job. It was a lot of hard physical labor, and I was always tired because after work I hung out with Patty, sometimes driving him around until the early hours of the morning. But I ran into another problem. The shop steward who ran our loading gang liked to bet, and one day he talked about the upcoming mayoral election in Newark. He thought that Kenneth Gibson was going to win, and I didn't. We each bet $100 and agreed to give our money to a third guy to hold. Come election day, the shop steward didn't show up for work. Since he hadn't put up his stake, I assumed he had changed his mind and we had no bet. Gibson won, and the next day demanded his hundred. I said no way; you didn't put your money up, so no bet. He got nasty, and I said we would straighten things out right after work. He said the hell with that, we were going to settle it then and there, and he came at me swinging. The fight was a draw, but this guy figured he would have the last laugh: He fired me on the spot.

I thought I was in the right. If you don't put up your money, there is no bet. I was pretty steamed, so I went to Patty and told him what had happened. He said he would speak to the guy and I should go back to work in the morning. I never knew exactly what Patty said, but the next morning the steward welcomed me back with open arms. He even apologized. He hadn't known I was connected; now he did.

But the fight had been the last straw. I just wasn't cut out for the nine-to-five life. No matter how good the money was, I was tired of getting up at the crack of dawn every day and stumbling down to the Port. I was dead tired all the time. I started to leave work earlier and earlier to do things for Patty. Amazingly, the boss never said a word, and my full paycheck came every week. Then I simply stopped going to the job and started hanging with Patty all the time. My dream had started to happen. I was now in the mob.

2

COMING OF AGE
IN THE MOB

For me the seventies were good times. I mean for a guy still in his early twenties, in New Jersey, what could have been better than being young, having money, and being a wiseguy.

I was now driving Patty full-time. He wanted to get a new car, so he gave me the money to buy it and to register it in my name. I bought a few-years-old sky-blue Buick Electra from a numbers guy who needed to change cars about every six months so the cops couldn't tag him by the car he was driving. It was a good car, clean and well maintained, and it came with an added bonus. The numbers guy had installed a hidden compartment that could be reached through one of the backseat armrests. We used it to stash money or betting slips or occasionally a gun. Buying the car for Patty taught me a lesson right off: Have as few assets as possible in your own name—house, cars, whatever of value that the Feds or the state might try to seize someday. The idea is to keep everything in other people's names. Patty followed this policy and had most of what he owned in his father's name, his sister's name, his brother-in-law's name, his girlfriend Anna Marie's name, and now, since I was just a kid, in my name.

So I drove Patty around. Driving a guy like Patty was not like you were the chauffeur and he was the guy in the backseat; it was more like you were his assistant. Patty always sat in the front seat, and he would talk about what was going on. He told me everything so I would understand and learn. I would run errands for him and take messages to guys and bring messages back. Fear of wiretaps made organized crime very much of a direct, person-to-person operation. It is not likely that you can be bugged if you whisper directly into a guy's ear. I spent a lot of time doing that on Patty's behalf.

I would pick Patty up at his house in the morning, and we drove to one of the places he hung at, either a club or a business that was owned by his cousin. Patty spent the whole day doing business. Mob life is not like a regular job. You have to create your income every day; you're always on the hustle. Every day is different, a different scam, a different hustle. At times it was swag—stolen merchandise. For a while, it was cigarettes. We got them by the carload from a guy who was stealing them off trucks. We actually set up routes. Other times it was other things. People would pay money for Patty to do them favors—get them jobs or city contracts, whatever. But in Down Neck, gambling was the thing. So day in and day out, above everything else, we made our basic money gambling. Hour after hour, day after day, we would hang around some club or street corner waiting for something to happen. People would come in to see Patty, or we would go out to meet them. Then at night we usually joined some guys for dinner and sat around a club or bar drinking. I might drop Patty off at midnight or 2:00 A.M., and then we would start all over again the next morning.

There were a couple of exceptions. One was Saturday nights. In the mob, Saturday nights were for families. On Saturday night you and your wife, and maybe your kids, went out for the best dinner you could afford, usually with some of the other guys and their wives. After I got married, I fell into this habit. Now, though, I hung out with the guys on Saturday nights because Patty was out with his wife.

The other exception was when Patty was with his broads. For many of the guys in the mob, wives were for raising the children. They were to be respected and provided for, and possibly even to be loved, but broads were for screwing. I never subscribed to this philosophy, but Patty sure did. He always had several girlfriends on the side—several at the same time. Eventually he settled into a long, "monogamous" relationship with Anna Marie, and in the end she was the only one he wanted to be with. But when I first started hanging with him, he saw three or four girls regularly.

And he was embarrassed by it, I think, because he wanted to keep it a secret. So he would drive himself whenever he went to see one of them, and that was three or four times a week. Usually we would have dinner with some guys. Then he would take the Buick, and I would either be free for the rest of the night if he was going to stay over, or else I would meet up with him a few hours later.

Patty was great to work for. He was more like a friend than a boss. He was teaching me everything there was to know about being a wiseguy. He let me in on everything that was going down. Things in our family were a lot more relaxed than in some of the New York families. A young guy could learn quickly. He could meet the right people, and if he was smart, he could get himself accepted. And he could start going out on his own.

About all I did at first was drive. I drove Patty every day and every night. Several times a week we held a card game or a crap game at some secure location. So there wouldn't be too many cars around the place, the house or apartment, I drove guys to and from the game. But gradually I started to do other things. Patty had a pretty good shylocking business going, and I delivered money or made collections. I did the same for his bookmaking operations— collected the money or brought bookies money so they could pay off their customers. I was a driver and a messenger, and in some ways what I did for Patty was not much different from what I had done for my father when I was nine years old.

Patty paid me a couple of hundred a week, and I got tips from the guys I was driving to the games. Since I was still living at home, I really didn't need a lot of money. A couple of hundred was plenty. But I was anxious to do more than just carry money around, so Patty put me to work in his numbers business. Actually, I went to work for Anthony "Slicker" Attanasio, a guy who got his nickname from the slick way he dressed and the slick way he could handle a deck of cards. Slicker was running Patty's numbers business, and I became a controller for him. I had a bunch of numbers writers under me, and it was my job to see to it that their packages were in on time, that their accounts were in balance, and that they were doing a good job serving their customers. In many ways I had graduated to doing what my father had done for many years, and for this I was paid $150 a week by Slicker, in addition to what I was getting directly from Patty.

At one point back then, Slicker gave me a hint of the every-man-for-himself attitude that I soon learned was so prevalent in the guys around Patty. One time I needed $500 to buy something or other, so I went to Slicker and asked him for it. I thought he would just reach into his pocket and give it to me; he certainly had it. But instead he "lent" me the $500 at five percent interest per week. Over the next ten weeks he held back $75 a week, half my salary, so I ended up paying him back $750 for the $500. He saw me as another shy customer, not as a friend or colleague. I didn't think much of it at the time, but years later I remembered it when it came time for me to make some hard decisions about Slicker.

I had been driving Patty for about two years when both of us decided it was time that I started getting out on my own. It was 1975, and I had just turned twenty-two. So I began doing what I knew best, what I had learned as a kid from my dad: I started making book and running a small numbers writing operation for myself. Patty wasn't into bookmaking at the time, but he thought it was something I would probably be very good at and something that would earn money for us all. He introduced me to Pee Wee DiPhillips, a made member of the Genovese crew, who had an established book. I became an agent for Pee Wee, handling some of his accounts while I developed my own. I stayed with Pee Wee for about a year and then, with Patty's blessing and Pee Wee's, I went out on my own. I was quick and honest, and I started to draw in good players. Pretty soon I had a list of about sixty customers, and Patty and I were clearing a few grand a week during football season.

I also started representing Patty at a monte game that Tony "Bananas" Caponigro was backing in the Bronx. The game was held several nights a week in the back of a massive old parking garage on 181st Street. The place was perfect, solid brick and built like a fort, with a front door of cast iron that could be bolted from inside. If the cops had raided it, it would have taken them hours to break in, and by that time we would all have been long gone through any number of other exits.

Like Patty, Tony Bananas was a made member in the Bruno family, but he had power and authority much greater than any captain. His was probably the most powerful organization in Jersey, more powerful than any of the New York families' New Jersey operations. The power came from the money he made, the number of guys who were loyal to him, and his willingness to do the dirty work for most of the New York families.

Monte is a kind of street version of the casino card game baccarat; it's a made-for-gambling game where the action is incredibly fast and furious. As in baccarat, one of the players acts as the "bank," betting against the other players. This meant that, as the house, we were not playing against the bettors the way a casino does in craps or blackjack; instead, for holding the game and providing drinks, food, and other services, we took a "cut" of every pot. "Cutting" the game is actually what made it illegal. We were profiting by running the game, and the profits were big. Our game drew many of the most active Hispanic drug dealers in Spanish Harlem, and these guys would walk in with paper bags full of hundred-dollar bills. It was not unusual for $10,000 or even $20,000 to be on the table, hand after hand, for hours at a time. Our cut of the pot could add up to $50,000 or more per night.

I had a couple of jobs at the game. I acted as a kind of referee to settle any disputes between players. I was also there to lend money —Bananas' money, of course—to any players who needed short-term cash. And I was there to play occasionally or to act as the bank. I remember one night when I got lucky and won about $90,000. I split it with Patty, $45,000 each. My share, though, went to pay off some players in my book who had a particularly good weekend.

The game was actually run for Bananas by Joseph "Scoops" Licata. Scoops was about ten years older than I was, and he could easily have passed for Hollywood's idea of a gangster. He was short, fat, and mean. His nickname was actually a kind of hand-me-down from his older brother Tom, who was the neighborhood gossip. If you wanted the straight "scoop" on anyone or anything, you asked Tommy Licata. So he became known as Tommy Scoops, and Joey naturally became known as Joey Scoops, even though he was as tight-lipped as any guy you will ever meet.

By the time I started hanging with Patty regularly, Scoops was already well established. Like many of the guys, he got his start in the Bruno family's numbers business. Down Neck, that meant working for Tony Bananas. He graduated eventually to loan-sharking, putting Tony's money out on the street and helping to do the collection work. He was always carrying some of Bananas' money and would constantly flash his roll. Patty never completely trusted Scoops because he was very close to the Luccheses and their boss Michael Perna. But Scoops appeared to be very close to Tony Bananas, and he liked to brag that this was because he was such a big earner. He really thought that Bananas liked him. But Tony often told Patty and me that he really didn't like Scoops much, and he agreed with Patty that Scoops should not be trusted.

Who Bananas really liked was Scoops's wife Jackie. Bananas used to tell us often about how he wanted to bang Jackie. And the reason he wanted Scoops close to him was so that he could send him places. That was probably the main reason he put Scoops in charge of the monte game. Most times the game went all night, and we would not get home before daylight. That left Tony plenty of time to go after Jackie. I don't know if he succeeded in his conquest, but he often bragged he did. And his and Patty's distrust of Scoops was one of the reasons Patty put me into the game. I was there to keep an eye on Scoops.

I was making good money. About half went to Patty. He passed half along to Bananas, who in turn passed along a taste to Bruno in Philadelphia. At times I felt as if I were supporting half the mobsters in the Northeast. Even so, I was able to support my mother and my little brother, and help out my older brother who had just gotten married and was struggling. And I still had enough left over to wear the best clothes and walk around with thousands in my pocket.

I was still living at home, the few hours a day I wasn't with Patty. Patty was my life. Except on a Saturday night when he might be out with his wife and I would have dinner and hang out with some of the guys I had known since high school, I was with Patty or running some errand for him. I had almost no social life. I really didn't date. I had no time. I went out occasionally, but it wasn't dating in any sense of the word. One thing I was gaining, though, was stature. I was about the newest guy among the so-called associates, guys who had not yet been made, but I was accepted as an equal because of my relationship with Patty. Younger guys in the neighborhood began to look up to me.

Money was pouring in from everywhere. Besides the monte game, we were involved in bookmaking, loan-sharking, protection rackets, vending machines, and all kinds of scams and hustles. One of the strangest situations I was ever in involved the two best sports gamblers I ever met. Davey Battista and Dominic Iavarone, who was known as LuLu, were from Philadelphia and connected to some guys in our family there. These two guys could bet football, basketball, baseball, and the horses, and almost never lose. I couldn't believe it. About ten guys worked for them, gathering information from all kinds of insiders, and they knew more about everything that was going on than any bettors I have ever seen.

But they had a problem. They were known to just about every big bookie in the country, and they were running out of places to bet. So Patty got a call one day from one of our connections in Philly who knew these guys, and they came up to meet us. They had a simple proposition: We would find bookies for them and front the action, and they would supply the bets. They would put up the money at first, but later, once we started to win, we would have to put up the dough. We would split the winnings. They assured us there would be no losses.

They were right, at least for three years. Their schtick sounded too good to be true, but I have never seen anyone who was as right, as often. One year our share of the winnings from placing bets for these guys was $250,000. But once we started having to front our own money, we almost immediately ran into a cash flow problem.

Unfortunately, even with these guys, you lost some bets. It sometimes happened that you would win with one bookie while losing with another at the same time. On a given week—and such situations might happen quite often—with one book we would win $50,000, and with another we would lose $30,000. Bookies have different settlement days. Maybe the guy we lost to settled on a Tuesday, and the guy we won from did not settle until Friday. In situations like this, we needed the $30,000 until we could collect the $50,000. So we took in a partner, Joseph Pico, who ran a numbers bank and had quite a bit of cash going in and out. He could easily front us ten or twenty grand for a few days or a week, and we would pay a couple of points a week in interest.

Pico also had another terrific scam. He took junkets to Vegas, to the Sands Hotel, maybe once every month or six weeks. There were always a couple of big players on these junkets, but there were also other guys who just wanted to go out and party, get the free airfare, stay in the free room, eat the free food, and see the shows. But to go on these junkets you had to play at the tables, and they had to see you play. The casino gave each of Pico's guys $5,000 in credit, hoping they would lose that and more. So what Pico did was take ten or twenty guys out, most of them freeloaders who wanted to party and not play. They each signed markers to get the $5,000 in chips, and then they paired off and bet against each other: red-black, odd-even, pass–don't pass. Every time one lost, the other won. With few exceptions it was a break-even proposition, but at the end of the weekend these guys each gave Pico their $5,000. His deal with the casino was that his players did not have to repay their markers until the next time he brought a group out. This meant that he got the use of maybe $50,000 to $100,000 of the casino's money, interest free, for a month or six weeks. He then put it out on the street in shy money or used it to finance his numbers, or Patty and I used it for the float in our betting operation for the Philly guys.

Hardly a week went by that we didn't win big with this operation. It got so we were having trouble finding books who would take our bets. Actually, there was another thing about this operation that was almost as odd as the fact that Davey and LuLu would always win. While we spread our bets around all over, we bet heavily with a top New York bookie, Joe "the Butch" Corrao, a Gambino family captain and an important member of John Gotti's crew. It was really weird, at times almost supernatural. As often as we won with just about every other book we were betting, with Joe we almost always lost. On a given Sunday we might bet ten football games and win seven of the ten. Somehow, the three we lost were always the three we bet with Joe. There was no real explanation for this, it just happened. We just had no luck with the Butch. It seemed that every Wednesday night we found ourselves in Little Italy in New York paying off our loses to Joe. On Wednesday nights the Gambinos threw these huge dinners at Taormina, a restaurant on Mulberry Street across from the club where Gambino boss Paul Castellano hung out. There were often a couple of hundred guys there from various crews. Patty and I would eat and drink, meet a lot of guys I later worked with, and then after dinner I would hand Joe or one of his guys a very fat envelope with anywhere from $20,000 to $50,000 in it.

Our deal with Davey and LuLu went on for four years. We made money, a ton of it. But finally during the fourth football season, for whatever reason, Davey and LuLu simply lost their magic. Where before they couldn't do anything wrong, suddenly they couldn't do anything right. We bowed out of the operation, but it was a terrific run while it lasted.

During this time we developed what was one of my favorite hustles. Patty and I figured out a way for the Catholic church to make us big money every year. Italian Catholics love to celebrate the feast days of their patron saints. Each May in Down Neck the Catholics, which was about the whole neighborhood, celebrated the feast of Saint Michael, the patron saint of our parish, Our Lady of Mount Carmel. Some guys who were in the Father's Club of the parish came up with the idea of holding a street fair like the big celebration of the Feast of San Gennaro in Little Italy in Manhattan. Patty turned the idea over to me, and before you knew it, the Bruno family was in the church fair business.

The clubs we hung out at, the 3-11 and the East Side Social Club, were at the intersections of Chestnut and Adams. The church was one block over, at Oliver and Adams. I set up the booths along Adams Street between our club house and the church, and rented them to the vendors who wanted to sell the food or novelties or run games of chance at the fair. That first year we started out small, renting maybe a city block's worth of booths at about $5 a front foot for a single weekend. The next year we expanded slightly to five days, Thursday to Sunday, and had maybe two blocks' worth of booths. By the time we finished, we were going for ten days, including two weekends, and were renting out booths that filled seven to eight blocks. They ran all the way down Oliver Street to Independence Park, and we filled the park with amusement rides. By then the booths were going for $30 a front foot for two solid weeks. In addition to that, we ran our own gambling games, including a large crap game in the back of the 3-11. And we held a big raffle on which we split the profits with the parish's Knights of Columbus chapter. We also ran the amusement rides. The first couple of years we lost money on those, but over the last few the rides became a gold mine. One weekend, the last year I was involved, we made $40,000 from the rides alone, and that was after we paid for the rental.

This was not all found money. We had to work hard for about a month setting everything up and then actually running the fair, and we had a lot of costs. Before we saw our first dollar in income, we had expenses of about $30,000. We rented most of the equipment from various mob-related companies, including lights, which were our biggest expense. In those days we owned Newark, we owned the city government, and most of all we owned the police. Whatever we wanted, we got. But it was expensive. We constantly had to make all kinds of payoffs. For the fair, in order for the police to ignore the gambling that was rather open, we had to pay off a top police official and a local captain, who in turn gave ten of his officers $60 a night to act as security guards for us. We paid off a local council member to get the permits we needed. We paid top dollar to I don't remember how many inspectors to overlook various code violations. Then we had to kick some of the money back to the parish, usually about 30 percent of what we netted. But when it was all over, especially in the later years, we had quite a nice pot to split. We sent money down to Philadelphia; we gave a good share to Bananas; we probably gave $5,000 each to fifteen or so guys who hung around Bananas and Patty; and Patty and I still had a tidy sum to share when all was said and done. The good parishioners of Mount Carmel thought they were helping the church. And they were, but they were also lining the pockets of the Bruno family.

Patty knew a lot of people; it seemed he knew everyone. He knew wiseguys and the bosses from all the families. He knew politicians and cops. He knew sports figures. And he knew people in show business—among them Frank Sinatra. Over the years I probably saw Sinatra perform a dozen times, in Vegas, in Atlantic City, or at the Latin Casino in Cherry Hill. Each time I was front row center or at the best table with Patty or Bananas or later with Nicky Scarfo, and we were always Frank's guests or the guests of his manager.

One time a bunch of us were out in Vegas, and we were walking through Caesars, where Sinatra was appearing. We ran into Jilly Rizzo, who was Sinatra's close friend, a kind of alter ego, and a guy we knew pretty well. He invited us to Frank's dinner show that night and made a big deal about our sitting at his booth. But then a little while later we ran into "Louie Domes" Pacella, a Gambino captain Patty knew, who was very close to Sinatra. Louie Domes told us that Sinatra had fixed him up for the dinner show that night and asked us to join him. Domes must have told Sinatra that we were in the hotel because Patty got a call from him during the day, and Sinatra said he hoped we would be joining Domes for the show. So that night we went to the room and gave our names to the headwaiter, who fell all over himself taking us down to the number one booth. We were barely seated when the champagne started flowing. Domes showed up, and as we were eating, I turned around and, in the far distance, maybe ten rows of booths behind us, I saw Jilly in his booth. He was sitting alone.

But Sinatra should have showed Patty that respect. Over the years Patty had done him more than a few favors. One time Pat got a call from one of Sinatra's people, who said Sinatra was leaving the West Coast on his way to Atlantic City, where he was beginning a tour.

Sinatra needed an opening act, and he wanted Sam Buteria and the Witnesses, which was a big act in those days. But Buteria had a problem: He had signed a firm contract to do a month at a club, and they were not about to let him out of it after they had done all kinds of advertising and had big bookings. Sinatra's people had called them direct and had gotten nowhere, so now they were calling on the chance that Patty could help.

It took Pat all of five minutes. He made a call to the club and said that he would consider it a personal favor if Buteria could be released from the contract, and Mr. Sinatra would make good on any losses. The reply was immediate: For you, Pat, of course, and there will be no expenses. So Pat called Sinatra's people back and told them that Buteria would be waiting in Atlantic City when Sinatra got there.

I met Ann on Thanksgiving night in 1976. Patty was with his family, so I had no obligations that evening. I had actually heard about this Ann long before I met her. One guy I hung with, Jeff, was dating her best friend. Then another guy who hung around our clubhouse, a guy named Danny, was always talking about Ann. Danny's problem was that he was painfully shy and could never work up the nerve to ask Ann out. On Thanksgiving night I went to this high-class club, Creations, mainly to hear Tramps, a band I liked. I really didn't go expecting much from the evening, but almost as soon as I arrived, I ran into Jeff and his girl and her girlfriend, the Ann that Danny was always talking about. She was wearing a tight black dress with a sheer back, and she looked gorgeous. I can still remember that dress. I ended up hanging out for the evening with the three of them, and Ann and I danced a few times. I really enjoyed the evening.

The next day I ran into Danny at the club. I told him I had met the Ann he was always talking about and that she and I had really hit it off. One thing led to another, and I ended up betting him I could get a date with her before he did. That turned out to be quite an effort. It took my asking her again and again over the next couple of weeks before she finally agreed to go to dinner with me. And to her great surprise, I now know, we hit it off.

They say opposites attract and, with Ann and me, maybe that was what happened. Although we lived only about twenty miles apart, we quite literally were from two different worlds. I grew up street smart and tough. She was from what passes in New Jersey as a relatively small town, and she had led a rather sheltered small-town existence. Ann was the youngest of four, her parents were the caretakers at a church, and the family lived in a large house the church supplied on its grounds. By the time I met her, she had graduated from high school and was out on her own. Even though she was then only twenty-one, she had a good job, her own car, and, kind of unusual for those days, her own apartment. Another thing that made us different was that she liked to go to clubs to dance and hang out, and I didn't. I hung out with Patty and the other wiseguys, and when I went to a club, it was not to dance but to gamble.

I would like to say it was love at first sight for both of us. It might have been for me, but I know it wasn't for her. I would like to believe I swept her off her feet, but we went out for six months before it became serious, and another six months before she said yes to my proposals. Since I was always hanging with Patty, dating was logistically difficult at times, but Patty was thrilled that I had found someone. For years he had been saying that I ought to find a girl, and now that I had, I half-think he was enjoying it as much as I was. Ann and I would go out on Saturday nights when Patty was with his wife or whenever he was spending the evening or night with one of his ladies. Sometimes we had an early dinner, and then I would meet up with Patty later. Other times he all but ordered me to go out with her and had Slicker or someone else drive him for the night so I could get away. Ann and I ended up together for at least a few minutes every day, and we went out on "dates" at least four or five times a week.

Why did she finally agree to marry me? If you ask her, she'll tell you that while I might not have been the suave Casanova that I pictured myself, I was very different from the guys she had been meeting in the clubs, all pick-up lines and little more. I was very attentive toward her and a lot more mature than most of the guys she knew. Although it was not all that important, I had money and was willing to spend it. I treated her very well, and she appreciated it.

When we first started going out, I told Ann I was in the trucking business. She really didn't question me too closely about what I did. Later, when things began to get more serious, I told her that while I "fooled around" a trucking company, my main source of income was from gambling. I said that I was good at it and that I was able to earn a good living doing it. Still later I admitted that not only did I gamble, but I also accepted bets and ran card games.

After we had gone out for more than a year, but still before we got married, Ann started to help me during football season when I was running a big pool card business. Every week the pool card listed most of the major college games and all the professional games with point spreads, and the player would pick from three to sixteen games, betting from a dollar up. If the player won all the games he picked, he would get a nice payoff. But it was very hard to pick that many winners without a loser. Week after week I made big money from these cards, but it also made for a lot of paperwork. Every Saturday and Sunday night I had to go through each and every card to see who won and who lost. It took hours even with Ann's help, but it was worth it. When there were very few winners and I really cleaned up, she would get excited.

Ann and I dated for almost two years before we got married. When she finally said yes, Patty could not have been happier. He was my best man. A year later, 1979, our first son was born.

It was right after our son was born that I got into real deep trouble with Tony Bananas. Under most circumstances Patty was about as easygoing and as nice a guy as you would ever want to meet, but if you pushed him too hard, he would push back even harder. He was "willing to do what had to be done" on occasion. It was near Christmas when a friend of ours who ran a numbers bank for Patty was being hassled very hard by a guy who wanted to muscle in. He knew the numbers bank operator was around Patty, but he pushed anyway. This was a major affront to Patty and something he had to deal with strongly and immediately. One day we were over at the Upstairs/Downstairs Club when Patty heard that this guy had just come into the 3-11. Patty called me and told me to take a couple of the guys over to the 3-11 and hurt the guy, hurt him real bad. "Georgie, don't kill him," Patty said, "but make sure he don't walk too good anymore." So four of us got into the car and went speeding over to the club. I ran in, and this guy was sitting there. I jumped him and started to bang on him real good. I remember I used a bat on his legs, and then I was banging his head against the jukebox for what seemed like ten minutes. The other guys finally came in and pulled me off him. I guess I lost my head and went too far. They took the guy to the hospital.

The guy then ran to Bananas. By this time Bananas had become the Bruno family consigliere, the number three man in the organization after the boss and the underboss. Patty was an important man among all the families operating in northern Jersey, but he was under Bananas and had to answer to him. Bananas had long commanded respect and fear—even when he was only a made guy—because of his power and because he was a stone-cold killer. He had started out in the early days as a killer with Albert Anastasia in Murder Inc. Over the years he had built up his own mini-family, guys who were loyal to him first and foremost. In time he became a multimillionaire, but he still liked to kill people and did it as a kind of hobby. He killed people for all the New York families, and he was the one guy who was feared by even the most powerful bosses. So when Bananas sent Joey Scoops to bring Patty and me to him, all the way over I was quaking. Patty kept telling me not to worry, that everything was square; but I honestly didn't know if I would be coming back alive.

Bananas was really angry. He screamed at me, and he screamed at Patty. He wasn't so much angry that we had beaten on this guy, because he agreed with Patty that that was business, but he was angry that Patty had not cleared it with him. He was even angrier that I had done the beating in what he considered "his" club—the 3-11. Coming into his club to do that kind of business made him look bad. I remember him screaming: Would I go into his house, into his living room, to do that kind of crap? If not, why then did I think I had the right to do it in a joint he owned? Patty ended up calming him down, and the whole thing eventually blew over. I found out later that Bananas actually liked me, and I ended up doing a lot of things for him. But his temper and his habit of killing people to solve problems would eventually catch up with him.

As 1979 passed into 1980, things could not have been going better as far as I was concerned. I was making good money. I had a wonderful wife and son at home. I wasn't a made guy yet, but when I was, I knew I would be set for life.

Then on Friday night, March 21, 1980, Angelo Bruno was whacked in Philly, and mob life would never be the same. According to many so-called mob experts, the hit was done because the New York families were feuding with Angelo over Atlantic City. That is completely wrong, exactly 180 degrees backward. Angelo was not killed because he was keeping the New York families out of Atlantic City. He was whacked because he was letting them in.

Patty and I had seen it coming. As soon as we heard the news on the radio, we knew it was Bananas who had whacked Angelo, and we knew why. Bruno was never a strong leader. During part of the 1970s he had spent three years in jail for refusing to testify before the New Jersey State Commission on Investigation. Then, too, it was simply not in his nature to be aggressive. Known as the "Docile Don," Angelo hated violence and valued negotiation and peace above all. So Bananas was pretty much allowed to do his own thing in northern Jersey. Bruno simply did not bother to worry about his consigliere's empire building. Any of the other bosses would have seen it for what it was—a direct threat—and would have had Bananas killed, but as long as money continued to flow down the New Jersey Turnpike from Newark, Bruno let Bananas have his way.

In 1976, Bananas went to jail for assaulting an FBI agent. Ducking a federal warrant, he had been an absent figure, hiding out with his girlfriend in New York City for almost a year. I used to drive Patty into the city to meet with him, and sometimes Patty would send me with messages or money, or to pick stuff up. Finally, during the Christmas season in 1975, the FBI staked out his house, guessing correctly that he would try to visit his family during the holidays. He came out, and when he saw the Feds, he tried to run. A car chase ensued, and it ended when he crashed his car into an FBI car. That's how they got him for assaulting an agent.

When Bananas got out in 1978, Bruno did not simply make him a captain, he promoted him to consigliere, the third most powerful position in the family. For the first time Patty and our guys officially had to report to him. Bruno hoped that the promotion would buy Bananas' loyalty. It didn't. Bruno's low-key ways frustrated any number of the powerful family members. Bananas was constantly angry, and so was Bruno's underboss Phil Testa. And there was one thing in particular that really made them mad: Bruno was renowned for his dislike of the drug trade. He even gave interviews and said that all he did was make gambling available to people who wanted to bet and that he would do almost anything to keep drugs off the streets of Philadelphia. A lot of people thought that Testa and the other "young turks" in the family were angered because Angelo wouldn't let them go into the drug business. Well, not exactly. Angelo was personally against drugs, and he would never personally profit from the drug trade, but if drugs were going to be sold, he saw no reason why some people in his organization shouldn't profit.

What actually was happening was that, with Angelo's permission, a number of Carlo Gambino's blood cousins—including three brothers, Rosario, Giuseppe, and Giovanni Gambino—opened pizza shops in Cherry Hill, Philadelphia, and Delaware. They were actually fronts to move heroin, and many of the sales were to Bruno family members in Philadelphia. They in turn sold the drugs to non-Mafia distributors who sold it to street dealers. The problem was that the Gambinos were making huge profits on the transactions. Many of the Bruno family members, especially those buying the drugs from the Gambinos, believed that if our family had been in the drug trade in an organized manner, we would have developed our own lines of supply directly through the old country and be making two or three times the amount.

That was at the heart of Bananas' problem with Bruno. He was simply too complacent, too willing to go along with what Gambino and the rest of the New York families wanted. That was especially true about what was happening in Atlantic City. The Bruno family had long controlled Atlantic City when it was a down-at-the-heels resort town not worth much mob interest. But then along came legalized gambling, and suddenly Atlantic City was a prize. Bruno realized that he did not have the muscle to keep the New York families out, so he closed his eyes and let them in, and asked almost nothing in return. To Bananas, this was cowardly, and he believed being spineless was in Bruno's genes. Bananas was a Calabrian; Bruno was from Villalba. Generations of old-country feuds required that Bananas look down on Angelo, so finally he had enough.

But you don't kill a boss like Angelo Bruno without permission. Patty told me that Bananas had told him he went to Frank "Funzi" Terri, the head of the Genoveses, to get the Commission's permission for the hit. He did not move until he got it, and for the last weeks before the hit, Bananas was telling Patty that he was going to become the new boss and that Patty would become his underboss. Patty said if this happened he would straighten me out first thing and make me the youngest captain our family had ever had. But in the meantime we should keep a very low profile.

Actually, a couple of days after Bruno was whacked, something happened that confused both Patty and me. The night that Bruno was killed, he had had dinner with three other guys at Cous' Little Italy, a small, but popular restaurant in South Philly. Bruno never drove himself, of course; he arrived with Raymond "Long John" Martorano, a family associate who owned a large vending machine business that carried Angelo on the payroll as a salesman. A lot has been made of who ended up driving Angelo home that night, as if it was somehow a part of the grand scheme, but the reality was that Angelo's driver that night was the result of absolute happenstance. Angelo went to dinner knowing that Long John had an appointment after dinner and would not be able to drive him home. He assumed that one of the other guys at the table would, but they begged off, saying they wanted to get home to listen to a live opera broadcast on the radio. An opera lover like Angelo understood that, and it said a lot about his docile personality that he would not think twice when a guy in the family said he had somewhere else to be and could not take him home.

Actually, Angelo knew all he had to do was ask and half the guys in the place would fall all over themselves to drive him. What happened was that Long John went out to the bar to see who was there who could drive Angelo. Several guys volunteered, but Long John chose John Stanfa, who had just come in and was having a drink. Stanfa was relatively new to Philadelphia, having arrived a few years earlier from Sicily where he had been connected. He had come to Philly because he was being sponsored by a relative who lived there. Carlo Gambino, who apparently knew Stanfa's people back in the old country, had personally called Angelo and asked if we could take him in. Angelo said sure, we would be happy to, so Stanfa came, began a small home repair business, and was starting to be with our guys.

The two drove away in Stanfa's old Chevy. After making a stop to let Angelo buy a paper, they pulled up in front of Angelo's brownstone at 934 Snyder. John later told me that they sat there for a few minutes talking about Sicily when suddenly the shooter came up behind the car, stuck a double-barreled shotgun through the window, put it to the back of Angelo's head, and pulled both triggers. Some of the pellets passed through Angelo into John, but the moment he heard the shots, John was out of the car and running. He was young, and I guess he had really good reflexes. In any case, the shooter did not go after him, and John spent a day or two in the hospital and was questioned by the police.

Much was made later out of the fact that the window had been open, it being a cold March night and all. Stanfa had supposedly been in on the hit and had lowered the power window on Bruno's side with the controls on his side. This was a nice theory, but the problem with it is that Stanfa's car did not have power windows, and the window was not wide open. It was down only a few inches, but that was enough. As anyone who had ever driven with Angelo knew, he had a habit of lowering the window a few inches and then hooking his fingers over the top. I'm sure that is exactly what happened that night.

Despite the fact that Patty and I were sure Stanfa was not involved, a day or so later Patty got a call from Bananas telling him that Stanfa and Frankie Sindone, a family captain in Philly, were coming up. He told Patty to bring them to him, and they would go together into New York to meet with Paul Castellano. The Gambino boss had been close to Angelo and, we were told, was very angry about his being whacked.

That made no sense. Based on what he had been hinting at for weeks, we just assumed it was Bananas who whacked Angelo. It was natural to suspect Stanfa, because he was driving; as for Sindone, if I hadn't known what Bananas had been saying the past weeks and had to guess, Sindone would have been among the top two or three guys I would have picked to have made the hit. Logic does not always rule in the mob, and reasoning can get very cockeyed. But I picked Sindone because he was very close to Angelo and might be considered the best choice to succeed him.

The family had been badly fractured for a long time. Angelo had not spoken with his underboss, Phil Testa, for almost two years. Testa was the leader of the faction that was not happy with the way Angelo had been running the family. That obviously would make Testa suspect number one; but right behind him would be Sindone because if the Bruno faction retained control, he would likely be chosen the next boss.

Given what we knew about the hit and our assumption that Bananas had cleared it with the Commission, Patty and I could not understand why Castellano would now be leaning on Stanfa and Sindone. Even stranger was that Patty told me to be prepared to do some "work" that night. "Bananas says that if Paul does not believe these guys, they ain't going back to Philly," he told me. "We'll have to do it, so I want you to be ready by the time we get back."

The two of them drove up from Philly and met Patty and me at the 3-11. Then the four of us went over to a diner on South Street owned by a guy who was with us. (At that time the diner was still under construction and not yet open for business.) There we met Bananas, and I stayed behind while the four of them got into one of Tony's cars—with one of his guys driving—and they all headed for New York. I went back to the 3-11 and got a couple of heavy plastic tarps, the kind house painters use, and I went to Happy Bellini, a guy who was connected to us, and picked up a couple of guns. I waited for Patty to call. Several hours later they all came back laughing and carrying on like no one had a care in the world. We had a couple of drinks, and they headed back to Philly. Patty later told me that Castellano had been ready to have Stanfa and Sindone killed, but Bananas saved them by assuring Paul that neither of them had been involved. So I returned the guns to their owners and put the tarps away for another day. John Stanfa is now the boss of what is left of the Bruno-Scarfo family. I wonder if he knows how close he came to dying that March day in 1980.

As for me, I had come pretty close to spending probably the rest of my life in jail. I later found out that the Feds were following Stanfa that day because they, too, thought he was connected with the hit. They followed him up from Philly right to the door of the 3-11. They had surveillance photos of Patty and me coming out with them, and they followed us to the diner and then tailed Bananas' car into New York. The plan Patty and I had made was that, if Castellano ordered it, when Stanfa and Sindone came back to the diner, we would kill them right there, roll up their bodies in the tarps, and dump them somewhere. If we had done it—and I'm sure I would have been one of the shooters—the whole thing would have been played out almost in front of the FBI cameras.

But Stanfa and Sindone went back to Philly, and I kept wondering what was going on. I half-wanted to ask Bananas, but Patty had long ago warned me, "When one of our friends leaves us suddenly, don't talk about it, and above all don't ask questions of nobody. You can keep your ears open and take in everything that is said, but don't ask questions because you never know who you are talking to and whether he might think you're butting in where you don't belong." I remembered that and kept my lips buttoned. But keeping your nose out of things did not mean that you were prevented from speculating quietly about what was happening. Two things didn't make any sense to Patty and me. Number one, why would the Commission okay the whacking of Angelo when he had opened Atlantic City to them? He was so easy to get along with, and he never stepped on anyone's toes. The New York families would have to be crazy to want to have to deal with Bananas as boss. And number two, if they had given Bananas permission to make the hit, why call Stanfa and Sindone in and rake them over the coals? We couldn't figure it out— that is, until we saw how it all ended, and then it made perfect sense.

On the night of April 17, when I heard over the radio that the cops had found an unidentified body in the trunk of a car in New York, I knew right away it was Bananas. It was a Thursday, and I had spent the morning at the 3-11 playing gin rummy with him. In those days Bananas may well have been the richest gangster in the metropolitan area, richer than most of the big bosses. But even though he was a man worth millions, he loved playing cutthroat gin, and he reveled in winning. He loved to beat me, and although I often saw him carrying $50,000 or $100,000, he would collect every cent I lost to him—and then he loved giving it away in front of me. That morning I lost $200 to him. Then he asked me to drive him to the train because he had to go to New York. On the way to the station he explained that his no-good brother-in-law Freddy Salerno was in some kind of trouble over a jewelry booth he owned in the diamond district, and he was going into the city to meet with some guys and straighten it out. The last thing Bananas said to me as he got out of the car was "I'll call you about what time I'm coming back so you can be here. And take the $200 you owe me and give it to the barmaid back at the 3-11 from me."

Bananas always hosted a major mob dinner at the 3-11 on Thursdays. Guys would come from Philly, Atlantic City, and New York for an evening of good Italian food and drink, and sometimes we fed forty or fifty guys. It was the high point of Bananas' week, and he wouldn't miss it for the world. But he did miss it that Thursday night. We sat around waiting for him to call for his ride from the train, but he never did. When I heard on the car radio, driving home from the dinner, that a body had been discovered, shot gangland style, I just knew it was Bananas, but it would be almost two weeks before anybody knew for sure. For reasons that have never been entirely clear, the FBI identified the body almost immediately but didn't notify the family for eleven days. All we knew was that Bananas had disappeared. We were reasonably sure it was his body that had been found, but there was some possibility he had simply gone underground.

We later learned from the undertaker who was a friend of ours that as many as a half-dozen guys must have opened up on Bananas the minute he walked into that meeting. But the FBI guessed that the initial barrage had not stopped him. He was in terrific shape for a man over sixty, and he went after some of his attackers. That accounted for numerous stab wounds on the body as well as the dozens of bullet holes. Bananas had been shot so many times, his body was almost not identifiable. Then they had stuffed money in his mouth and other body cavities, the sign that the murder victim was too greedy. And to wrap things up, they shot Freddy, too, and stuffed him with money. They were sending a strong signal.

Actually, Freddy getting whacked along with Bananas was quite an irony. Even years later a lot of people thought that it was Freddy who was the shooter in the Bruno hit, and that was why he was whacked. That's nonsense. Angelo Bruno was personally whacked by Tony Bananas. Tony himself was the shooter. That's how he grew up. He loved that kind of stuff, and he wasn't about to let anyone else do something he wanted to do so badly. Besides, as he told me more than once, Tony absolutely hated his brother-in-law. The guy was always getting into scrapes that he had to bail him out of. Time and time again Bananas had to call some guy or go to New York, to get Freddy out of some jam or another. About the last thing in the world he would do was trust Freddy to whack Angelo. In fact, as we drove to the train the day he was killed, Tony was bitching about having to save Freddy once again. "I'm going to whack that son of a bitch one of these days," he told me. "I'm getting tired of him screwing up." It was ironic that in dying, Bananas got his wish. Freddy was killed, I'm sure, just because he was there. And he was there because they needed him to lure Tony.

I was scared to death the night I heard that Bananas had been whacked and for the week or so following because we still didn't know what had happened. Since Patty and I assumed Bananas had the Commission's permission to whack Angelo, then Bananas' death in New York could only have meant that one of the New York families was moving in on us and perhaps was trying to take over the entire Bruno family as well. If that was true, then Patty was a prime target. In times like this a family is supposed to stick together, but I began to get an inkling of exactly how many of the guys around us thought of themselves above all else. Basically, most of them simply disappeared. They should all have gathered around Pat, but instead they went into hiding. Patty and I armed ourselves and went into hiding, too, but only for a couple of days. Finally, Patty said the hell with it; if they want us, they're going to find us. So we went back to the club and resumed our normal schedule. Truthfully, we were not as calm as we wanted to appear, but we began to relax after Patty was ordered down to Philly about three weeks after Bananas was whacked.

This meeting of all made Bruno family members had been called by the Commission—the heads of the five New York families—so no one dared miss it. It was held in the back of a restaurant—with no little irony, Cous' Little Italy, the same South Philly joint where Angelo had eaten his last meal the night he was whacked. Everyone tried to appear calm and casual, but the tension in the air was thick. Since I was not yet made, I couldn't get into the back room for the meeting itself, but Patty told me what had happened as we drove back to Newark.

The meeting was run by Bobby Manna, the consigliere of the Genovese family. He first tried to settle everyone down by guaranteeing that none of the New York families was trying to make a move against the Bruno family. He indicated that the killing of Bananas had been a personal thing and that nothing extended to the people who had been around him. He said that the Commission approved of Phil Testa assuming the role of boss and that as far as the Commission was concerned all other matters were a closed issue. There was some grumbling among the old-timers that it was up to us and not the New York families as to who should be our boss. If it had been left up to them, they probably would have chosen Sindone. But since Testa had been underboss and this naming of him by the Commission prevented any kind of war breaking out over succession, it was grudgingly accepted.

A short time later Patty and I found out how Bananas had effectively been tricked into signing his own death warrant. He had gone to the Genoveses and told them of his problems with Angelo. The answer he got was "Take care of your problem." Bananas understood this to mean that he had a green light to kill Bruno. But after he did it, the Commission met, and Funzi Terri said he had told Bananas to work things out with Angelo. So as far as the Commission was concerned, Bananas had made an unauthorized hit on a boss, and that was an automatic death warrant. The bottom line was that the New York families knew Bananas was a danger to them and would be even more so as the boss of the Bruno family. But he was simply too powerful to hit without a reason. He had a hundred soldiers in his crew, and there would have been an ugly war. So Funzi simply let him have more than enough rope to hang himself.

Bananas' whacking of Angelo had a big impact on our family. Maybe Angelo wasn't aggressive enough for Bananas, but everyone was making money and there was peace. Now peace was something we would be without for quite some time.

Once Testa took over, he moved quickly to cement his hold. First he had Angelo's cousin, Johnny DeSimone, whacked. Then in a move that almost anyone could have predicted, he had Sindone killed. A lot of people speculated that these two guys were done in retaliation for Angelo's hit, that somehow they were involved. Again, that was exactly backward. DeSimone and Sindone were hit because they had been close to Angelo and now might pose a threat to the new leadership. Phil Testa was simply house cleaning.

He might have expanded this to other guys who had been close to Angelo, but they got him first. Just a week short of a year after Bruno was killed, Testa was also killed. He was whacked by his underboss Pete Casella. Casella had served a seventeen-year prison sentence for drug dealing. He had done his time in a stand-up fashion, not ratting on anyone, not agreeing to any of the many deals he had been offered by prosecutors. He thought this entitled him to some consideration, including being named boss instead of Testa for whom he had little good to say. He was also a friend of John McCullough, the longtime head of Local 30 of the Roofers Union. Testa had McCullough whacked when he tried to organize in Atlantic City and wouldn't take no for an answer. Casella planted a bomb on Testa's front porch and blew him up late one night as he returned home from making his rounds. The killing threw the family into turmoil, and it looked as if a war was in the offing.

Actually, when Testa was killed, Patty and I were hiding out in Florida. The New Jersey Crime Commission had gotten it into their heads to investigate Bananas' murder, so they issued a subpoena for Patty, who didn't want to talk to them or appear in front of any grand jury. So he ducked the subpoena, and we screwed to Florida where we were sitting in the sun at the Thunderbird Hotel when the call came telling us that Testa had been whacked.

Several weeks went by with not much news out of either Philly or Newark. We heard that "Harry the Hunchback" Riccobene, an old-line Bruno captain and ally, was pushing to succeed Testa. Harry, who was heavily into the drug trade, had started to talk with other family captains, drumming up support. We assumed since Testa had left no clear-cut successor that the family captains would meet to select the new boss. It looked as if the Hunchback was gathering the necessary votes.

Then suddenly the phone started ringing. Another meeting had been called in Philly by Bobby Manna. Patty considered going, but he assumed the meeting would be staked out by the Feds and by local police, and that he would be picked up if he showed his face. He considered sending me as his emissary, but since I wasn't made yet, this would not have been well received. So we sat in Florida and waited. Within minutes after the meeting we got a call with the startling news that Little Nicky, Nicky Scarfo Sr., was our new boss.

Manna had told the meeting that the Commission was extremely unhappy over the whacking of Phil Testa. Given the abrupt nature of Testa's leaving, there was no clear-cut successor. This was a bad situation, and the Commission was therefore stepping in to prevent a war. Manna told the gathering, just as he had with Testa a year before, that he was there to indicate that the Commission was "recommending" Nicky as the new family head. A lot of guys thought this was wrong. It was the second time in a row that a new boss was being named from New York, and it was starting to look as though the Bruno family was being run by the New York families. But things were so unsettled they didn't feel they could challenge Manna. And in a way he was correct: If things were left to work themselves out, there probably would have been a war between Scarfo and Casella. But they were angry because they believed that Manna had manipulated the whole thing with the Commission. He and Nicky were very tight.

In a show of good faith and out of deference to the stand-up way he had served his time, Casella was allowed to retire to Florida (where he died of natural causes). His brother Tony, also involved in whacking Testa, was allowed to retire, too. He became a virtual recluse, rarely leaving his house in South Philly. The guys who actually planned and carried out the hit, including Chickie Narducci, were told they owed their total loyalty to Nicky, or else. So it was now the era of Little Nicky, and things were never the same.

In a way Nicky Scarfo became Angelo Bruno's worst mistake. His parents were Calabrian; they had emigrated to Brooklyn, where Nicky was born. Shortly thereafter they moved to Philly, and Nicky and his two uncles, who were actually about his age, grew up in the Bruno family. All three were made while they were still in their twenties. About the kindest thing you could say about Nicky was that he was completely crazy. Maybe it was because he was so small, but he was deeply paranoid and liked to kill people, which made for a bad combination. Bananas liked to kill people, too, but at least he was rational.

Bruno learned about Nicky one day in 1963 when the then thirty-two-year-old Nicky walked into a crowded diner in Philly. All the seats at the counter were taken, so Nicky marched up to one Joseph Duggan and demanded that he give him his seat. Duggan quite naturally said no. Nicky then reportedly screamed, "Don't you know who the fuck I am?" Duggan said he couldn't care less. Nicky pushed him. Duggan threw a punch. Nicky pulled out a knife and plunged it into Duggan's heart, killing him instantly.

Bruno was enraged when he heard of the incident. You simply did not kill civilians in public for no reason other than their resisting your throwing your weight around. But since Nicky was a made member, Angelo felt he owed him some measure of help. Strings were pulled, and the case landed before a very friendly judge. Nicky's plea of self-defense was rejected out of hand, but he was allowed to plead to a lesser offense and received three years. When he got out, Angelo effectively banished him, sending him to Atlantic City, which in those days was a virtual wasteland. Angelo could have saved himself and the world a lot of grief—and a lot of guys would still be alive today—if he had simply had Nicky killed back in 1963 when it became apparent how out of control he was.

Nicky was gone and all but forgotten in his exile. He had put together a small crew aided by his nephew, "Crazy Phil" Leonetti, and the Merlino brothers, Salvatore, called "Chuckie" by everyone, and Larry, called "Yogi." These guys eked out a small living by charging protection to bar owners, running some gambling operations, loan-sharking, and labor racketeering. But then Nicky caught a break by going to jail.

At the same time the New Jersey State Commission on Investigation called Angelo to testify about his knowledge of organized crime, they also called others from various families active in Jersey, including the Genoveses, the Bonannos, and the Gambinos. Among the guys dragged before the SCI were both Nicky and Bobby Manna. Like Angelo, they also refused to talk, and they, too, were sent to jail. At various times a total of nine guys went to jail for contempt of the SCI. The assumption was that they would serve only a year or so, but the state meant business, and all of them ended up serving anywhere from three to seven years. They did their time housed at Yardville, the New Jersey state prison system's reception center in Trenton. Although nine men were eventually sentenced for contempt, only seven were in Yardville at the same time. A newspaper story of the day dubbed them the "Yardville Seven," and they have been known by that handle ever since.

All of the Yardville Seven grew very tight, and being a member of that elite group boosted Nicky's standing in the eyes of almost everyone else in the family. And because Nicky did his time in a stand-up fashion, Angelo was forced to allow him back into family affairs even while keeping him in Atlantic City. Quite probably Nicky would have abandoned Atlantic City and gone back to Philly if legalized gambling had not been on the horizon. On the day in 1977 that it was approved, Nicky emerged as a major player, not only in our family but in organized crime on the East Coast.

Nicky was quick to respond to this newfound stature. After years of keeping a Bruno-enforced low profile, he and his crew began to act the part of mob big shots right away. First they killed a local judge, Edwin Helfant, whom they had paid off to give a light sentence to one of the crew and then saw him throw the book at the guy. Then Crazy Phil Leonetti whacked a guy who owed him loan-sharking money and was refusing to pay. The cops had an eyewitness, and they put Crazy Phil on trial. But he walked when the witness suddenly had a serious and complete memory loss. Then Nicky ordered a Philly dope dealer who owed him money killed, with the hit carried out by Chuckie Merlino and Salvy Testa, Phil Testa's son.

Finally, Nicky got into a beef with a guy who was associated with the family, Vincent Falcone. It got back to Nicky that Falcone had called him crazy—actually an astute observation. Nicky went nuts. He called and invited Falcone to a Christmas party, and he sent Philip Leonetti and Yogi Merlino to pick him up. When Falcone got to an apartment in Margate, just outside Atlantic City, he found out that he was the party. Crazy Phil shot him in the head while Nicky stood there laughing and screaming at the guy. Then when it looked like Falcone was still breathing, Nicky tried to take the gun away from Philip and finish the job himself. But Philip pulled away and shot Falcone again in the chest. Philip later told me he had looked down at the guy and shouted, "If I could bring the motherfucker back to life, I'd kill him again."

People have always tended to write Little Nicky Scarfo off as a stupid thug. Sure, he was a thug, a killer utterly without conscience, but he was not dumb. I first met him one night at the 3-11 in Newark in the mid-1970s. He had come to town to meet with some union guys. He cut quite a figure, a cocky and dapper little man always dressed in a very expensive suit. You knew right away that this guy was no dummy. Nicky was quick and he was cunning, and he proved it by the way he outsmarted the New Jersey Gaming Commission.

When legalized gambling was first suggested in the state legislature, there was an immediate outcry that it would be taken over by organized crime. So the legislature went to extraordinary lengths to protect against the mob through a complex and rigid system of licensing and oversight. If the mob had tried to go into Atlantic City through the front door, it would have been met with force, and the effort would likely have failed. Nicky was smart enough to realize that it was probably fruitless to buck the system head-on, so he decided that if he couldn't go in through the front door, he could find a back door. The back door Nicky found into the Atlantic City casinos was through the labor unions.

Nicky reasoned that within a short time there would be thousands of workers in the casinos and hotels, and these workers could be quickly organized. He also reasoned that if he controlled the union that controlled these workers, he could hold the work stoppage sword over the heads of the casino owners. And as a plus, he would get access to all the health and welfare funds that would be flowing through the new union.

The key was Frank Lentino, a retired Philadelphia Teamsters Union executive who was an associate of the Bruno family and for years was involved in the systematic shakedown of contractors in Philadelphia. At seventy Lentino retired and moved to Atlantic City. There he was recruited by Nicky, and it was arranged for him to sign on as a consultant to the existing Bartenders Union, which was run by Al Daidone and closely allied to Bartenders Local 170 in Camden, which was run by Ralph Natale, a Bruno family member. Within short order the small Atlantic City local was expanded into Local 54 of the Hotel Employees and Restaurant Employees International Union, and when membership climbed from about four thousand hotel and restaurant workers in the pre-gambling days to more than thirty thousand with the arrival of the casinos, Nicky was on his way.

Nicky was not subtle. With control of the union he had the power to call hotel or casino workers out on strike. Since one night's wildcat strike could cost a casino a million or more, the owners were very anxious to avoid any labor problems. Nicky was anxious to accommodate them. But he wanted a few things in return, service contracts foremost among them. In exchange for labor peace, hotels and casinos made mob-connected companies the providers of everything from garbage hauling to supplying meats, poultry, and liquor.

Nicky also made another decision, and that was to stay out of the construction trades. With the coming hotel-building boom, it would have been a natural to try to tie up the building trades unions. But Nicky knew that the New York families were into the construction trades, so he left these for them. Obviously millions could be made from construction contracts and shakedowns, but in showing deference to the New York families in the area, he won for himself the right to be left alone with the employees union. And as Nicky told me once, "The employees union is going to be around long after all construction has been completed."

But Nicky was not left out of the building boom altogether. He owned and Phil Leonetti ran a company called Scarf, Inc., that was in the cement business. Much of the cement that was poured in the new hotel and casino construction came from Scarf. Then Nicky had a big piece of two other companies, Batshore Rebar and Nat Nat, Inc., that were in the steel and steel-reinforcement business. They were run for Nicky by the Merlino brothers, and these companies provided the structural and reinforcing steel for most of the new casino projects.

When Angelo Bruno made the decision in 1978 to allow the New York families into Atlantic City, Nicky made a big scene of being enraged. He complained to Bananas and Phil Testa. But here again Nicky showed how cunning and smart he was. He effectively played both ends toward the middle. If the New York families were going to be allowed in, they would have to come to him if they wanted into the unions. He used his old Yardville Seven connection with Bobby Manna and his Calabrian heritage to set up a working arrangement with the Genoveses and the Gambinos.

As Nicky explained to me and Patty, this move was crucial to winning over the Commission to back him for boss of our family. He told us this a few days after the Philadelphia meeting when he and Phil Leonetti went down to Florida to pay a courtesy call on Patty. He explained that the moment he heard Testa was dead, he was on his way to New York to meet with Manna. Through Manna, Nicky posed a question to the heads of the New York families: Did they want to risk a new boss of the Bruno family declaring Atlantic City a closed territory? The New Jersey Gambling Commission had gone to such lengths to try to protect against organized crime that the last thing the families needed was some kind of war over Atlantic City. The New York families would undoubtedly win, but at what price? Back me, Nicky said, and the arrangements we have been working on will continue. Manna agreed, and the Commission agreed with Manna. Little Nicky was now the man.

3

BUSTED

The Commission said its purpose in making Nicky the boss of the Bruno family was to avoid war, but a long and bloody war is exactly what Nicky gave them. Over the next couple of years twenty-seven guys died, many senselessly.

What happened initially has been called the Riccobene war. Harry "the Hunchback" Riccobene was a squat, powerfully built man who by 1981 was well into his seventies. But that appeared to be the prime of life for the Hunchback. He had a mistress in her early twenties, and he boasted she could barely keep up with him. He was still very active in the drug trade, and he was angry, very angry, that Nicky had been made don.

A year earlier, when Phil Testa had been elevated after Angelo was whacked—even if it was by the order of the Commission—it had been a natural progression. Testa was the underboss, and he was Angelo's most logical successor. But not so with Nicky. Not only was he not in line to succeed, but to the old Mustache Petes who had surrounded Angelo, his succession was almost unthinkable. And there was no one who thought this more than Harry the Hunchback.

In the weeks following his accession, except for the quick trip to Florida to see Pat, Nicky stayed in Atlantic City—for a reason. It was up to all the made guys, all the captains, to make the trip to

Atlantic City to pledge their loyalty to the new don. All the young guys in the family went to pay homage. The guys from our area made the trip, but very conspicuous by his absence was Harry Riccobene, his brothers, and the guys around him. As far as Nicky was concerned, that could mean only one thing: They were now his enemies, and that meant war. To Nicky it was simply kill or be killed. As he saw it, he had to get Harry and his guys before they got him.

It was at this point that I got my first orders to whack someone. Just before the Christmas holidays in 1981, Nicky ordered most of the made guys he trusted to a big meeting in Atlantic City. I drove Patty and a couple of the other guys down and dropped them off on a corner. I was told to pick them up there in three hours. I went and played cards, and three hours later they were standing at the corner. On the way back to Newark, Patty told me I had some work to do.

"Nicky wants Chickie Narducci done, and it's going to be our job to do it. It will happen sometime in the next month. I'll need you to get ready."

Frank "Chickie" Narducci was one of the old-line family captains who had been around Angelo Bruno. He had been in charge of all the family's gambling operations under Angelo, and now Nicky figured he was going to throw in with Harry Riccobene; this meant he had to be taken care of. As Patty explained, Nicky figured that Chickie would be on his guard, so the easiest way of doing him was for Pat to invite him up to Newark for a holiday or post-holiday gathering. Chickie would not be expecting any trouble in our neck of the woods.

"This thing has to be done, George. It's business," Patty said, "and I want you to be the shooter so you'll have this behind you." What he meant was that eventually I was going to have to kill someone "to make my bones" before I could become a fully made member of the family. This would be my opportunity to get it over with.

I received the news without thinking much about it. I wasn't excited about whacking someone, but if Patty said it was business and that it had to be done, then I would take his word for it. When the time came, I had no doubt that I could pull the trigger.

Patty told me that Nicky had spent some time talking about his plans for the family, about how he was going to expand it. One thing he wanted to do soon was straighten some new guys out, both in Philly and in Newark. "He likes you, George," Patty said. "We talked about you tonight. He knows you'll be doing this thing. When the time comes, he'll remember."

In the end I didn't have to pull the trigger on Chickie. Nicky changed his mind. He figured that Chickie might get suspicious if an invite from Pat came out of the blue. So Nicky gave the contract to Salvy Testa, Phil Testa's trigger-happy son. Salvy hit Chickie on a Philadelphia street as he was getting out of his car on January 7, 1982.

For Nicky the big problem was still Harry Riccobene. Killing him was not going to be an easy matter. Not only did Harry have about twenty-five guys around him, but he was in the drug business with the Pagan motorcycle gang. But Nicky was determined. He gave the contract to his consigliere Frank Monte who brought in Long John Martorano. The two of them figured the best way to get to Harry was through his younger half-brother Mario, who they believed had long chafed at living in Harry's shadow. But Mario refused to turn on his brother. Instead, he went to Harry and told him about the plot. Harry's response could have been expected: He decided to kill Monte and Long John before they could kill him.

He succeeded with Monte. His guys shot Monte to death on the night of May 13, 1982. I was in Atlantic City that night, and I can personally attest that Nicky went nuts when he heard about it, not only because his guy had gotten whacked but also because the police immediately gave out a statement that they thought Monte had been killed by Nicky because he had been holding out. That was not true. He had been killed by Riccobene, who was angered that Monte, as consigliere, had not stayed neutral in a family fight and had sided with Nicky.

Nicky became obsessed with killing Harry. He tried to get some of the Pagan motorcycle gang to do it in exchange for taking over completely the drug business they shared with Harry. But for reasons that Nicky could not figure out—to him, loyalty could not have been a reason where business was concerned—it never happened. So he kept upping the ante until finally one night Salvy Testa and Wayne Grande came upon Harry sitting in a phone booth.

Grande ran up to the booth and just started shooting. He hit the Hunchback five times. This apparently annoyed Harry quite a bit because he came charging out of the booth and was all over Grande. Finally, Harry passed out, and Grande and Salvy took off. Harry went to the hospital but was there for only a short time before checking himself out so he could recover at home.

Harry's first try at revenge came a few weeks later. His guys caught Salvy Testa in the open. Salvy was hit by a shotgun blast but took most of it in the arm. He escaped with only a minor injury. Then Nicky had another chance a few weeks later. This time his guys caught Harry sitting in a car. They shot up the car real bad but missed Harry. This war was starting to look like a contest between two gangs that couldn't shoot straight.

The war came to a screeching halt for a time while both Harry and his half-brother Mario went off to jail to serve gambling sentences, and Nicky went to federal prison in Texas on a nickel-and-dime illegal weapons charge. But in a matter of a few weeks after Nicky's release, his guys killed two guys around Harry, including his brother Robert, and wounded a third. Both murders were particularly vicious, and both were committed in front of the victims' mothers.

The war finally ended when the Philadelphia police got two of Harry's shooters to flip, and then flipped Mario who was still in prison on the gambling beef. They testified against Harry in the Monte killing, and the Hunchback was given a life sentence. Mario also testified against Long John Martorano and Al Daidone at their trial for the murder of union boss John McCullough. They, too, were convicted.

Harry the Hunchback's life term ended the Riccobene war but not the killing. By now, early 1984, Nicky was back from his jail time in Texas, and he was angry. He perceived that his hold on power was not as strong as it had been before he left. And much of his anger began to focus on Salvy Testa.

What happened with Salvy typified Nicky's ruthlessness. To begin with, Salvy was Nicky's godson. Then, too, he was Nicky's chief hit man. Salvy ran a group of guys who became Nicky's hitters. The police and the media, and even us, began to call them the "Young Executioners." It was a badge that Salvy wore with great pride, and he would have killed just about anyone Nicky asked him to without giving it a second thought.

But Salvy also did other killings. He tracked down and killed everyone who had been in on the whacking of his father. A year to the day after his father's death, Salvy got hold of Rocco Marinucci, who had planted the bomb, and tortured and killed him. In so doing Salvy won a great deal of respect around South Philly. By the time Nicky returned from prison, it was Salvy who was running the organization in Philly, not Chuckie Merlino, Nicky's underboss, whom Salvy used to dismiss as a "dumb drunk" even though at the time he was planning to marry Chuckie's daughter Maria in the mob wedding of the decade. Salvy was starting to make big money, and even though he was passing Nicky his share, with the money came power. More than that, with big money came an increasing number of guys around Salvy whose loyalty was to him and not to Nicky. They were becoming a family within the family, much as Bananas' crew had been. Bananas' power is what had killed Angelo Bruno, and Nicky was not about to let it kill him.

The straw that broke the camel's back, so to speak, was that Salvy jilted Maria Merlino on the eve of their wedding. That enraged Chuckie, and he went to Nicky who was only too glad to hear that Chuckie now wanted revenge. It was settled in Nicky's mind. Despite the fact that Salvy was his godson and despite the fact that it was Salvy's gun that had helped propel Nicky to power, he was a dead man.

Nicky gave the contract to kill Salvy to Tommy DelGiorno, a bookmaker and numbers boss who had become a big earner for the family in Philly. Tommy Del had really come into his own when Nicky took over the family. Nicky had straightened him out after he had killed Johnny Calabrese, a drug dealer and gambler who had been refusing to pay tribute to Nicky. Tommy Del had prospered to the point that he bought two South Philly restaurants, including Cous' Little Italy, the place where Angelo ate his last meal and where the family met to hear Bobby Manna put first Phil Testa and then Nicky into the boss's chair.

Tommy Del was a friend of mine because, like me, his whole life had been in bookmaking and numbers. I used to see him all the time in Atlantic City when I went down to play blackjack or to bring Nicky money from Patty, and Tommy Del often bought me dinner in Philadelphia. Tommy had a problem that he talked about a lot. You can't kill someone you can't find, and Salvy was lying very low. Just about everyone in the family knew that Salvy was a target. Salvy knew it, too, but incorrectly thought it was Chuckie who wanted him whacked because of Maria. So while Salvy was playing it very close to the vest, he was ducking Chuckie and guys around him, not guys around Nicky, who he still thought was his friend.

After several murder attempts failed to come off because Salvy would not show for a meeting or a dinner, Tommy decided that he had to get somebody around Salvy to set him up. He brought the idea to Nicky who told him to get Joey Pungitore, one of Salvy's closest friends. Tommy made Joey Punge an offer he couldn't refuse:

help set up Salvy or die yourself. But even with Joey helping, it was still several months before they could lure Salvy in front of a gun. On September 7, 1984, Salvy went with Joey Punge to a candy store on the belief that as capo he was being asked to settle a numbers territorial dispute between Joey Punge and Wayne Grande. As soon as Salvy walked in, Grande shot him twice in the back of the head. All three of his killers were members of his own crew.

At about the time of the shooting, Ann and I were arriving in Atlantic City, me for a weekend of blackjack and seeing some of the guys, Ann to get a little late summer sun. I heard the news almost at once and was surprised by my reaction. I really didn't know Salvy all that well, and he was not the kind of guy you wanted to turn your back on even if you knew him pretty well. But I was saddened by the news, more than a little revolted, and a little scared. If Nicky would kill his own godson, who was loyal to him to a fault, where would this killing ever stop? I also noted that Atlantic City was very quiet that night. Most of the guys around Nicky had disappeared. The next day I found out they had all gone to Philly for a victory party thrown by Tommy Del for the shooters and for Nicky at LaCucina. He did not use either of his own two places because he thought the cops would be watching.

I saw Nicky briefly the next day when he got back. It seemed as if he couldn't stop smiling. Philip Leonetti told me, "George, it was a bad thing, but it had to be taken care of. Salvy would have become a major problem."

My only thought was that I hoped Nicky didn't see me or Patty as a problem.

Thankfully, he didn't. Despite all the bad stuff that started to happen in Philly and Atlantic City with the arrival of Nicky as boss, things were pretty good for us in northern Jersey. Nicky and his Atlantic City crew were really only interested in what was going on there and in Philly. They were involved in what they saw as a growing power struggle, and they had little time to worry about us. As long as Nicky got his cut from Newark, he was just as happy to leave us alone.

There was one problem, however, and that was the reason Nicky had gone to Florida to see Pat immediately after he was installed as the new boss. With Bananas gone, there was no question that Pat should become the Bruno family captain in northern Jersey, probably with the same title of consigliere that Bananas had held. But Nicky had some bad news for Patty. As part of the deal he had struck with Bobby Manna, Nicky had to elevate Ralph "Blackie" Napoli to captain. Blackie had been another of the Yardville Seven and had grown very close to Manna in the joint. He had been over sixty when he went to jail, and now he was in his seventies. In a way he was kind of an elder statesman, and he acted senile half the time. But he was also mean, very mean, and he was bitter because he thought he should have gotten more, much earlier. In the mob, mean and bitter is not a good combination. But Nicky said it was something we were all going to have to live with and that Patty should not worry.

Actually, it was not Patty who was worried. Given his stature, there was really not much Blackie could do to him or about him. The guy who was really in Blackie's cross hairs was Scoops Licata. To put it simply, Blackie absolutely hated Scoops. Maybe he didn't much like me and maybe it would not be too strong to say that he hated Patty, but Blackie's dislike for Scoops ran much, much deeper.

At this time Scoops was not even a made guy, and Blackie, as a captain, held absolute power over him. He utilized it constantly and made Scoops's life miserable. He abused him physically, mentally, and financially. Blackie hated Scoops because he had been around Bananas and had grown rich around Bananas. Blackie had spent much of the 1970s in jail for refusing to talk to the crime commission. He believed if he had been out, he was the one who would have gotten rich. In a way he thought that Bananas had made what should have been his, and so had Scoops.

Bananas had kept Scoops very close to him so that he had a way to stay close to Scoop's wife, Jackie. But Scoops was also smart, and he was especially smart with money, so Bananas had taken advantage of that. He had not only put Scoops into the monte game but had also put him in charge of the considerable shylocking money that he always had out on the street. Scoops did very well while Bananas was alive. He had a big house, new cars, and expensive clothes, and Jackie had her furs and jewels to keep her happy. But we all believed that Scoops did even better, much better, when Bananas died.

Tony Bananas had been a very closed-mouth type of guy. No one really knew everything he was into. No one knew for sure except Scoops how much shy money he had out at any one time—it might have totaled a million or two million or three million—or who his borrowers were. It was in $5,000 and $10,000 amounts to local guys, and it was in six-figure amounts to guys in the garment district in New York and to the drug dealers who played in the monte game. With Bananas gone, this money now belonged to the family, and it was Scoops who controlled these millions and had the only real knowledge where they were.

We all assumed that when Scoops made an accounting to the family, he had held back. Rumors were that he had given them an undercount of as much as a million dollars and had taken this money and simply dropped it into a hole somewhere. He denied this, denied it loudly and everywhere, but no one believed him, least of all Blackie. The thought that Scoops was holding out threw Blackie into —pardon the expression—a black rage.

While Bananas was alive, Scoops had little time for Patty, but now he started hanging around him day and night in the hope that Pat could protect him from Blackie. It got to the point where Scoops was sure it was only a matter of time before Blackie would have him whacked. He begged Pat for help, and Patty finally agreed.

Patty was already starting to become ill, and he really didn't want to move around very much. So he told me to go down to Atlantic City to see Philip Leonetti. I was to pass the word through Philip to Nicky that the situation between Blackie and Scoops had worsened and that Pat would consider it a favor if Nicky would intervene and get Blackie away from Scoops's throat.

I was playing blackjack at Resorts while I waited for Philip and our meeting. I looked up and saw Philip and Nicky approaching. This put me in kind of a bind. I was not a made guy, and under mob protocol I could talk with Philip because it had been arranged by Patty, but I could not just go up to a boss like Nicky. To my surprise he waved me over, slapped me on the back, and said he had come along to hear what it was that Patty wanted.

That was the way it was between Nicky and me. He liked Patty, and he knew I was the closest guy to him. So he always accepted me as if I were already a made guy.

Nicky listened as I explained what Blackie was doing to Scoops. He just kind of shook his head. "Yeah, I know, the guy's both stupid and a prick," he said. "But you know I can't really do nothing yet."

Nicky said his hands were tied because Blackie had Bobby Manna's backing. "I can't do nothing about Blackie now," he told me, "but he's old and he's stupid, and eventually he'll do himself in. We just have to be patient. But tell Pat I will talk to him about Scoops. I'll tell him to lay off."

. . .

Despite the fact that Blackie hated Patty and didn't like me much either, things went well for us. Starting in 1980 I went on what amounted to a two-year winning streak. I was still working at the monte game. In the late 1970s we had moved it from the Bronx down to Mulberry Street in Little Italy, and we were running it in partnership with the Gambinos. Our partners were a couple of captains from John Gotti's crew. The game was bigger than ever. Not only did the drug dealers from uptown come down to play, but we added a whole new cast of players including businessmen, some rich artists and gallery types, and a lot of wiseguys from various crews. We were making money hand over fist, but it got split up so many ways, between so many crews and guys, that relatively little ended up in my pocket.

My earnings came mostly from my bookmaking operation. I was only twenty-seven years old, but putting false modesty aside, I was running one of the largest and most profitable bookmaking operations in northern Jersey. My partner was Don Hingos, a guy I had first connected with shortly after leaving Pee Wee DiPhillips in the early 1970s.

Patty's and my relationship with Don was complicated. Don was a former cop, a huge man about six foot four and three hundred pounds. He had left the force and now owned a sandblasting and cleaning company that cleaned truck trailers. He wanted to get contracts with some of the big shipping companies at Port Newark to clean their trailers before and after they came off container ships. To do that he had to come to terms with the Genovese family. But Patty and I couldn't simply go to the Genoveses on something like this because if it looked like a good thing, they would simply take it for themselves. So we had to put it in terms of them doing us a favor, but they really didn't owe us a favor. We knew they owed several favors to John Riggi, the boss of the DeCavalcante family, so Patty and I went to John, who in turn went to Michael Coppola, who ran the Port for the Genoveses. Don got his contracts, and he paid us $1,200 a month, of which Pat passed along half to John. That's how business was done.

Don was also a big-time bettor. But rather than simply losing to some book, he thought it would be better if he was a book himself. So he and I became partners. The big problem was that Don tended to lose money as fast as we made it.

During football season we averaged about $300,000 a week in bets. If we had played it safe, we could have made between $15,000 and $20,000 a week on the vigorish alone, the premium that gamblers pay just to bet. It works like this: Say you have a football game, and one player bets $5 on one team and another bets $5 on the other. In this situation the bookie would use one player's money to pay off the other no matter which team won. But to win $5, a gambler must risk $6. Bets are made over the phone on credit. When it comes time to pay off the winner and collect from the loser, the bookie pays $5 to the winner while collecting $6 from the loser. The extra dollar from the losing bettor is the bookie's commission. Thus, the ideal is to have even bets on both sides so you have none of your own money at risk, and you pocket the vig.

It didn't exactly work that way with us. Don was a good guy and really knew the bookmaking business, but he was also a degenerate gambler. He just loved to bet against the guys who were playing with us. Say we had a Miami-versus-Jets game on the boards. By Sunday we might have $100,000 bet on Miami and $50,000 bet on the Jets. If Miami covers the point spread or the Jets don't, we could be out $50,000. The logical thing to do in that case is to lay off at least $30,000 to $40,000 of the Miami money with other books or in Vegas. But not Don. Often without my knowing it, he would carry such a bet into the kickoff because he was sure he knew better and that the Jets would cover. At one point in the 1980 season, I remember we were down $1.5 million. That in itself didn't worry me because we could make that up within a couple of weeks. The problem came in finding the cash to pay off the players and the interest it cost us to come up with that kind of cash.

But even with Don losing us tens of thousands of dollars, the book was still highly profitable. Don and I were both associates of the Bruno-Scarfo family, and as such we were working under Patty. It was in effect a three-way partnership. Every week the three of us took maybe $1,000 out of the operation for walking-around money. At Christmastime we took another $15,000—$5,000 each—for holiday spending, and then we spread another $20,000 or so around in joint Christmas gifts to associates in the mob and sent packages down to Philadelphia and Atlantic City. Our big payday came the week after the Super Bowl when we balanced out the accounts at the end of the football season. At that point we would split another $150,000 or so, and we would take our families down to Florida for a little vacation and to see if we could work a scam or two in the sun.

. . .

One time Patty and I almost killed for Don Hingos. One night Don went to dinner with Patty's son-in-law Joe Reggio and one of Patty's girlfriends, Santina Spagnola, at the Stone Crab in Bloomfield. Also at the restaurant that night was Michael Taccetta, one of the Lucchese family captains in northern Jersey. It seems that Don, who had quite a temper, had slapped around one of Michael Perna's nephews. Perna was a made Lucchese member, and the family had been looking for Don in order to settle things. When Taccetta saw Don, he put in a call, and a Lucchese goon squad responded. Don was sitting in the bar drinking while Joe and Santina were in the dining room in back having dinner. The goons jumped Don right in the bar, and there was a bloody battle. Don was outnumbered four or five to one, and given his size, it went on for quite a while. The Luccheses finally overwhelmed him and gave him an awful beating.

Joe called Patty from the hospital, and when he found out what happened, he went nuts. Don worked for him, so Patty considered an attack on Don an attack on all of us. Joe said he recognized the guy leading the goon squad, James Fede, a guy from the neighborhood. Patty said this could not be allowed to happen. "Get a couple of guns, Georgie," he told me.

Patty and I sat in my car outside Fede's house the rest of the night. Had he come home, he would have died before he got to the top of the stairs. But either he was too smart or he had been warned. He didn't come home. The next morning Perna called Patty, all apologetic. He said he was sorry that the beating had been done in front of Joe and the girl, and he told Patty that it had been done because Don had slapped around his nephew—a fact Patty had not known. Finally, the whole thing blew over. Perna made sure it was over from the Lucchese side, and Patty made sure Don did not try to retaliate. But if Fede had decided to sleep in his own bed that night, I would have killed him.

It was also during this period that I discovered exactly how well my old gym teacher Greg Notti had taught me to play blackjack and count cards. I started to hit Atlantic City in a big way, spending three or four nights a week there, never playing in the same casino two nights in a row so people wouldn't notice me. I would play for only a couple of hours, betting between $200 and $800 a hand. Some nights I won big, other nights I lost some. But week in and week out I pulled about $5,000 from the tables. I guess that in a ten-year period I won about half a million playing blackjack in Atlantic City, and I got to be a big deal guy in the casinos. They were all trying to woo me to gamble with them. They would give me free suites, free food, and whatever. They knew I was connected, and this got me even more respect. Here I was, not yet thirty, with these casino guys rolling out the red carpet for me. And on top of that I was beating them bad while I was staying in their free suites and eating their free food. It was a heady experience.

And of course the book and the tables were not my only sources of income. I still had my no-show job on the docks, and I was involved in a number of other hustles including stolen credit cards. I was making big money for myself and for Patty, and I thought it would never end. When you couple that with the thousand or so I was taking out of the book and the five grand or so in weekly blackjack winnings—tax free—it was a pretty nice living, even with half or more going to Patty and the organization.

I actually needed the money. With the birth of my daughter, my family was growing. Then, too, I was still supporting my mother and my younger brother, and helping out my older brother when he needed anything. I was probably making more money than ninety-nine percent of guys my age anywhere, and I was really happy I could provide for everyone I had to provide for. I thought I was going to be on easy street forever. But easy street, I soon discovered, is a dead end.

The biggest drawback about running a bookmaking operation is that you are always at the mercy of the players. You depend on them to bet, you depend on them to lose, and then, most important, you depend on them to lose graciously.

In the movies when a bookie is owed money, he sends the leg breakers out to collect. This does happen occasionally in the real world, especially when a bookie thinks a player is trying to cheat him. But if a guy doesn't have the money, beating on him isn't going to get it for you. And if you lean too hard on a player, he will seek to get out from under by turning you in to the cops. That is always the ultimate danger. So when you're running a book, you try to insulate yourself from the players. You have someone else write the bet and collect and pay off. You hope that if anyone gets turned in, it will be him and he won't roll over on you. But keeping the players at arm's length is not always possible. Some of them bet with you and only you because they trust you. You don't want to discourage someone who is losing thousands of dollars a week to you. You are both in an illegal relationship, so if he trusts you, you have to trust him. That trust often doesn't hold up.

On Sunday, December 12, 1982, I was arrested for the first time. It was just a combination of bad luck, bad timing, a couple of screaming kids, and a business partner who was too lazy to walk to the corner and use a pay phone to make a call.

I had frequently told Don to never, never make a business call from his house. But it turned out that in early November the state police had gotten onto a guy named George Ziggler, who was handling bets for Don. They bugged Ziggler and from his calls got to Don. They then established a wiretap on Don's home phone. On Thanksgiving Day it was cold and raining. Don was dying to find out how one of our big bettors—Harry Serio, a union guy who got whacked a few years later—had done on the Detroit game. Harry was the kind of bettor who always seemed to lose. But that year he was killing us, and it was making Don crazy. He had to know if Harry's lucky streak had broken, but he didn't want to know badly enough to get wet in the rain. So he called me from his house, and now the state police had me—or, more properly, they had the phone I was using.

At the time I was writing bets out of an apartment in Newark rented in the name of a girlfriend of a guy who was around Patty. Karen really didn't know what was going on. All she knew was that I had a phone installed in her apartment, that about twelve weeks a year she had to clear out for a few hours on Saturdays and Sundays, and that in exchange for her forced absences she was getting free rent. Sometimes I went to the apartment and did my work. Other times, when I was lazy or had some other obligation, I had Karen call-forward the phone calls to where I was.

That's how I started that particular Sunday. Ann and I and the children were going over to my in-laws for a big Italian midday meal, and I had Karen call-forward the calls to my in-laws' number. That was the phone the state police had got from bugging Don's house. Had things gone the way they should have, the worst thing that might have happened that day was the state police bursting into an empty apartment, or an apartment containing a very frightened young girl, and they would have found absolutely nothing. I expect that Karen would have immediately led them to me, but so what? They most likely would not have had enough evidence to prosecute.

I had taken my bets for the one o'clock games, and then we ate. The kids were just too noisy, so I decided to drive over to the apartment to find some quiet to take bets on the four o'clock games. As I was walking up the stairs, three or four guys with guns suddenly jumped out of the bushes and rushed me. One jammed a gun into the back of my head and started screaming in my ear that they were state police. To tell the truth, they scared the shit out of me. Years later I ran into the guy who was jamming the gun into my neck that Sunday afternoon, and he couldn't apologize enough for the way he had acted. But he and the others were actually part of an anti-drug team that spent its days taking down violent drug dealers. They really didn't understand the difference between a drug dealer and a bookie. But they had me shaking in my boots for a few minutes.

We went up to the apartment, and Karen was there. They started to search and found nothing. I had a piece of paper in my hand with the one o'clock bets I had taken. But it was in code, and that was probably not enough to prosecute me. What the cops needed was a live bettor making a bet. While they were searching the apartment, the phone kept ringing; but since it was still set on call-forwarding, it rang only once, and before anyone could pick it up, the call was gone. Finally, one of the cops got wise and told me to take the phone off call-forwarding. It was about 4:05 P.M. by now, and I figured that everyone who wanted to bet the four o'clock games had called. So I thought I was safe. I had not banked on Steve Rizzo.

If I could nominate someone for the dumbest human on earth, it would be Steve Rizzo, a guy I talked with several times a week over a two-year period. I knew his voice instantly and assumed he knew mine. I had talked with him twice already that day, early in the morning and again when he bet the one o'clock games. So I took the phone off call-forwarding and it rang instantly. One of the cops picked it up, said hello, and the person on the other end—who I later learned was Rizzo—quickly hung up. But a few seconds later the phone rang again, and again the cop picked it up and said hello. I could only hear one side of the conversation, of course, but it was obvious what was going on. The cop said hello, and Steve did not recognize the voice and said something. The cop said, "I've got this damn cold." Well, wait a minute. Did Steve stop to consider how George had developed this terrible cold in three hours? Of course not. He just plunged ahead and bet three of the four o'clock games for a "dime"—a thousand dollars each. The cop hung up in triumph. He had me. But he showed he didn't know much about gambling when he announced that some guy named Steve had just bet a hundred dollars a game. Then, adding insult to injury, he wouldn't tell me what games Steve had bet, so I would never know if I beat him for three grand or not. The least the cop could have done was let me salvage something for the weekend.

This arrest was no big deal; it was just part of doing business. I was a first-time loser, so I was not too worried. First-time bookies almost always got probation. The state cops took me to the South Orange lockup, I used my phone call to speak to Patty, and he came straight down and bailed me out. I went home to total my wins and losses for the day. Except for not knowing about Steve Rizzo, I ended up doing pretty good.

The problem was that I didn't stay a first-time loser very long. A month later to the day, on January 12, 1983, Ann and a friend were out shopping when her parents and her sister dropped by our house to bring a present they had bought for one of the kids—a parakeet. They let themselves in with a key, and what they found was a houseful of Essex County cops ransacking the place. My poor in-laws were terrified. They had guns placed to their heads and were searched by the cops and held until they were convinced as to who they were. They were then released, and my sister-in-law headed straight to a pay phone to beep me. Thus warned, I went into hiding. Ann's sister could not get hold of her, so Ann and her friend arrived home late in the day with the kids to find the place in a shambles. The cops were gone, but the house looked as if a bomb had hit it. I was finally able to reach Ann, and she dropped the kids off at her parents' and then joined me. We hid out for a few days, but I realized that was not going to do me any good. On Monday I called my lawyer, and he arranged for me to give myself up.

The funny thing about this was that we had known something was going to happen. One of Ann's friends who worked in the Essex County prosecutor's office heard that a raid was going to take place, but she could never find out who or where. Now it was obvious that the who was me and the where was our house. I later learned that one of my players who owed me a bundle had decided it was easier to go to the police than pay up, so he rolled over on me, and the cops had torn up my house looking for evidence.

In those days a lot of guys kept their records on rice paper because it was highly flammable. If the cops came through the door, you could just light a match and the evidence was gone. But since I was a smoker and was afraid I would accidentally burn up my only copy of who owed me money, I kept my records on a special water-soluble paper and always kept a bucket of water handy. I figured if the cops came, I could just dump the list in the bucket, and there would be no more evidence. The cops had spent hours tearing up the house, and in the end they found the players list I had hidden between the cracks of the basement steps. These cops had not been very neat, but they certainly had been thorough. Weeks later when my lawyer and I were reviewing the evidence, a cop was standing by to make sure that neither of us tried to light up. They thought the paper was incendiary. I said I felt faint and asked if I could have a glass of water. I wish I could say it worked. It didn't.

I was still not really worried. Yes, I had been arrested twice in a month's time, but it was all the same case. The state police arrest had technically been in Union County, New Jersey, and now the Essex County police were arresting me. So I hired Tony Rinaldo, a lawyer who had great political connections in Essex County. He told me not to worry, that the two cases would be combined into one. Patty also told me not to worry, that we had moves in Essex County. I listened to them, didn't worry, and went about my business. But since my business was bookmaking, that turned out to be a mistake.

With our problems in Jersey, Don and I decided to move our wire room to New York City for the basketball season. On March 12, 1983, I was with Alan Pincus, who ran our New York wire room for us, at an office we rented in Manhattan. Suddenly Alan received a strange call, and he thought it best if we vacated the premises. We put the phone on call-forwarding to his apartment in Queens and went up there.

We had been there about forty-five minutes when we heard several pairs of feet coming up the stairs. Alan knew immediately what it was. "We're about to be raided" was all he said. There was a knock on the door, and in came several members of the NYPD. They couldn't have been nicer. They told us the raid had been requested by the Monmouth County (New Jersey) police. I later learned that one of Don's players, a low-level drug dealer, had been pinched. The cops asked what he could give them in exchange for a free pass. He gave them his supplier, and when that was apparently not enough, he offered them "the biggest bookies in Jersey." They got a wiretap on Don, and from that wiretap they learned the phone number in New York. They called the New York cops, who went to the location in Manhattan where the phone was registered. They saw us leave and tailed us.

It was obvious that a bookmaking bust was very low on these guys' priority list. They told us they wanted no trouble. If we had any guns, they said, throw them out the window. We didn't. If we had any money we didn't want introduced into evidence, give it to Alan's wife and tell her to take a walk. We did. So we went down to the precinct, were booked, made bail, and a couple of weeks later I pleaded guilty to a misdemeanor bookmaking charge in Queens County (New York) Court and was fined $1,000. No big deal. Case closed, I thought. Boy, was I wrong.

About two months later, in May 1983, I was indicted by prosecutors in Monmouth County on the basis that some of the bets that went into the New York City wire room had been placed from Monmouth County. I was surprised by this indictment. I assumed that my guilty plea in New York had taken care of this case. I called Tony Rinaldo, and he assured me there was no problem. He immediately filed a motion in Monmouth County asking that the indictment be thrown out on double jeopardy grounds. I figured I had a good shot at winning this motion when New York State refused to extradite Alan, who had been indicted with me, because of double jeopardy.

I started to get a little nervous when Rinaldo told me that the motion had been rejected. It was only later that I found out what happened. It was never heard on its merits; it was treated as withdrawn after good old Tony did not appear to argue it.

Later, when I was in jail, I had some jailhouse lawyers file a writ of habeas corpus for me, seeking to reverse my conviction on the grounds that I had not had adequate legal representation. Federal appeals courts get hundreds of such writs every month, and almost all are rejected in a single paragraph with no explanation. In my case the Third U.S. Circuit Court of Appeals went on for seven pages, giving serious consideration to my contention that I had not had proper representation and that the double jeopardy motion should have been granted. But the court said I had undermined my position by retaining Rinaldo after the trial. Had I not used him to file an appeal with the State of New Jersey, then the federal appeals court might have reversed my conviction on constitutional grounds and granted me a new trial.

At the time I knew none of this. All I knew was that my double jeopardy motion had been "rejected." And while that alarmed me, I was still not overly worried because things were going so well in Essex County on my other two arrests. True to his word, Patty had the moves in Essex County. We were told that if we gave $3,000 to the right person at the right time, the judge would do right by me. So we passed the money along, and on the prescribed day, I appeared before the judge and pleaded guilty to both charges.

The judge came through. He sentenced me to 364 days in the Essex County jail plus a fine of $1,000. Then he ordered that I not spend any time at all behind bars. Instead, my entire sentence was to be spent in a work-release program. That meant all I had to do was find a job that would pass muster with the county probation office, and I could do that with any of a dozen no-show jobs at the Port of Newark. Basically, the judge was releasing me with a $1,000 fine.

I was elated. Despite the fact that I still had to show up for trial in Monmouth County, I now believed that I could beat this rap. I became sure of it when I learned that we had worked out what amounted to a plea agreement with the Monmouth prosecutor.

What with motions and pre-trial this and pre-trial that, the Monmouth County trial did not begin until October 10, 1984, before Judge Alvin Milberg. A week earlier I had started to serve my Essex County time behind bars and not on work release because with the Monmouth County case still pending, I was not eligible for the work-release program. I could have delayed the start of my Essex County time, but I wanted to begin serving it so any time I picked up in Monmouth would be concurrent, and I could serve it in the very friendly Essex County jail where we had all kinds of moves. I entered Judge Milberg's courtroom fully expecting to be back in the Essex jail for dinner and then into the work-release program and back on the street in a matter of days.

Everything got off to a lousy start. My case was to be called at 9:00 A.M. Tony Rinaldo didn't show up. He got his calendar confused and arrived at one o'clock in the afternoon. The judge was clearly steamed. I stood up, and the judge read the charges against me and asked how I pled. I said guilty. He asked if I knew that meant he could send me to jail, and I looked over at Tony, who nodded. I said, "Yes, Your Honor." The judge then looked at me with cold, cold eyes and asked if I realized that he was not bound by any agreement I might have made with the prosecutor. That should have set off all sorts of alarm bells in my head, but I again looked at Tony, and again he nodded. So once again I said, "Yes, Your Honor."

I was getting awfully uncomfortable until the prosecutor stood up and said, "Your Honor, you should know that Mr. Fresolone has been sentenced and has started to serve 364 days in Essex County for these activities. Monmouth County does not believe that he need serve any additional time. We ask that he be sentenced to the same term, to run concurrently. What the state wants, Your Honor, is that Mr. Fresolone be taught a lesson. We ask that he be fined the maximum ten thousand dollars for this offense."

Okay, I thought, that was the deal. Monmouth would give me a concurrent sentence with Essex, which meant since I was going into work release in Essex, I would not have to serve any jail time in either place. But I would have to pay ten grand. That's all right, I thought. It was simply a cost of doing business. I would make it up in one weekend.

Then Tony got up and launched into a Clarence Darrow defense of me, not only arguing that I should do no time but that I shouldn't even have to pay the fine. I could see that the judge was getting even more steamed. To this day I do not know for sure whether he ended up throwing the book at me for what Tony went on and on about or whether he would have done so anyway if Tony had not said a word. But in any event, when it came time for Milberg to have his say, he jumped in with both feet.

To him I was the scum of the earth. As he saw it, given my state arrest and my Essex County arrest, I was now a three-time loser. The only place for me, he said, was behind bars and away from society. My sentence: the maximum four years, meaning I had to serve at least half. The prosecutor's mouth dropped open. Tony began to stammer. Don't worry, he said, we would appeal. He would get me released right away on bond while that happened. It would be all right, he assured me. But I really heard none of that. All I knew was that I was going to jail for two years.

Given the three convictions I now had on my record, things got a little complicated. I could appeal my sentence in Monmouth, but even if I was out on bond, there would be a detainer on me, which meant I was no longer qualified for work release in Essex. So I now had to serve my minimum time on the Essex charges in jail. They took me from the courthouse directly to the Essex County jail.

While I was in Essex County I got some great news. One morning Turk Cifelli called and told me to wish my friend Pat "a happy birthday." I knew it wasn't Patty's birthday, so I guessed what Turk

meant. It was confirmed later in the day when the two of them came
to visit. Blackie Napoli had finally screwed up one time too many. It
seemed that as the family's captain in northern Jersey, Nicky was
using Blackie to take important messages to representatives of other
families in New York. To Nicky this showed a sign of respect, sending a captain on such missions. But Blackie thought such duty be-
neath him, so instead of going himself, he sent somebody else, and if
that wasn't bad enough, he often sent his driver Caesar, who was
not even straightened out. Here Nicky thought he was showing respect to the guys in New York by sending a captain to deliver messages, and Blackie was turning it into an insult by sending an
unmade guy.

Several people warned Blackie not to do that. Patty tried to talk
with him. But Blackie was not big on listening to anyone. Finally,
Nicky found out, and he was furious. Given Nicky's track record,
Blackie was very lucky he didn't get himself whacked. But he was
really too old to be killed, and he was still too close to Bobby Manna.
But even Manna agreed that this could not be allowed to pass. So
Nicky suggested strongly that the time was ripe for Blackie to go
into retirement in Florida, and Manna backed him up when Blackie
started to bitch. So he was gone, and, even better, Nicky was elevat-
ing Patty to captain. It was long overdue.

In mid-December my no-good lawyer finally did something right.
He got a three-judge state appeals court panel to grant me an appeal
bond while they reviewed the Monmouth conviction. Patty put up
the $2,500 cash. Because the bond had the effect of lifting the Mon-
mouth detainer, I became eligible for the Essex County work-release
program. I got out within a couple of days. By January 4, 1985, I had
served the minimum required of me on the 364-day sentence—91
days. I was now paroled by Essex County.

Ann, I must say, took all this quite well. She always knew what I
did for a living. She had helped me with the football pool cards and
often watched me book bets at home and at her parents' house on
some Sundays. From the very first I had told her that a cost of my
being in the business was that someday I might have to go to jail. I
had never thought it would happen, or if it did, I thought I would
probably be facing a couple of months of county time somewhere.
But now I was facing two years, minimum mandatory, and this was
serious time.

Ann stood by me like a rock. With three babies to take care of, she knew it was not going to be easy for her. I could tell she was not happy, but she was resolute. We still had hope that I would win my appeal and get a new trial in Monmouth County. At the very least I knew it would be quite some time before my appeal ran out and I would actually have to start serving any time. I convinced Ann that when and if I had to serve this time, above all, she and the kids would be taken good care of. This I promised her because I believed it. I promised her because I was promised by guys like Scoops and Slicker. I told her we would make it through this, and in the meantime, while I was waiting for my appeal, life went on.

If I did win my appeal, it would look better for me—if and when I had to stand trial—if it appeared I had a real middle-class job. So, on paper at least, I became the office manager of the Tectonic Construction Company, a company run by Mike Salimbene, a guy who was around John Riggi. Actually, I did nothing except pick up my paycheck once a week. I would cash it and immediately give 15 percent back to the boss. I would then split the rest with Patty. But if it ever came to a pre-sentencing hearing at some future trial, I was gainfully employed in an honest job with considerable responsibility.

Even though I was out on bond, I continued doing what I had always done, gambling and scamming and leading the life of a wiseguy. The funniest thing about my Essex County arrest was that at first the cops thought I was a drug dealer. In one of the intercepted phone conversations, I was overheard telling a guy I wanted "twenty-six pounds of sausage." They knew I didn't make pizza, so naturally they thought—they later told me—that I was ordering twenty-six ounces of some controlled substance. It took me forever to talk my way out of that one because I could not really tell them the truth: I had been speaking in a code, and what I was ordering was twenty-six stolen credit cards.

In those days stolen credit cards—we called them "muldoons"— were a big thing. In the early 1980s, stores and restaurants didn't yet have the electronic devices that automatically read the magnetic strip on the back of the card to get an approval code. When you charged above a certain amount, a merchant called into a phone bank at Visa or American Express and received verbal authorization. So if the guy you were dealing with was dirty, you could run any number of scams without even having the actual card.

What we did was buy actual, active credit card numbers from some guy we knew in a restaurant or store. We would cut the number into a blank piece of credit card plastic. You could use the blank, with the name and number of the account holder and the interbank code number in the right place, to make an imprint when you ran it through a regular card machine. You could only use this phony card with a merchant or waiter you knew, of course, because it was clearly not a real card. So we would go to stores we knew and buy dinners or goods, and the guy would ring up extra. For example, we bought our clothes at a store called Suit Yourself, run by a guy who was around the Luccheses. We might go in with one of these cut plastics and buy two suits. The owner would get authorization for four. We would get our two suits, the owner got the money for four, and everyone was happy. If the credit card company came calling, the owner would say he didn't remember who had made the purchase or what I.D. he had seen.

The beauty of the scam was that the person who owned the credit card did not know the number had been stolen because he still had the card in his wallet. Sometimes a number would stay good for a week, sometimes for a month. You might get a number that was already maxed out, but sometimes you got a card with thousands of available credit. You would just use the card until it didn't clear and credit was denied.

One time during the period I was out on bail, I was down in Florida with Patty and Scoops. Anthony "Tumac" Accetturo—a Lucchese captain we knew well—had a good friend who was an assistant manager at the Diplomat Hotel in Miami Beach. In season, oceanfront rooms were going for $250 a night in the early 1980s. This guy would give us the rooms for $60 a night, and we could pay with muldoons.

Nicky went down to his home in Hallendale with a bunch of guys from Philly and Atlantic City to celebrate getting out of prison in Texas. One night he decided to host a dinner for a whole bunch of guys from various crews at this Italian restaurant in Miami where we knew the owner very well. When it came time to pay, Nicky turns to Patty and says he should pick up the tab. Patty then turns to me and Scoops. Often at dinners like this the check sort of rolls down the table, and on this night it was me and Scoops who were sitting at the bottom of the table.

Now what Nicky meant by picking up the tab was not that he would reimburse Patty for this rather sizable check. He meant that Patty should pay for it. To Nicky, being the boss meant never having to pull a dime out of your pocket if your crew was around. This very expensive meal was going to have to come out of Scoops's and my pockets, and out of Patty's, too.

Patty knew we were carrying muldoons and were using them at the hotel, but the possibility of embarrassing Nicky by trying to use one here that wouldn't go through panicked him. It was not very good for your health if you embarrassed Nicky, especially in front of the kind of guys we were eating with that night. On the other hand, we were looking at a two-grand tab. So I went into the back, slipped the owner a couple of hundred in cash, and asked him to quietly run the bill on a stolen number. If it didn't go through, I had the cash to pay for dinner. But it sailed right through, and Scoops and I walked out of that place with big smiles. Patty was pissed that we hadn't listened to him and had risked getting turned down on the bad plastic. But he was not really all that pissed; we had saved him a thousand. Oceanfront rooms and great meals on bad plastic: That's how a wiseguy goes on vacation.

Despite the war and all the bloodshed, Nicky Scarfo was really starting to prosper in Atlantic City. Few people gave Nicky credit for being as smart as he was. His hold on the Atlantic City unions was beginning to pay off big time. For years he had supported himself and his crew by taking a few hundred a week from every bar and restaurant in town to guarantee that the union would stay out, or if the place was already organized, that there would be no union trouble. After Nicky got HEREIU Local 54 reorganized, Bobby Manna put him together with a big Chicago organization guy who had the head of the national union in his pocket. That gave Nicky the final leverage he needed. But more than owning the key hotel employee union, Nicky also owned the city government. The mayor, Mike Matthews, was bought and paid for, and Nicky also owned others in the city government. If you wanted to deal in Atlantic City, you had to deal with Nicky. Everything was set for a maximum cash output for Nicky and the organization, and the money started to flow both to Manna in New York and to the guy in Chicago.

One day Patty sent me to Atlantic City with some money and some messages for Nicky. As was usually the case, we met at Resorts, and when I first saw him that night, he had this huge smile on his face. This, I can tell you, was unusual. He was with Philip Leonetti, and the three of us went into the lounge for a drink. I gave Nicky the money and the messages, and he gave me a couple of things to take back to Patty. Then the talk turned to why he was in such a good mood that night. He said this rich guy Trump from New York had just paid him a bundle to acquire a parcel of land near a hotel he was opening.

One of the things that Nicky had done years before, when he had seen gambling on the horizon, was to use his knowledge of the area and his in with the unions and the city government to start buying up what would become key parcels of land. Some of this land he bought in his own name or Philip's; other parcels were bought in partnership with guys from Philadelphia. Still others he bought and then put them in the names of guys from his crew, or guys in our family in Philly.

One parcel that Nicky controlled was in the name of Salvy Testa, Phil's son, and Frankie Narducci, the son of another of our oldtime captains. It was the La Bistro, a rundown old bar on a nice-sized lot at the corner of Pacific and Missouri avenues, diagonally across from what was becoming Trump Plaza Hotel and Casino. Nicky had bought the place five or six years earlier for about $100,000. The purchase price may have been higher, because Nicky once told me that in many of his deals a big chunk of the stated purchase price was kicked back to him under the table, laundering it.

That night Nicky was positively glowing. He boasted that Trump had agreed to pay him more than a million dollars for the parcel. The total came to more than $230 per square foot, making the old bar some of the most expensive land in Atlantic City. Trump has said he was willing to pay a lot because he had obtained the required approvals to build his casino-hotel without a plan for parking, so he needed land where a garage could be built. Trump acquired other nearby parcels as well. "This guy Trump, he wants no problems," said Nicky. "Putting out this kind of money, he won't," Philip said, laughing.

They were both clearly on a high. They bragged that the new hotel was going to be a fountain of money for them, that they were going to get into the construction deals and the steel and concrete contracts for the new hotel. They laughed about how complicated the La Bistro deal would be, with the title to be held first by some lawyer's secretary for a while and then transferred to a corporation Trump owned.

Some time later I noticed that Trump announced he had bought the parcel, along with others on the block, as a site for the Plaza's parking garage, but all it was ever used for was parking for the construction trailers while the Plaza was being built. Whatever the eventual use of the land, Trump got his money's worth. He owned so much prime property that the zoning officials rolled over for him on countless key matters.

Actually, my evening in Atlantic City ended on a down note. Nicky and Philip knew I was waiting to hear about my appeal and that things did not look good. "You'll do this time quick," Nicky said, "and we'll keep things for you out here while you're inside. When you get out, we'll straighten you out. Don't worry, you're one of us."

The string finally did run out for me on July 9, 1985. I had been free on the appeal bond since my Essex County time was up the previous January, and I guess both Ann and I fooled ourselves into believing it would somehow last forever. Of course it didn't. My appeal was rejected, and my bond was revoked. I was told to report to the state processing center in Trenton on July 12 to begin serving my sentence. I guess you could say that the mood around my house was like a funeral.

I said my good-byes to various guys. I made a final trip into New York to say good-bye to the Gambino guys I was with in the monte game. I said my good-byes to my brother and my in-laws. By the night of July 11, I was ready. I still had a storybook view of my life in organized crime. To a great extent I thought I was about to embark on a kind of noble adventure, something I had to do, had to get behind me, before I could really be a mobster. I knew very few guys who had risen to the level I hoped someday to achieve who had not served some time behind bars. Many guys had served bids of six or eight years or longer, and I was going away for only two years. I figured I could do it standing on my head.

And I was bound and determined to do it right. Even before we knew the result of my appeal, Tony Rinaldo had said that he could work out a deal for me to get probation if I rolled over on even a few guys. The suggestion had incensed me. No way, I thought. I looked upon myself as a stand-up guy. Yes, it would be hard on Ann and the kids. Yes, it would be hard on me. But I was not about to turn on my friends, certainly not on Patty or the guys around him. I would do my time the way I was supposed to, and when I got out, I would be looked up to. I would be owed a debt, and someday I would collect on that debt.

The night before I left for jail I wanted to stay home with Ann and the kids. Patty was going to drive me to jail the next morning, so I was not with him that night. The kids had been told that I was going into the army the next day. We had a nice family dinner, and then after we got the kids into bed, Turk—Nicholas Cifelli—came over to say his good-byes. We sat in the living room, Ann, Turk, and I. He was representing the whole crew, he said. They all wanted me to know how much they admired the stand-up way I was doing this. They knew that I had been under pressure to give some of them up in exchange for my freedom, and they wanted me to know that I could put my mind at ease and that every day I was gone they would be there for my family.

Then he looked directly at my wife. "Ann, you are one of us," he said with sincerity. "While George is gone, you and the kids will never want for anything. If you need anything, all you have to do is pick up the phone and call, and we'll be here. George means a lot to us. What he's doing means a lot to us. You mean a lot to us. We're here to take care of you. We won't let either of you down."

I believed him. After all, that is exactly what I would have said to his wife if the tables were turned. I would have meant it, and I would absolutely have lived up to my word. If the tables were turned, I would have given to his family as if they were my own. I expected no less of him. Now he was saying that we could count on him and Scoops and all the rest. And we were counting on them.

His words gave a lot of comfort to Ann. She was placing her faith in him and the other guys. This was not easy for her. She never liked them, and she never liked me hanging with them. But she had come to accept that that was how I led my life, so she tolerated them and, to a lesser degree, their wives. Now I was going to jail, and they had come forward with an offer to help. It took a lot for her to agree to accept that help and become dependent on these guys, which is why she grew to hate them with such passion when they turned their backs on her. Ann remembers this one evening probably above all the others she ever spent with any member of my crew. She remembers exactly what Turk said and the way he said it, and she remembers how he rejected her out of hand when she finally did go to him in desperation.

But all I knew was that night I was worried, not for myself because I was about to embark on something of a holy mission—proving once and for all what a stand-up guy I was—but for Ann and the kids because I would not be able to help them where I was going. That's why Turk's words of assurance meant a lot to me. I had a surprisingly good night's sleep. I was ready to go.

4

JAIL

Jail is not bad if you approach it in the right frame of mind. They say that most people in the can will tell you they are innocent. Not me. I didn't believe I belonged in jail, but I was certainly not innocent; and I was determined to do my time in the right frame of mind. So I wasn't all that depressed when I reported to the Riverfront State Correctional Institution, which was still under construction, at Camden in southern Jersey, to begin serving my two-year bid.

Relative to other medium-maximum security facilities in New Jersey, Riverfront was actually a pretty nice place. It was all high-tech. There were no bars on the windows or doors. Windows were made of space-age plastics, four inches thick with wire mesh in the middle. They let in light and you could see out of them perfectly, but you couldn't put a bullet through them. The one-man cells had no bars, just a thick steel door with a window in it. Inmates had keys to their doors and could lock up their possessions when they were at meals or recreation during the day. At night the doors were locked tight using magnets. You couldn't possibly budge them. I always wondered what would happen in a general power failure, but we never had one while I was there.

The warden was a decent guy named Tom Hundley. But he was a

warden, and all corrections guys tend to be very authoritative. And the higher up they go, the more authoritative they get. I guess I should say Hundley was as good a guy as a warden could be—or, put another way, he was a good guy as long as you did what he said when he said it. Riverfront wasn't Club Fed, one of those federal minimum facilities with tennis courts and room service. At Riverfront your day was very regimented; you had to do what you were told and do it when you were told to do it. You were not free to come and go, of course, but in its way I guess it was not that much different from being in the army.

It should not have been difficult time to do. I had this theory about going to jail; for me it was an occupational hazard. I was a bookmaker. If I had lived in Vegas and was doing what I was doing in connection with one of the casinos, it would have been perfectly legal. However, I lived in Jersey, so what I was doing was illegal. To be honest, I didn't feel it was in any way wrong or immoral. But it was against the law, and I had always assumed that sooner or later I would run out of luck. The authorities would come calling, and I would have to go away for some period.

Riverfront was a brand-new joint, so all the cons, including me, were also brand new. What they did was transfer a lot of long-timers in from various facilities around the state. Now for these guys Riverfront was the next thing to paradise compared to what they were used to, and the officers made it clear that they should do exactly what they were told or else they would be on the next bus back to the hellhole they had come from. Then the prison administration assigned these guys to the PRC—the Prisoners' Reception Committee—the organization that represented the prisoners' interests in dealing with the officers. In this way the warden had a captive PRC, guys who would not make waves and make his job difficult. I was not a real quiet kind of guy in jail, and shortly after I got there, one of the guys on the PRC left for some reason, so I was elected to the committee. Sort of overnight I became the thorn in Warden Hundley's side.

It was mostly small stuff, things that are of great importance to men in prison—like food, access to postage stamps, and telephone privileges. And there were special problems because construction was still going on. They couldn't let us go into the yard for exercise because it was filled with construction equipment, so we stayed in our cells, in lockup, twenty or more hours a day. For the older guys who had transferred in, twenty hours a day in a Riverfront cell was still better than where they had been, so they kept quiet. Not me. I bitched, and I bitched loud. Finally, they worked out an arrangement where part of the yard was cleared, and everyone got outside for some period each day.

Our biggest problem occurred near Christmas. The heating system wasn't completely installed yet, and the wing I was in was freezing cold. It was so cold, you could see your breath in the cells. We asked for extra blankets until they could get the heating system fixed. The guards ignored us. The PRC as a whole did nothing because even ice cold the Riverfront cells were still better than what they might get sent back to.

We endured the first night without extra blankets. But when it looked as if we were going to have to spend a second, I went to the night shift tier captain and told him that unless we got blankets, we were going to refuse to lock in when 10:00 P.M. came. That was big trouble for him. If he went by the book, he would have to declare something approaching a riot and bring in guards from other shifts. That would cost a fortune in overtime, and everyone would be unhappy.

His first response was to threaten to ship me out that night. I told him to go ahead, but he would still have thirty guys refusing to lock in until they got blankets. There was a lot of muttering on his part, a flurry of phone calls, and somehow, about 9:45, a huge pile of blankets showed up.

But that still didn't solve the problem of no heat. I talked with the tier captain to no avail. I talked to the assistant warden to no avail. I talked to Warden Hundley, who basically said the system would be fixed when they got to it, and it was not a top priority. So when all my yelling did no good, I resorted to something unheard of: I called the head of the Department of Corrections in Trenton.

Now in jail, any jail, you can usually make only collect long-distance calls. So the Department of Corrections refused all collect calls, and prisoners could never get through. But what I did was call Ann and then had her conference in the call to Trenton so they didn't know I was a prisoner when I called and asked for the assistant director. When I got him on the line, I lodged a formal protest based on a health emergency. He knew if he did nothing, he would hold himself and the state open to a lawsuit. So he thanked me for the call and said he would look into it. I was a little surprised when he acted immediately.

A small army of heating guys descended on the jail, and within forty-eight hours the heating system was working just fine. Everyone was happy except Warden Hundley. I had gone over his head, and that was a major sin. This wasn't one of those "B" jailhouse movies where the wicked warden seeks revenge and has the prisoner beaten or killed. To his credit, Hundley didn't seek any kind of reprisal against me. But I could tell he was really mad, and I was careful to make no missteps that would give him some excuse.

I liked Riverfront, but being so far away from Newark made it very hard on Ann. She was bound and determined to see me every time they would let her, but that meant a two-and-a-half-hour drive in each direction from the house. It took an entire day. Occasionally she would bring the kids. Now we had three. The baby was born while I was awaiting trial in Monmouth County, so on these trips to Riverfront, Ann was bringing a six-year-old, a four-year-old, and the baby. We still told the two oldest that I was in the army, and they were both still too young to realize that a prison was not an army post. On trips when Ann left them at home, she would have to make elaborate arrangements for someone to take care of them.

After a few months of this I could see that Ann was getting really run down. I tried to talk with her, but sometimes she could be very stubborn. She believed we had to see each other regularly for our marriage to stay strong. I certainly couldn't argue with that because I agreed with her, but I could see that coming two or three times a week was starting to wear on her.

There was another problem. When Riverfront opened, they needed guards, and so they got many of them from a nearby youth facility. Most weren't bad guys, but they had spent their entire careers dealing with unruly fourteen-year-olds. They didn't understand that dealing with adults was different. In the facility they came from, they knew they had to be uniformly rigid to maintain control; they brought that rigidity with them, and it affected the way they dealt with us.

On visits they would pull up folding chairs around inmates for their families. Visitors had to stay put. All well and good for adults, but a very difficult proposition for young children. On one visit the older two got antsy and started to fidget in their chairs; then they played around them, and finally they ran around a bit. One of the guards told them to stay put. They did for a while, but then they started to roam again. Finally the guard grabbed my six-year-old and physically dragged him back crying to the chair. I came close to punching the guy out, but knowing the consequences, I held back. But it was clear that Ann could no longer bring the kids. In fact, I suggested that she stop coming down for a while.

She resisted that idea. When I talked with Patty about it, he suggested that I go to the warden and get her visits terminated for her own good. That would force her to stop coming and might be better for her, I thought, but it would have been too high a price for me to pay. There had to be another way. I talked with some of the guys who had been around the prison system for a while and learned there was another way. The solution carried with it a high price that I would have to pay.

"You want to do what?" Warden Hundley was dumbfounded when he heard my request.

"I want a family hardship transfer to Rahway," I answered.

"You can't be serious," he replied. "People kill to get out of there. Nobody in his right mind wants to get in."

I did, I said, and I was serious about the hardship request, which made it a priority. I said I knew exactly what I was getting into.

Rahway was New Jersey's hellhole. It was a one-hundred-year-old, overcrowded, maximum-security institution, filled to overflowing with the dregs of the state's penal system. I could understand why Hundley did not believe anyone would actually ask to be transferred into Rahway, especially from the state's new showplace prison. But Rahway was an easy fifteen-minute drive from our house, and Ann could spend an hour or so with me three times a week instead of once a month.

After spending another few minutes in a halfhearted attempt to talk me out of it, Hundley agreed to sign off on my request and to put it through. Actually, he was probably pretty relieved that he was losing me; the memory of the heating system situation was still fresh in his mind. Since mine was a hardship request, it got top priority, but even then such a request could take weeks or months. I suspect Hundley called Trenton and applied more than a little grease to the wheels. The request must have rocked from desk to desk at the Department of Corrections picking up the necessary signatures, and ten days later I was on my way.

I arrived at Rahway on January 28, 1986, the day the Shuttle Challenger lifted off on its short and ill-fated flight. I have to admit

I was apprehensive. As I waited to leave Riverfront, it seemed that every guy in the joint wanted to tell me one horror story or another about Rahway. But in the end it was really very simple. You can survive in jail if you know the moves because in jail everything is moves, but you have to learn the moves quick if you're going to make it. In this I was lucky. The word got out quick in Rahway that I was connected and that I had transferred in from Riverfront, so everyone was looking at me with suspicion.

Whenever you enter a prison, you're initially put into classification. It can take a couple of weeks before you're assigned a permanent place in the general population. My initial assignment was to an eight-foot by four-foot cell in 4 Wing, the oldest and the worst that Rahway had to offer. A made guy in the family, Red Pontana, was a close friend of Dennis Steo, an inmate in Rahway with a lot of moves. When Patty found out I was headed there, he had Red call Dennis, and as soon as I got out of the processing, Dennis was there waiting for me. From that moment on, Rahway became survivable.

In my whole life I've met few men as honest and honorable as Dennis. He had originally caught a seven-to-twelve-year bid for being the driver of the getaway car in an armed robbery. But while in jail he had killed a guy in a fight. For that he caught a life bid, and when I first met him, he had already been in for twenty.

As a way of keeping sane, Dennis had founded an organization inside the walls called the Society for the Handicapped. It collected small donations from other cons and with the money it sent holiday cards—Christmas, Easter, birthdays, and the like—to old folks and shut-ins all over the state. It arranged for birthday parties for the elderly in state homes (Ann eventually got involved and went to quite a few of these parties). It helped out the elderly who needed help and even arranged for presidential greetings to be sent from the White House to people all over the state who were turning one hundred or were celebrating some other special day.

I suppose the White House Communications Office would have been shocked to learn that those requests were coming from a state prison and the contact they talked with all the time was a convicted murderer. But as far as they knew, they were dealing with an organization that was trying to make old people's lives a little happier—and they were. Dennis actually cared about the Society. It wasn't a scam even if it got us quite a few privileges that were not available to the general population, and it looked good in your file when you went to see the parole board.

The Society really did good works, and the prison system right-fully helped out by providing it with an office in an area of the upper tier known as the Inmate Group Center. The office came equipped with a private phone, an answering machine, and some other really nice privileges. Dennis brought me into the Society, and having a place to go away from the general prison population helped me get adjusted. I could talk with Ann and Patty whenever I wanted, and they could always reach me quickly. We could even get decent Italian food brought in.

But Dennis did much more than simply bring me into the Society, he introduced me to all the right guys. I started out working in the prison laundry. It was not the best of jobs, but with Dennis's help I was able to get a job in the library, which was very good duty. It was clean and quiet, and it gave me a lot of free time. Then I started to make book, since it was something I knew well how to do, and I ended up with a nice profitable operation in no time. In the joint, cigarettes are currency. Lucky me, one of my biggest players—and a real lousy bettor—was a guy who worked in the commissary. He and I came to an understanding: He was willing to steal anything in the commissary. He would pay off his loses in the two major currencies in prison, cartons of cigarettes and postage stamps.

With an ample supply of both, I could buy almost anything I wanted. If I had been into drugs, it would have been a simple matter to get a fix or to get high or to score some downers. It was absolutely amazing. There were more drugs of every variety in Rahway jail than there are on the streets. Anyone could watch the drugs flowing in, but the guards simply turned a blind eye and let it happen. On visiting days, which were Wednesday nights, Saturdays, and Sundays, visitors would come in, wives or girlfriends, with a condom filled with drugs in their mouths. They would kiss their guys and pass the tied condom mouth to mouth. The inmate would swallow it, and when he got back to his cell, he would either vomit it up or wait until it passed in his stool. He would then have drugs to use or sell. When I first saw this happening, I really couldn't believe my eyes. It was incredibly dangerous. In my year in Rahway, three guys died doing this. The condoms would break or come undone in their stomachs, and they would die of overdoses. It's not a pretty way to die.

But I didn't do drugs—never have, never will. With my cigarette and stamp score I was able to get done what was important to me. I could pay someone to do most of my chores, I could eat well, and I could stay out of danger.

One of the most dangerous places in Rahway was the huge mess hall. Every group in the place—redneck whites, blacks, Latinos, homosexuals, and so forth—sat in its own section. About once a week there would be a major fight or disturbance, and guys would go after each other with shivs and pipes. The guards wanted none of it, so they would withdraw and shut the doors until the thing had played itself out. Then they would come back in to haul away the dead and wounded. An innocent bystander, which is what I considered myself to be, could easily end up in the wrong place at the wrong time. And if you were the wrong color—and generally speaking, in Rahway white was always the wrong color—you could end up being carted out with the dead and wounded.

Dennis knew the inmate who ran the officers' mess, a connected guy on the outside with the last name of Segal. Naturally we all called him Bugsie, and I don't know if I ever heard his real first name. For a rather large consideration in cigarettes, Bugsie brought us our meals from the officers' mess up to the Society's office in the IGC. We were therefore eating as well as the guards, and in peace and quiet and safety.

Disease was rampant in Rahway. The inmates' clothes were all washed together in huge machines. If the water was not hot enough, disease passed easily from one guy to another. But not for us. For a couple of cartons of smokes a month, we—Dennis and I and some of our friends—got our laundry done separately from the regular population. It also came back all pressed and hand-finished, not just thrown in a duffel the way everybody else got their stuff back. As things were, you could almost tell the guys with moves because they were the ones who weren't always wrinkled.

Eating well and looking good without worrying what you were catching from your undershirt was important, but your day-to-day safety was even more important. Being able to go about your business without anyone bothering you was crucial. In Rahway you could buy a lot of safety with ten cartons of cigarettes a month. But the place was completely crazy: Everywhere you turned, there was some guy who would just as soon kill you as look at you. Size didn't always matter, and toughness didn't always help. If a guy wanted you, he would get you, and little else mattered.

After classification I was assigned to a dorm in 5 Wing. I guess there were about sixty-eight guys in this dorm, of whom sixty-three were black. I knew I had to get this race thing under control right away or else I was in for some very long nights. So the first day I found out who the head of the blacks in the dorm was; there is always a leader. I went up to him and said that if there was going to be any trouble between him and me, let's get it over with right now, right here. He looked at me kind of funny and said he thought I was crazy. He had no problem with me, he said, and in the end we became friends. They treated me right, and I treated them right. So it was no problem.

Bunking next to me in that 5 Wing dorm was one of the few other white guys there, a real good guy by the name of Kevin Walsh. He was a little older than me and much, much bigger. He was about six foot three, weighed about 240 pounds, and was an absolute health nut. All he did all day, seven days a week, was lift weights. He was in almost perfect shape. I was glad he hung with me because I couldn't believe anyone would bother him.

The palace of Rahway was 6 Wing, actually a group of joined house trailers out in a corner of the yard. These were considered the best accommodations inside the walls. Dennis bunked there, and so did the other trustees. They had real beds, real bathrooms, more room, and, theoretically at least, a better quality of roommate.

You had to be in 5 Wing for six months before you could try for 6 Wing. Kevin and I applied the first day we could. He had a few weeks' seniority on me, so his application was reviewed first and he was transferred. In the cubicle next to him was a quiet little Hispanic kid in for murder. This kid was barely five foot five and 130 pounds. One hot night Kevin wanted to open the window they kind of shared. He opened it, and this kid closed it. He opened it and this kid closed it. Finally the kid stared at him and said, "If you open it again, I'll kill you."

Kevin blew the guy off and opened the window again. The guy just stared at him, and Kevin laughed. He went to sleep not knowing he had a problem. He woke up to find the guy working on him with an ice pick. He was stabbed eighteen times. The only thing that saved his life was his tremendous physical conditioning. He was in surgery for thirteen hours and ended up losing a kidney. The only good to come from it was that he was so injured that they released him as soon as he was recovered enough. But I couldn't help thinking that if they had reviewed my application first, I would have been bunking next to this kid. And God knows I might well have said something that would have set him off. He was a walking time bomb and Kevin just happened to push the wrong button. It could easily have been me. That was the problem with Rahway—they just threw you together like cattle, a thief next to a multiple murderer. I honestly believe the moves that Dennis had are what kept me alive.

. . .

Going to jail wasn't all that hard on me, but I wasn't sitting with three young children, almost nothing in the bank, and no job. Ann was, and it was starting to prove quite an ordeal for her.

I had been doing good, making a bundle, but when you're in the mob, earning money is a far cry from being able to put much of it away. I had been earning big, but money ran through my fingers like water. Living a life of organized crime is spending countless boring hours sitting around clubs or corners with a bunch of guys you might not like very much, and shelling out huge amounts of money just living high. There was a time when I was spending an average of maybe $500 a day, six days a week, just buying drinks and picking up tabs. I might have been earning thousands a week, but I was also spending thousands a week.

Then there were my lawyers and my legal bills. Criminal lawyers for guys like me are expensive, and they want their money up front and usually in cash. My trials and then my appeal ended up costing me tens of thousands of dollars. I had a little something in the bank and a little more under the mattress, but it all went to the lawyers.

At first I was sure Ann would have enough money to get by on. There was still some money in the bank, and I figured that should last a while. But what I was really depending on was the continued income from my share of the bookmaking operation, the monte game, and a bunch of deals that were still in the works when I went in. Things would be far from flush for my family, I had concluded, but there would be more than enough to tide them over for the next twenty-four months.

What is really amazing is how long it took me to find out what was going on. Ann figured I had enough problems of my own just trying to survive inside without her telling me how desperate her situation was becoming. She had lived as frugally as she could; she lived off the money in the bank, and she waited for money to come in from my friends. But it didn't come. I knew that for the first few months I was in, Patty would send her a few hundred a month. At Christmas he sent over $500 extra. But eventually this stopped. More important, the money she expected from my book and from my cut of the monte game and the other stuff never materialized. She asked her family for help, and she existed with the fear of being broke growing daily.

I got an inkling of what was going on shortly after I went to

Rahway in January 1986, but I didn't get the full story for another couple of months when Ann broke down during a visit. It was a typical visit. You sit there and talk with your wife while all around you a hundred guys are openly having sex with their wives or girlfriends. I am far from a prude, but it made me very unhappy when one day my young son literally tripped over a couple engaged in oral sex partially under a table.

Completely in tears, Ann finally told me the truth. She was living hand to mouth. In a nutshell, she and I were just about broke. "I got food stamps," she said. "And I'm going to have to apply for welfare. It's so degrading going down there, but the kids have to eat and I have got no choice. As far as your damn friends are concerned, I guess it's out of sight, out of mind."

I was dumbfounded. I was confused and angry at the same time. I had done what was expected of me. I had gone away, and I was doing my time in a stand-up fashion. It wasn't that I was expecting charity; they owed me, plain and simple, and they owed my family. This was my money, money that was coming to me from my business that I had left for them to continue running. They should have been paying Ann what was owed me.

"Have you gone to see Turk?" I asked, remembering the night before I left and his promise to look after them.

"Yes. Finally I did," Ann said. "At first I couldn't even reach him. Then when I did, he made all kinds of excuses about not having money. When I started hounding him, he said the state was building new public housing over in Elizabeth, and I could save money on rent if I went there. He said maybe he could help me move in."

It was like I was hearing someone else's story. This couldn't be happening to me and my family. I kept thinking my friends would never let me down like this. It must be a misunderstanding somehow. I felt almost physically sick. I tried to reassure Ann, and after she left I got to a phone as fast as I could. My first call was to Patty, and I wanted to know what the hell was going on.

"George, we're all going through a bad period," Patty told me. "Nobody's got any money. I ask these guys all the time, and all I ever hear is how the cops are all over us, how nobody is earning anything, how they are all on the verge of being broke."

I knew that money was a major problem for Patty because he was becoming so sick, he really couldn't do that much anymore to support himself. Guys like Scoops and Turk were only coming up with enough so that he could just get by. But because Ann was always so upbeat whenever we talked, because she never, never let on she was having any problems, I had no idea that she wasn't getting enough to get by.

I didn't blame Pat. If anything, he was in the same boat as Ann. Those guys should have been busting their humps for him, and they should have been helping my family. If the tables had been reversed, there was no way I would not have been helping their families. I didn't for a second believe they were all broke. I knew Scoops wasn't. He could have dipped into Bananas' shy money and supported Ann without even breaking a sweat.

Over the next couple of days I talked with them all. I talked with Scoops, with Slicker, with Turk, reminding him of the promises he had made sitting in my living room. I heard a litany of excuses:

"We're all broke."

"The cops are all over us, and we can't make any moves."

"The players have all moved over to New York books."

"I've never seen things so tight."

It all sounded like crap to me, but sitting inside Rahway with at least another nine months to go, I was really powerless to do anything. That was the worst—the powerlessness, the feeling of not being in control. It was a feeling I had never experienced before and something I vowed never to feel again. I was almost beside myself, but there was not much I could do. But from that day on, getting even with these guys became an important part of my life.

I was angry, I was in a rage, but I was angry at individual guys and not at the family as a whole, or not at the system that I still considered myself a part of. I didn't see that the system had let me and my family down; I only saw that Scoops and Turk and Slicker and the other guys had. When I thought about getting even, I thought about revenge in terms of gaining power in the family and then of using that power to get them. I don't know how many times I thought that if I were the captain, then they would suffer. If I were the captain and was given any excuse, I would whack them. But it never even occurred to me, not once, not for even a moment, that a way to get even would be by ratting them out. That would come later when I finally realized it was not individuals who had lost their honor but an entire system. That realization would eventually come, but now my thoughts of revenge were in terms of wiseguy against wiseguy.

. . .

In the New Jersey prison system there are basically three levels of inmate security: maximum, gang minimum, and full minimum. If you're in maximum, then you're behind the walls and have to work in a job behind the walls, in the laundry or in food service or in one of the make-work jobs they say teaches skills that can be used outside but that are basically a joke. The only real skill taught in prison is how to be a better criminal. It's a skill that most guys try to put into practice after they get out, which is why so many guys end up back in. If you're in gang minimum, you get to work in closely supervised groups outside the walls but still within the compound, which usually means some kind of maintenance work. Finally, if you make it to full minimum, you get to work outside the walls with only limited direct supervision.

Everything in prison is going from one stage to another. The only way I could be of real help to Ann was to get out of Rahway and into a halfway house in Newark. Then I could start earning again and bring some money into the house. But before I could even be considered for release to a halfway house, I had to get outside the walls and into a camp, and before I could be considered for transfer out to a camp, I had to work my way through the security levels until I reached full minimum status.

Everyone starts off in maximum. When I arrived in Rahway, I was in maximum. The way things are set up, if you're doing a two-year bid, as I was, you had to spend at least your first year in maximum. In maximum I was given jobs inside the walls first, in the laundry and then later in the library. Then I graduated to gang minimum, where I had to spend at least ninety days before I could be eligible to transfer to full minimum. In gang minimum I had an interesting job. Kevin and I were assigned to build a massive flower box just outside the main gate. Actually, it was two flower boxes, one on each side of the walkway up to the gate. They were forty feet long by about three feet wide and were made out of railroad ties that we had to bury three feet deep. It took us our whole ninety-day turn in gang minimum to put these boxes together. We later learned they were not so much decorative as they were "security measures." Still later we found out they were put up because some "political types" were being transferred into Rahway, and there was worry that somebody might try to break them out by ramming the front gate. These railroad ties, anchored three feet deep, would have stopped a tank.

Working in the sun all day digging holes was not nearly as enjoyable a job as working in the library, but it was a step up, and that was important. Finally, a year after I had arrived at Rahway and about a year and a half into my sentence, I made it to full minimum and got outside the walls and into the Marlboro Camp. The way I had it figured, I would spend ninety days at the camp, during which I would apply for and get released to a halfway house in Newark. I would spend another ninety days or so at the halfway house, and then I would be released on parole shortly after serving my two-year minimum. I had been close to a model prisoner, so I had no doubt that I would have to serve only the minimum.

As in most penal settings, there is always some prisoner who effectively runs the institution. At Marlboro Camp it was Sid Gnatowsky, a guy who had been inside for a very long time and was in his mid-fifties when I first met him. Dennis Steo called Sid and told him I was coming out, so when I got there, he tried to get me the best job available. Actually, I was slotted for food service, which was the worst job. To be cleared for food service you had to take blood and urine tests to make sure you had no disease. Sid kept my tests lost for about six weeks so I wouldn't get assigned, in the hope that a better job would open up. It didn't. I was assigned to work on a cooking crew that manned the kitchen in a nearby state mental hospital.

I enjoyed working in the hospital. It was not the most pleasant environment I have been in, but the job was easy and got me outside the prison every day. Another good thing was that we could cook our own meals using food that was brought to us from the outside. As a result, for lunch and dinner I was eating everything I wanted, cooked the way I liked it.

There were two kitchen shifts at the hospital. I worked the late shift. We went in about 1:00 P.M., helped clean up after lunch, then prepared, served, and cleaned up dinner. I missed hanging around with Dennis and the rest of the guys at the Society, but I had to spend at least ninety days at the camp before I could go to a halfway house. I looked at my time in Marlboro as a kind of necessary evil, time I had to do to get back to Newark, time I had to do to get back to Ann and the kids.

Things on the hospital kitchen detail improved for me after about my second week. The sergeant in charge of the dinner crew knew I was in for bookmaking, so on a Friday he brought me the next day's racing form and asked if I could handicap the races because he and some friends were going. I said sure, and I spent most of the shift buried in the form. The next time I saw the guy, I guess it was on

Monday, he ran up and hugged me. I had picked six out of nine winners including the double. He was only a $2 or $5 bettor, but he still won a couple of hundred dollars. For him that was good money, and he was overjoyed. From that moment on I got all the best jobs on the detail—no more washing dishes or laboring over a hot stove for me.

I was still very angry at Scoops, Slicker, and various other guys for not taking care of Ann and the kids as they should have and for not taking care of Pat, either. But my anger was starting to cool a little now that it became apparent Ann was able to get by. With three young kids at home she could not get a job, but she was getting state aid, food stamps, and money from her parents and my brother when they could. So she was hanging in there, and now that I could see the end of my sentence coming, I had settled down a little.

I still didn't blame the mob system for what happened; I was still blaming individual guys. I believed in the system; as I saw it, it was my only future. And I guess I proved it by what I did for Andy Gerrado, a Genovese family captain I had known slightly on the outside.

Being connected on the outside really didn't do you much good inside Rahway. If you were lucky, as I had been, being connected might put you in contact with some other connected guys, and they in turn could put you with guys who had moves, whether or not they were directly connected. Andy was not a good candidate for long-term survival inside. He was a guy in his fifties who was very used to the good life outside, the kind of guy who would need help from the first moment he arrived.

One afternoon I got a "family emergency" call at the camp, just after I got back from the hospital work detail. The call was from Patty to tell me he had just been called by the Genoveses, who said that Andy was reporting to Rahway that day. Actually, by the time I got the call he was already at the prison going through the intake workup before being assigned into the general population. I felt a responsibility. I wasn't going to let any friend of ours come into the can without some moves being prepared for him. It just wasn't right. Despite everything, I still felt I had to do the right thing, and time was of the essence. I had to get back inside to make the contacts and the introductions for Andy so his way into the population could be smoothed.

But I had a problem. I couldn't just pick up the phone and call Dennis in the Society's offices and tell him that Andy had arrived and that he should be taken care of. It was all part of the culture of prison. If mob life involved protocol, there were even more rituals inside the walls. Something like this could not be done over the phone. Dennis would not even talk with Andy, no matter what I might say over the phone, unless I was there in person to make the introduction. This was something I had to do, and I had to do it immediately.

I had to get to the main prison, but the last bus had already left, and there was no easy way to get back. So I went to the sergeant and told him I suddenly had an awful toothache. I figured it was easier to have a dental emergency than a medical emergency—the only reasons I could think of to get a camp car to take me back to the main prison. The sergeant was more than a little suspicious since the toothache had come on the heels of an "emergency" call from home, and he gave me some dire warnings about what I could expect if I was faking. When I assured him I could barely think or talk with the pain, he shrugged and put me in a car.

I got back, went to the medical facility, and immediately sent word to Dennis that I needed to see him. As good fortune would have it, while Dennis was on his way down, who should walk by but Andy. He had come to the facility to get his arrival physical, and what might have been a very complicated meeting to arrange with no notice became very easy. When Dennis arrived, I simply made the required introduction. Dennis said that of course he would be happy to take Andy under his wing, just as he had done for me when I first arrived. He would also make a bunch of introductions for Andy with other guys he would need to know. My duty was done. Andy, and through him the Genoveses, would owe a big one to me and to Patty. Not only had I done the right thing, but now I could call on the Genoveses for repayment. All in all, a good day's work.

But now came the hard part. The sergeant was still waiting for me back at the camp and would be more than a little upset if he believed I had scammed him. He could easily have me transferred back inside the walls, and that would mean I couldn't get to the halfway house as I had planned. There was only one thing to do. I had to see the dentist.

"It doesn't look as if there's anything wrong with that tooth," the dentist said after looking long and hard into my mouth. But what else could he say? It was, after all, a perfectly healthy tooth.

"The pain is terrible," I told him. "Pull it."

"That's crazy. There's nothing wrong with that tooth."

"Pull it."

So he did. He gave me a shot of Novocain and pulled a perfectly good tooth. But I figured it was a small price to pay to get back to Newark three to four months earlier and to start bringing in a few bucks for my family. I took the car back to the camp and, first thing, showed the sergeant the empty hole in my swollen mouth where the tooth had been extracted. He was satisfied and even gave me the next day off from work detail to recover.

In the end I almost lost that tooth for nothing. I applied for release to the Newark halfway house, and my request was denied. Murderers, rapists, virtually everyone in the state system who had reached the end of their sentences could qualify for a halfway house if they had been good prisoners, but the powers that be suddenly decided that guys with organized crime ties weren't eligible. It seems that too many wiseguys were getting released to a halfway house and then falling into their old habits while still technically in custody. This was causing some people in the penal system a lot of headaches, so suddenly a new rule was put into effect: no goodfellas in the halfway houses. I was therefore denied the right enjoyed by murderers and rapists. I wasn't pleased about that and told the assistant warden I was filing suit against the state system immediately. That apparently gave them second thoughts. He asked me to hold up on the suit, and my application would be "re-reviewed." It was, and in short order I was released to the halfway house in Newark.

At the halfway house, either they got you some kind of job or you could get your own and they approved it. I asked if I could work as a bookkeeper with Giordano Waste Haulers. They said sure, that was a very acceptable job. In fact, the firm was owned by Pat Giordano and Danny Fasano, two guys we knew, and it was a no-show job. I would punch in and out every day and go by once a week to pick up my pay; they would certify to the halfway house that I was working forty hours a week. If anyone called to spot-check or even came by, they would say I had gone out to a client's for an audit or something like that. Instead I spent my days at home with Ann and the kids and hanging with Patty. And about twice a week I would make a run down to Atlantic City to deliver money or messages to Nicky or Philip. I had to be back in the halfway house by 7:00 P.M. every night, but I got forty-eight-hour passes every other weekend. It was a most tolerable situation.

I almost didn't get out when I was supposed to. I ended up in a bitter fight with Judge Milberg in Monmouth County to get credit for the sixty-three days I had served in Essex County waiting for my appeal bond to be approved. I had to file three separate motions before he finally agreed to give the credit.

Finally, on June 16, 1987, I walked out of the halfway house a free man. I'd like to believe that my two years in the joint had made me older and wiser, but I immediately went back to my old life.

5

BUGGED

After I got out of jail, I tried to put my life back together within the mob. Despite a lot of second thoughts and some very insistent and not very subtle signals from Ann, I largely succeeded. It took most of the year, but I again had money in my pocket and a new car, and Ann no longer had to worry about where food for the family or the next rent payment was coming from.

I had made a vow in jail: I would never again be a bookmaker and place myself at the mercy of some player who wants to get even for losing or get himself out of some kind of scrape by dropping the dime on me with the police. I knew I could make a very good living by running the monte games, by playing cards myself in Atlantic City, and by participating in various other scams. I figured it out: I could probably pay my street taxes to those higher up and still clear a few hundred thousand a year without breaking much of a sweat. It would take me a while to become a millionaire, but in the meantime I would be making more than most and would not have to worry about ending up back in jail. As a three-time loser, my next time would likely be under the habitual criminal laws, and that would mean a very long stay indeed.

After Ann finally told me about her money problems when I was in Rahway, and I had talked to Patty and a couple of the others, I realized that the business I had built up over the years had foundered while I was away. But I hadn't realized the full extent of the situation until I got out of Rahway and into the halfway house. Basically, I was broke. It was like the last ten years had never happened. It was like I was nineteen again.

When I went to jail, so had my partner, Don Hingos. The way things worked in the mob, our bookmaking business reverted to Patty. He wasn't a bookmaker, so he parceled it out—some to a bookie who was around us by the name of Steve Blum, but most to a made guy in the family named Joey Sodano, who had his fingers in a lot of pies and had another guy named Ray Springer working for him as a bookmaker. Most of the business went to Joey because he had lent Don $100,000 at two points a week shortly before we got busted.

When I say parceled the business out, what Patty actually did was assign Joey and Stevie to take over certain players. I had figured that both of them were honest bookies who provided good service, so my players would be in good hands while I was in and would be waiting for me when I got out. But allowing your players to go elsewhere is a very dicey proposition in the bookmaking business. A player goes with a particular bookie because he likes him, because he trusts him, because he develops a relationship with him. It's a lot like a doctor and patient. A doctor can retire and sell his practice, but that doesn't mean that all his patients, or even most, will go to the new doctor. That's what happened here. When I met Joey with Patty while I was still in the halfway house, to hear Joey tell it, most of my players had drifted away to some other book, or else he had been forced to drop them because they were winning too much or because they were in so deep he had to cut them off and just try to collect the old debts.

I had this vision that while I was away Joey and Stevie would protect my operation. They could take the profits while I was gone—after they gave Ann a share—and when I got out in triumph after serving my time in such a stand-up fashion, I would have the option of taking over again. If I didn't want to book bets again, I could parcel out my players and still get some of the income at the end of the football season. But Joey was there to tel! me that nothing was left to take over.

That was, of course, if I believed him. I didn't—not for a minute. I called a couple of my bigger players and found they were still playing with Joey. I also knew he was paying Nicky Sr. $3,000 a month in street tax. It was not a huge sum, but it showed he was doing okay. But there was not much I could do about the situation. He was a made guy, and I was just back on the streets. I was not yet in a position to challenge him.

I knew he was paying Nicky because I was the one who took the money down to Atlantic City or Philly. That started when I was still in the halfway house and holding down the no-show job at Giordano Waste Hauling. Once a month I would arrange to pick up the $3,000 from Joey, $1,200 from Scoops, and a grand from Vito Fresco, another book who was around us. I should have been picking up at least twice that amount, with half going to Patty and the other half going south to Nicky Sr. But these guys kept poor-mouthing, and Patty was sick a lot, with the result that all the fire seemed to desert him. Rather than fight, and rather than cut back on Nicky's take, Patty simply sent it all south.

Nicky Sr. had gone to jail the previous January, so the family was being run by his blood cousin Anthony Piccolo, who had been his consigliere and who everyone called Cousin Anthony for obvious reasons. What no one else knew but me was that when Nicky was arrested, he offered the job of acting boss to Patty. It was not the kind of thing you turned down easily, but Patty said that if he had accepted it, he would have had to either move to Philadelphia or spend a lot of time there. He didn't particularly like Philly. It would also have meant that in short order he would become a major target for the Feds. Patty just wanted to stay a low-keyed guy, so he said that while he was greatly honored, no, he had to refuse. He blamed his failing health. He told Nicky truthfully that he didn't have the strength or the stamina for the job. Nicky was not the kind of guy you said no to, but he understood and passed the leadership to Cousin Anthony.

But the money we were sending south every month did not go to Anthony; it went directly to Nicky Sr. through either his son Nicky Jr. or his underboss Phil Leonetti. I suppose most of it went to pay Nicky's huge legal bills. When it came time to deliver the money, I would call Phil McFillin, a guy who had been around our family in Philadelphia for years acting as a high-level advisor but who would never be straightened out because he was Irish. I would tell McFillin I had a package to deliver, and he would tell me where and when to deliver it. Occasionally it was some bar or restaurant in Philly, but usually it was in an Atlantic City casino—more often than not Resorts—and usually Nicky Jr. was there.

We called him the Kid. He was about ten years younger than me, about twenty-five, and before I went to jail, he really was a kid. Physically he was good-looking and bigger than his father, but then who wasn't? He was soft-spoken and unusually polite, but at the same time he was ambitious and—as I would learn later—he had a real mean streak in him just like his father. Now he was trying to be a mobster. Like me, he wasn't made yet, and he was really hungry for it. It was the first time I had spent any time with the Kid, and we quickly became good friends.

It was Patty who had arranged for me to have the no-show job at Giordano Waste Haulers. Most of the garbage companies in the New York City area are either mob-owned or mob-connected. Pat Giordano and Dan Fasano, the co-owners of Giordano Waste Hauling, Giordano Recycling, and G&F Recycling, were connected with the Genovese family through Joe Polo (actually Joe Parlivecchio), a Genovese captain. At first I punched in every morning, maybe had a cup of coffee before leaving to pick up Patty and hang with him the rest of the day, then go back to the company and punch out in the afternoon. When I received my paycheck every week, I would simply endorse it back to Giordano. It became tax-free money for him. After I got out of the halfway house, I was on probation and needed a job to show my probation officer I was on the up-and-up. So I kept the Giordano job, and if ever the probation officer called or showed up during the day to check me out, he would be told I was running an errand or something. I would get a page on my beeper and rush back.

For a couple of months I actually earned my salary. On paper I was supposed to be working in the bookkeeping department, and its accounting practices were a mess. Bills were going unpaid simply because they got lost, and jobs were not being billed to customers because drivers' logs were not being checked. One morning Pat asked if I could try to figure out what changes had to be made. I spent a few hours a day at it, and we eventually got things straightened out. During this time I got to keep my check. The guy thought I was earning it, and that made me feel pretty good. It was as close as I ever came to earning an honest living unless you count the few miserable months I spent working on the docks after I got out of high school.

While I really did some honest work for Pat Giordano, I also did a little dishonest business for him. Patty had reached out to Joe Polo to get me the job, and that meant Patty and I owed both Polo and Giordano a favor. Later on they called on us for repayment.

Giordano received an offer for the building his company was in from some developer who wanted to combine it with other property and put up a shopping center. At the same time Giordano made an offer on a larger piece of property down the block, which he needed because the company was growing so fast they didn't have room to park all their trucks. But to use this new property, they had to put up a building and make some other changes, and to do so they needed a use variance from the Newark Zoning Board. Giordano had tried through channels, but it got him nowhere. It appeared the board was not going to budge. The chairman of the Zoning Board was John Mavilla, a guy I had grown up with Down Neck who was still close to Patty. Pat Giordano found this out and asked me if Patty and I could get to him on behalf of his variance. We talked with Mavilla, and a couple of days later he called me back.

"George, for two thousand dollars we can get this thing done."

In other words, for $2,000 he would be willing to sponsor Giordano's use variance application and guarantee its passage.

I told him I was sure that would not be a problem, but I had to talk with my guy.

I called Giordano. "Pat, the guy wants six thousand dollars. Can you handle it?"

"So much, George?"

"Yeah. We tried to get him down, but he wouldn't budge."

"Okay, if that's what it has to be, that's it. Come by in the morning and pick it up."

The next day I picked up $6,000 in hundred-dollar bills. I gave $2,000 to Mavilla, and the use variance was approved at the next Zoning Board meeting. Giordano and Fasano were happy. So were Patty and I—we split the other $4,000.

As much as I enjoyed that brief experience making an honest living with Giordano, straightening out their accounting problems, I guess old habits, even bad old habits, die hard. I kept my vow of not going back into the bookmaking business and still got into enough action right away to begin getting back on my feet financially. Actually, I don't know who was happiest when I got out, me or Patty or Ann. The other guys, like Scoops and Slicker, were not producing for Patty, and he needed me to resume bringing in the money. So he pushed me to do more and to branch out. He put me in charge of supervising some of the shy business, and I was able to pull a couple of hundred a week out of that.

But the big money I started making again was from the card games. Before I went to jail I had been working the New York City monte game that had moved from Harlem down to the Lower East Side where we were partners with some guys from John Gotti's crew with the Gambinos. I thought we could do better with our own games in Newark, so we started a monte game at the Cage Club on Tenth Street and a big baccarat game at the East Side Social Club at Adams and Chestnut streets. Our partners in the monte game at first were the Genoveses—Joseph "Joe Z" Zarra, Phil DeNoia, and Ronald Catrambone. It shut down for a while, and when it reopened, we went partners with the Gambinos—Robert "Cabert" Bisaccia, Charles "Blackie" Luciano, Joe "Rackets" Casiere, and Anthony "Babe" DeVino.

What really surprised me was the number of new scams we had gotten into while I was in jail. We still did some business in stolen credit card numbers, but it was becoming a problem because the verification process was growing more and more electronic and we were not equipped to create the coded magnetic strips on the back of the cards. We still did some business in stolen goods and had started to fence goods on the East Coast that had been stolen in California and shipped back to us. And we were just starting to get into the video game and video poker business. Eventually it would become as big a money maker for us as bookmaking and the card games, but that was still to come. Now it was something for me to learn. And another new thing I got into was almost funny. The mob had figured out how to make big profits from what was essentially a kid's game.

I don't know what the game is called, but it's a large glass box crammed full of small toys and stuffed animals. There's a small crane in the box that you work from the outside with some hand controls. You get a small amount of time for a quarter or a half-dollar to lift an animal or a toy with the crane and drop it down a chute to the outside. It seemed so easy, but of course it wasn't. The stuffed animals were packed in so tightly, you practically had to dynamite them out. And even if you did win, you and others had probably put in $10 in quarters to get out a prize that cost less than a dollar.

The damn machines were a gold mine. If it was in a good location, you could take a couple of hundred dollars a month in profits out of every machine. That was our job, to persuade arcades, convenience stores, and other places where kids went to install the machines. The really big grossers were machines in Atlantic City and down on the Jersey Shore where families vacationed. At one point I heard the family as a whole was taking more than $10,000 a week out of these machines, and even more in the summer months.

Some things had changed, though. In June 1986, while I was still in Rahway, Nicky had straightened out six guys including Scoops, Slicker, and Joey Pungitore. I had felt good for them at the time, but I had also felt cheated because I knew that if I had been out, I would have been in the group. Now these guys were made and I was not, and at least theoretically our relationship was fundamentally different. I had to show them, as made guys, respect. We were all under Patty, and I still answered directly to him, but I was expected to show these guys respect. I knew that was going to be a problem for me.

In the mob, Christmas is a big time of year. Guys who were expected to give up some money every year to their bosses did so around the holidays, it being a nice touch to call a street tax a Christmas present. I'm not talking about the regular street tax a bookmaker, money lender, or drug dealer might pay for protection or the "tribute" that was paid by a member to the boss. That was a regular thing, paid weekly or monthly, or sometimes the boss was really a silent partner and took a split of the profits on a regular basis. Christmas money was almost voluntary.

A guy around Patty named Beeps Centorino was a good example. He was basically a fence, a guy who dealt in stolen property. Patty was not really a part of his business, he hadn't financed him or anything, but Beeps was around Patty and could come to him if he had a problem. So every year at Christmas he gave up $2,000 to Patty. It was certainly only a token, but if a couple of dozen guys gave such tokens every year, it ended up being a nice piece of change.

Christmas was also the time of year when payoffs were received from various honest businesses who needed protection or some favor or another. For example, the DeCavalcante family, founded by "Sam the Plumber" DeCavalcante, controlled the building trades unions throughout New Jersey. If you were a builder or a contractor, you could not do business unless you made annual payments to John Riggi, who was the boss of the family and also the business agent for Local 394 of the Laborers Union. A guy by the name of Mike Salimbene owned the Tectonic Construction Company headquartered in our part of Newark. Every year Salimbene paid Riggi $15,000. We had the job of collecting, which was not much of a job because Salimbene always paid on time; he knew he would be out of business overnight if he did not. But for our efforts, we got half—$7,500 every Christmas. Patty would keep half of his half, and we would send the rest down to Philadelphia. John Riggi gave us half of this payoff because he and Patty were close, and because we had been doing him favors for years.

I remember in early 1980 Patty asked me to pass along a clean gun with a silencer to John. So I did. A couple of weeks later, George Francenero, the brother of singer Connie Francis, got whacked. He was a bookie who had been around Riggi, and we heard the two had a falling-out. I never knew for sure if the gun I got did the job, but I had my suspicions.

So Christmas was a busy time for us, and every year Patty threw a big party at some restaurant. For the Christmas of 1987 the party was at Casa Dante, and everyone important in the Newark area was there. All our guys and guys from all the other families in the northern Jersey area were there. Cousin Anthony and some others had made the trip up from Philly, and Nicky Jr. and a couple more had come up from Atlantic City.

It was actually a wonderful night: good food, a lot of wine and booze, good company, and good conversation. At least one conversation I had that night was good. Another was not so good. And both involved Cousin Anthony.

Just after dinner I noticed that Patty was having a long conversation with Anthony. At one point I kind of walked by them, and Patty called me over. "George," he said. "Anthony and I have been talking about you, and he wants to tell you something."

"Yeah, George," Anthony said. "Pat is very upset and I feel bad that you ain't been straightened out yet. I want you to know that I know, and Nicky knows, that if you hadn't been in jail, you would have been taken care of along with Scoops and Slicker and those other guys last year. I'd do it now, but Nicky says wait until we see what happens with his appeal and things settle down some more. But we want you to know you are with us, you're one of us. Be honest, you are a lot more important to us than a lot of guys who have been straightened out. It'll happen, just be patient."

I found out later just how worried Patty was. He knew I was unhappy, he knew they had screwed up my business while I was in jail, and he knew I had done my time absolutely stand-up. Given all that, he was worried I was going to split. I had friends with the

Gambinos, the Genoveses, and the Colombos. It would have been unusual for a guy to move to another family. It would have been impossible for a made guy in one family to move to another. That was simply never done. But while it was unusual for someone who was around one family but not made to move to another, it was not unheard of, especially if a guy had no immediate prospects of being made. And since it did not look as if Anthony had been given the authority by Nicky to bring in any new members, Patty was worried that I might start looking elsewhere. His message to Anthony had been direct: They hadn't done right by me, and they needed me more than I needed them. Anthony had agreed that I would be straightened out as soon as possible, and he wanted me to know that as far as he was concerned and as far as Nicky was concerned, I would be treated as if I had been already formally made.

The whole thing pleased me a lot. I didn't tell Patty there wasn't a chance in the world that I would ever leave him—certainly not to join some other family. If I had been completely honest with him, I would have told him that Ann and I had begun to discuss what I could do and where we could go if I wanted to make an absolutely clean break. I thought about going to Vegas and getting work in one of the casinos. I certainly could have landed a top job as a pit boss or in one of the sports books, with my knowledge of the business and of the big-time players in the New York City–New Jersey area. But with my criminal record and my clear ties to organized crime, I could never get licensed. More important, at this point I just couldn't picture myself living a straight life or moving to some faraway place. I could never go straight in New Jersey or where they could find me. I knew much too much. They only let you retire alive when you were no longer useful. I could probably get away with becoming a Gambino, especially if John Gotti straightened me out, but I could never get away with becoming an average citizen.

Still, it kind of pleased me that I had them worried. I felt bad that Patty was worried, and later I laughed off the whole thing and told him I would be by him for as long as he wanted me. But the conversation with Anthony at the party seemed to be a kind of Christmas present. Later on, though, he had another present for me that was not very welcome or welcome at all.

I was standing with Nicky Jr. when Anthony came up to us. "George," he said, "there's some business Nicky wants you to take care of. I got word through Bobby that Nicky thinks it was Long John who flipped the Crow. He wants it taken care of. He wants you to do it. Nicky here will help you. Do it as soon as Long John is back on the street, or even better, if you can reach out, do it sooner."

When mob guys get together, they talk in a kind of shorthand or code, but I knew exactly what Cousin Anthony was telling me. He had received word from Nicky Sr. that he now believed Raymond Martorano—"Long John"—had persuaded Nick Caramandi—"the Crow"—to cooperate with the Feds. So Nicky wanted Martorano killed, and I was to do it with Nicky Jr.'s help. I was to wait either until Martorano got out of prison or, if I could figure a way, have it done in prison. If Martorano had been in a New Jersey lockup, that would have been easy. If he had been in Rahway, he would have been dead by New Year's. But he was in a federal institution.

That was the kind of message Nicky often sent us. Even though he was in the most secure prison the Feds have, he was still trying to run the business. He did it in one of two ways. There were strict limitations on who could visit him, and those visits were closely monitored. But he could have unlimited visits with his lawyers, and because of lawyer-client privilege, those visits were not monitored. So, as Nicky Jr. explained to me numerous times, his father would send out messages.

The other way Nicky kept in touch was even more ingenious. There was a list of people he was allowed to call, and he was limited to about one personal call a week, to a family member only. The guards would place the call for him to make sure he was not dialing some other number, and you can assume the call was either listened to or recorded. But Nicky was allowed unlimited phone calls to his lawyer, and again because of lawyer-client privilege, the guards were not supposed to monitor them. So what Nicky did was have the guards dial his lawyer's number, either Bobby Simone or one of the half-dozen others representing him on his appeal, and then as soon as the lawyer was on the line, he would conference in the third party Nicky wanted to talk with or who wanted to talk to him.

In the case of the message about Long John, it apparently came directly from Nicky via someone, who had been out to see him the week before. And why Nicky wanted Martorani whacked was a complicated story. It began when Willard Rouse and his Rouse Company, a major shopping center developer, announced he was going to Philly to build this huge $500 million shopping and entertainment center he was calling Penn's Landing on the riverfront downtown. When Nicky heard this, his eyes lit up. He knew Rouse was going to need zoning changes, legislation passed by the City Council, and the cooperation of a lot of labor unions in order to get this thing built. The way the project was structured, a bill had to be passed by the council before it could go forward. And the way the council worked, it would not even entertain such a bill unless it was introduced by the councilman in whose district the project was going to be located—in this case, Councilman Leland Beloff. Conveniently, Nicky owned Beloff, so a plot was hatched whereby Rouse would be asked to make a "contribution" of $1 million. In return, he would get his city ordinance, his zoning changes, and his labor peace. Nicky would take half, the councilman would take half, and everyone would be happy.

Nick Caramandi, called "Nicky Crow" or "the Crow," was a made guy who started out in the numbers and as a loanshark working for Dom DiVito. When Nicky had DiVito whacked, the Crow was working with "Pat the Cat" Spirto, collecting street tax from gamblers and drug dealers in Philly. But Pat the Cat had a falling out with Nicky and also got himself whacked. So Caramandi started running scams on his own and was involved in a couple of Nicky's hits. Nicky knew he could trust the Crow, so he brought him into the Rouse extortion.

Caramandi was given two responsibilities: to act as Nicky and Beloff's representative and collect the million dollars, and to make very sure that Rouse understood how bad it would be for his health if he ever told anyone about what was happening. So the bribe request was communicated to Rouse. He immediately went to the FBI. And when Caramandi started meeting with Rouse's "representative," the guy was actually an undercover FBI agent. In short order, the Crow, the councilman, and various others found themselves under arrest for extortion and other crimes.

The Feds needed Caramandi's testimony to be sure they would get Nicky Sr. and the councilman. They really didn't want Caramandi, who was small time, so they offered him a deal, but he refused. Enter Long John Martorano, one of the old Angelo Bruno guys. The Feds had him for ordering the hit on John McCullough, the union guy Nicky whacked for trying to organize in Atlantic City. Nicky believed the Feds had worked a deal: If Long John could convince the Crow to turn, then he would get a sentence reduction.

From talking with Caramandi I later learned that was exactly what had happened. The Feds put Long John together with Caramandi in the Philadelphia Federal Detention Center. Caramandi knew that Nicky was unhappy with him for not smelling out the fact that the guy he was dealing with was an FBI agent, so he was easy pickings for Long John, who convinced him that Nicky was going to kill him regardless of whether he talked or not. The only way he could save himself, Long John argued, was by getting himself into the federal Witness Protection Program, and the only way that could happen was if he rolled over on Nicky and the councilman.

He did, and he became the government's star witness. He ended up getting eight years, most of which was suspended. The councilman and his aide went to jail. And Nicky got fourteen years.

The order to whack Martorano showed the peculiar way Nicky's mind worked. If Caramandi had been standing in front of him or if Nicky had been standing there with his hands around Caramandi's throat, he would have killed him in an instant. But he basically understood the position that Caramandi had been placed in and that he had rolled over to try to protect himself. In a perverse way Nicky approved of this. What angered him was that Martorano would work with the Feds to get Caramandi to roll over when Martorano had no beef with him. So his message to me through Cousin Anthony was to be ready to kill Long John the moment he got out of jail. I was to know it was now my contract, and killing Long John would stay my responsibility for as long as it took.

Luckily for me and even luckier for Long John, he was in a federal lockup, somewhere where they keep snitches. And it looked as if he was going to stay where I could not get to him for quite a while.

In our family it was kind of a tradition, after the Super Bowl late in January, for all of us to head down to Florida for a couple of weeks. The purpose was to escape winter, spend some of the money we made from bookmaking during the football season, and, if we were lucky, make a little money by running one kind of scam or another in the Florida sun.

Before Nicky went to jail, this annual gathering was always centered around his house in Fort Lauderdale and the boat he kept there. In January 1988 we kept up the tradition even though Nicky would not be joining us. It was a much more relaxed gathering than it had been in years past. When Nicky was there, everything revolved around him. If he wanted to go over and lounge around a hotel pool, everyone lounged around the pool. If he was drinking that day, everyone drank what he drank. If he was hung over and not drinking, then no one drank. If he wanted to go out and cruise around on the boat, everyone went out for a cruise. If he wanted to go out to dinner, everyone went, and we were often left to pick up the check. Nicky's world absolutely revolved around Nicky. If you were missing, he might notice. If he noticed, he might think you were slighting him and get angry with you. And Nicky getting angry with you was decidedly bad for your health.

But with Nicky enjoying his enforced federal vacation, we all went south and had fun. We even took wives or girlfriends with us. I took Ann, and Patty took Anna Marie. We went to the track, we lay out in the sun, we ate and drank well, and we made one very nice score.

Patty's motto was that the best person to con was another crook because it left him no place to go. And his motto never worked better than during that vacation. One of the guys down with us knew a local who had ties to our family from when he lived in Jersey. About a week after we arrived, this guy tells us he has heard about a straight businessman from the Midwest who was down with a brief-case full of cash looking for a major cocaine connection. Our eyes lit up. We instantly determined that briefcase was going to be ours.

Another guy and I suddenly became two big-time coke dealers. We met this guy in a bar, and we had to keep from laughing during the conversation. The guy had been watching too much "Miami Vice." He was, in fact, a businessman who saw that all his friends were into coke in a big way, so he had a bright idea: He would buy wholesale in Florida, take it back home, and double or triple his money by selling to his friends. He figured he could make a couple of hundred thousand a year, tax free, and also be the center of attention back home as the supplier. "Set me up, fellas, and I'll be able to get laid forever," he said to us as we talked that night.

I have never sold a pill or an ounce of drugs in my life. I never wanted to, it was not my thing, and the risk was simply too great. But for three years I had spent every night at the monte game around some of the biggest drug dealers in New York. Talking with them and listening to them talk among themselves, I naturally picked up the lingo of the drug trade. I could talk ounces and grams, cutting, and wholesale value versus street value with the best of them. I just blew this guy away. He was sure I was the real thing and his ticket to riches.

"I only brought fifty thousand dollars with me," he said during our meeting. "Will you sell me fifty thousand dollars' worth?"

Of course I feigned insult. "How much?" I fumed.

"Fifty thousand dollars."

I sat there and sadly shook my head. "I was told you were a player.

Fifty thousand dollars is what I pay just for transportation on a shipment. This is not worth my time or the risk you're a narc."

I had him begging. He said he wanted a permanent connection and would spend three or four times that amount every couple of months in the future. It made me wonder exactly what kind of friends this guy had. But finally I asked him to step outside while "my colleague and I talk about this." When he left, we both burst out laughing. It's not every day you meet a guy who is begging you to take his fifty large. We let a couple of minutes pass, and then I went out to see him in his rented car in the parking lot.

"This is against my better judgment," I said, "but I've got a shipment coming in next week that's not completely spoken for. But I'm sorry, I just can't take the risk of selling you fifty thousand dollars' worth. I will only sell you multiples of one hundred thousand dollars' worth, but I'll give you full weight for every ounce. I'm only doing this because you were introduced to me by Tony, and he's heavily connected. I'm doing him the favor, not you."

This left the guy to hem and haw. He had brought only $50,000, he said.

"Fine, that's the down payment. You pay me half now and the other half when you pick up and test the goods. We'll meet here tomorrow night and start this. Can you get the other fifty thousand by ten days from now when you take delivery?"

"Sure, yeah, of course," he stammered.

"Okay. Here tomorrow night, say ten o'clock."

At that point we should have had some really sophisticated plan in mind, but we didn't. This guy was absolutely begging to be scammed. We were just going to take his money and tell him when to meet us with the other $50,000 to pick up his goods, then we would just get on the plane and fly home, figuring the guy would be too mortified to do anything. After all, what was he going to do, go to the cops?

We met the guy the next night, picked up the money, and told him to be in the same parking lot with a rental car in ten days. We asked if he was going home in the meantime. No, he answered, he would stay in Florida. "Don't worry," he assured us. "The other half is being wired down to me by my bank."

We expected to be in Florida another four days, which meant we were going to be out of there four days before this guy would be standing in a parking lot. We had a couple of conversations about whether we should try to get the other $50,000 by giving him a little actual coke and a lot of powder, figuring he wouldn't know the difference. But we figured it was not worth the risk. Besides, what if he was a cop? Actually, at times he acted so dumb and naive, that seemed the only answer. So we said the hell with it. We would just leave him poorer but wiser.

Then we caught a lucky break. The day before we were to leave, we woke up to banner headlines in the paper about this huge coke bust that had been made the night before by the Coast Guard. We couldn't let that pass. We called the guy in a panic and told him to meet us within a half hour. Our story was direct and to the point: It was our shipment that had been intercepted. We were sorry we had lost his $50,000, but we had lost $2 million of our own.

"Cost of doing business," I said, and I advised him to be on the next plane north in case we had been watched by the DEA. The last I saw of the guy, he was hurtling back to his hotel to pack. We had a nice dinner that night and left in the morning. It was a wonderful vacation, and it was more than paid in full. I only wish I had had a bridge to sell that guy. It was a good thing I was only a thief. I took his money, but the way he was stumbling around looking for a source, he was lucky I wasn't a narc. If I had been, he might still be inside.

It took about six to eight months, but I was finally beginning to feel comfortable financially. I was bringing in enough money every week to take care of things at home, allow me to start living the life-style again, and have enough left over to help Patty. There were ten or eleven guys around Patty, and none of them had been to jail. But I was his biggest money maker before I went in, and not six months after I got out, I was again the only one he could count on. It was really disgusting. This was truly the every-man-for-himself gang.

Even so, I was beginning to feel good about things again. There were strains, certainly, and a lot of it had to do with the fact that I wasn't straightened out, and Scoops and Slicker were. Slicker was okay about it. He hadn't changed at all. He treated me as a complete equal and would often defer to me to make decisions both big and small. But something had clearly changed in my relationship with Scoops. His whole attitude seemed to say: I'm made, and you're not. The change was subtle but clear. He became very formal with me, and he was visibly agitated when I resumed my place at Patty's side. Being around him made me feel very uncomfortable.

Ann watched all this without saying much, but I could tell she was not very happy to see me drifting back into my old habits. She had never been one to hang around with the other wives. Most of them were afraid of their husbands. Ann was never afraid of me, nor did she ever have any reason to be. She believed that most of the other wives put up with the crap their husbands gave them as long as there was a new fur coat in the closet every year, new jewelry at Christmas, appointments at the hairdressers twice a week, and summers at the shore. They didn't care what their husbands did or who they ran around with—male or female—as long as the gravy train did not stop. Ann had always held them in contempt.

Before my time in jail, I had thought she liked or at least tolerated Patty and a couple of the others. But she had come away from my jail experience and her months on welfare with both fears and hatreds, and my returning to my old ways just brought them to the surface. She didn't scream or yell; she didn't give ultimatums. There was no "get out" or "I'm leaving you." In a way I almost wish she had laid it on the line because then I might have been forced to make a choice to leave the life. She had too much class for that. She knew I had to come to my own decision at my own pace. But she showed how deeply bothered she was by what I was doing when she said one morning, "I'm going to get a job."

Even though our kids were in school all day now, for my wife to get a job was not just a big deal, in the mob life it was close to unthinkable. It was an insult to the husband, an admission that he couldn't provide for his wife and family. Wives took care of the children, wives stayed at home, wives had their place—to be seen when their husbands wanted them to be seen and to stay very quietly in the background when they didn't.

I knew exactly what Ann was saying. In making this announcement she was not asking me if she could go back to work, she was telling me. Ann was saying that never again was she going to be dependent on anyone if I was suddenly not there—whether in jail or shot through the back of the head some night. If I was going to stay in the mob life, then she would have to make plans for a life without me. I didn't disagree with her. She was a bright woman who had held a very good job before we were married. There was no reason she shouldn't now, and if it gave her security, so much the better. She had stood by me, and I would stand by her.

.   .   .

In late March I received a very disturbing phone call from one of the Lucchese guys I was with in the monte game. His family had a plant on the New Jersey State Parole Board. He in turn had a friend in the Attorney General's Organized Crime Task Force. From that friend he heard that about two weeks earlier the cops were able to place a bug somewhere near Patty, and he was being recorded. The Lucchese guy said he thought I should know about it quick.

It really didn't surprise us. Patty had been a special target of both the Feds and the New Jersey State Police ever since Tony Bananas had been killed. They were still angry that he had ducked the subpoena they had issued to bring him in and talk to the grand jury about Bananas. More recently we found out they had heard that Patty had been asked to head the family after Nicky was jailed in January. They had redoubled their efforts to get Patty, and we knew they had been watching him and the rest of us that hung with him. It didn't come as all that great a shock to hear they had planted a listening device somewhere; the question was where. We had to find it, or we would be doomed to speaking on street corners in a whisper for the rest of our days.

At first we were a little stumped. We searched as best we could with no luck. Then we borrowed an electronic bug-detecting wand from a guy who worked as an electronics consultant to the local cops. It was kind of ironic. We were using Essex County police equipment to find a state police bug. The wand was a high-tech gizmo that buzzed when it was placed near a radio transmitter. The guy showed us how to use it, and we set to work.

We swept the 3-11 Club. Nothing. We swept several other social clubs in the neighborhood. Still nothing. We swept Patty's house. Nothing. We swept Anna Marie's place on the off chance it might be bugged. It wasn't. We started to think we had gotten a bad tip, but we kept on looking. Patty had two cars at the time, one he drove occasionally and one his wife drove. We checked both of them. Still nothing. We were almost out of ideas. I was still too broke to afford more than one car, and that was being driven during the day by Ann because of the kids. Patty was never in it, but we checked it just in case. Negative. The only other place we could think of was Turk Cifelli's car which we had been using lately. We ran the bug detector through it, and it buzzed like crazy. Bingo.

The bug had been planted under the dashboard with a small radio transmitter hidden under the car frame. Our electronics consultant friend was very impressed. He said the system was absolutely state of the art, the latest thing and really expensive. He told us this as he was ripping it out.

It soon became clear that we had made the cops very angry. Turk took the transmitter to his lawyer, and about an hour later he was pulled over by a state trooper. Within a matter of minutes his car was surrounded, and the cops wanted the bug back. "Talk to my lawyer," said Turk. So for two days they did. The lawyer demanded to see the warrant under which they had planted the bug. The cops complied. It had been obtained based on the affidavit of a "confidential informant." The lawyer demanded to see the affidavit. The cops refused, of course. Finally, when the Attorney General's Office threatened to arrest both Turk and the lawyer on charges of receiving and possessing stolen goods, they got their equipment back.

When we discovered the bug, I started to do some very fast thinking. Since the information we had received about the bug from the Lucchese source in the Attorney General's Office had proved correct, we had to assume that the rest of the information was also generally accurate—that the bug had been in place for a little over two weeks. I tried to remember how many times I had been in the car during that period and what in God's name I had said. To the best of my recollection I had been in the car only three or four times, and I really didn't think I had been involved in any kind of incriminating conversation. I was spending most of my nights at the monte game, sleeping until early afternoon, and then heading back to the game after dinner. Turk and a couple of the other guys probably had some worries, but I figured I was in the clear. When nothing happened for a while, I thought we had gotten the word in time and the bug had done the police no good.

I learned years later how Turk's car had been bugged. I got the details from some of the guys who had been involved in the caper. It was one of the most expensive operations of its kind ever undertaken by the state police, and its failure when we found the bug had caused major ripples all the way up the line to the Attorney General himself. That they went to so much trouble and expense showed just how badly they wanted to get Patty.

The cops knew from a "confidential informant" that Patty was riding around in Turk's car. They knew Turk was driving a 1973 Cadillac Eldorado painted a really strange light orange color. In fact, the cops called the car "the Pumpkin" and referred to the tapes coming from the bug as "stuff out of the Pumpkin." Surveillance of Turk showed that a couple of times a week he would spend the night at the apartment of one of his girlfriends, Julie, whom we called Duckie. It was decided that on one of these nights the cops would take the car, install the bug, and return it to the same spot before Turk left in the morning. But that was not as simple as it sounded.

The first thing the cops did was buy an identical model of the Eldorado and have it painted approximately the same color. Then they had an identical set of license plates made so it would appear, even to Turk at a distance, that it was his car. They used this second identical car for practice; they learned exactly how to take the dashboard out, put in the bug, and replace the dashboard. It got so they could do it in their sleep. The plan was to block off both ends of the street in front of Duckie's apartment building, use a set of keys supplied by General Motors to start Turk's car, and drive it to a nearby state police barracks to install the bug. In the meantime, they would replace Turk's car in front of the apartment with the decoy car just in case he looked out the window. They figured they could take the car, plant the bug, and have it back in place within two hours.

On the appointed night, about twenty state troopers took part in the operation, and nothing seemed to go as planned. GM could only supply them with a ring of about a hundred keys, and they had to try them one by one until they could finally start the car. Then they had all kinds of problems installing the bug. It wouldn't work, and then they couldn't get the dashboard back on correctly. In the end it took over six hours, and by the time they got the car back, it was already daylight. Fortunately for them, Turk was not an early riser.

No wonder the cops got so angry when the bug was discovered only two weeks after they went to all that trouble and expense. They had planned to leave it in for six months or more. And from the methodical way we had gone looking for the bug, they knew we had been tipped off. That panicked them because it meant they had a serious security leak in their organization.

I also learned a few weeks later that Patty had caught a real break when we found the bug in Turk's car. As we were warned and as we suspected, Patty was the principal target of the operation. The state police had just begun presenting evidence to a grand jury, and when we were tipped to the bug, they were nowhere near ready to obtain an indictment or make an arrest. They figured that Patty would try to flee if indicted since that had been his pattern in the past. They intended to charge him under New Jersey law as a "leader of organized crime," which would carry a very heavy sentence if he was convicted. Given Patty's age, it would have meant life in prison. They were also going to oppose any bail, arguing that Patty was a flight risk, so the odds were that if he were arrested, he would never see the light of day again.

When the bug was discovered, the police went into a total panic. They rushed to Patty's house with the intention of following him closely while they quickly went into court and got an arrest warrant. They also went to Anna Marie's, figuring he would be there if he was not at home. But as luck would have it, Patty had not spent the night in either place. The cops missed him.

I knew he was spending the night at another girl's apartment. As soon as we found the bug, I hurried to a pay phone to call him. At the time I thought he overreacted to the news, but in retrospect he ended up doing exactly the right thing. The girl's place was around the corner from the house of Patty's son-in-law's mother. So he went there and began to make calls, and within an hour he had formulated a plan. He would leave the country that night and lie low until we could figure out exactly what was going on. His daughter brought him some clothes and his passport. He told me to meet him late that afternoon at Kennedy Airport and bring what money I could scrounge up. I spent an hour driving around, making sharp turns and constantly doubling back on myself to make sure I wasn't being followed. When I felt safe, I headed to Kennedy. I gave Patty a couple of thousand dollars, and he got on a plane to Argentina even before the cops realized he was not just hiding out in his house.

He picked Argentina because that's where his son-in-law was from, and he could stay with his son-in-law's relatives. Buenos Aires also has a large Italian community, and Patty had an aunt and uncle living there he could also turn to. Most important, he chose Argentina because its extradition treaty with the United States did not extend to gambling and financial crimes. Chances were that even if the cops were able to find him, they wouldn't be able to bring him back.

Over the next two weeks I talked with Patty several times a day. Although it was clear we were being watched and there was always a car with a couple of guys we assumed to be cops parked outside Patty's house, nothing had happened yet. They were looking for

Patty, but none of the rest of us had been arrested or even brought in for questioning.

"George, you can't take the chance they'll arrest you, too," Pat warned me over the phone. "With your record, any conviction will draw you hard time. Get on the plane and come down here. At least do it until we can see what happens."

I considered it, but I thought I had been in Turk's car so little, I was probably in the clear. Then when I talked it over with Ann, it was clear from her reaction that my fleeing the country would be about the same as going back to jail. There was no way she was going to pack up the kids and move to South America. I could leave, but she would not go with me.

But Patty kept hammering away, so about two weeks after he left, I made arrangements to take $10,000 down to him. When I told Ann I was going to Buenos Aires, but only for a few days, she gave me a withering look that said she didn't quite believe me. "Do what you have to do," she said, "but no matter what happens, we're staying here."

I went down, and Patty was insistent I not go back. But for one of the few times in my life I went against what he wanted. I stayed just a few days, and as I was getting on the plane, he still did everything he could to convince me I was making a big mistake. I didn't think so. I just couldn't believe the cops had enough on me from one or two recorded conversations to make any kind of arrest stick. I told Pat I thought he had done the right thing. I was sure I could play it out.

Wrong.

For a while I thought I was in the clear. The weeks passed with nothing happening. I pretty much went back to my normal schedule of going to one of the card games every night, sleeping in until late afternoon, having dinner with Ann and the kids, and then going out to the game again. Patty and I still talked just about every day, with him calling me at a different pay phone at a specified time. I tried to convince him that the planting of the bug had been a failure and they had not gotten enough on any of us to indict. I argued that he should come home, but he insisted on remaining out of reach until he was absolutely sure. He thought that if he was the main target, maybe they weren't making any move until they had him in their sights. It turned out he was exactly right.

Then came the night of May 31, 1988. It was a very long one for me. It started out with Scoops, Slicker, and me meeting Nicky Jr. and a couple of his friends for dinner at Lorenzo's Steak House in

Trenton. We gave him some money to pass on to his father, and we discussed some business. Then we took the train back to Newark, and I went over to the baccarat game at the East Side Social Club. It lasted until past dawn, and I was dead tired as I was heading home.

My beeper went off, not once but twice in rapid succession. One call was from my home number. Almost immediately a second page came in, and I recognized the number as a pay phone down the block from the house, a pay phone I often used to make business calls. I called that number first. It was Ann's sister. She had slept over at our house that night and was now in a panic. There were police at my house waiting to arrest me.

I sat in my car thinking for a few long minutes. My first reaction was to head to the airport and hop a plane to Argentina. But then I said to myself, no, I can't leave Ann and the kids. Over and over I kept coming back to the same conclusion: Based on the bug in Turk's car, they couldn't have enough on me to make any kind of an indictment stick. The only thing I could conclude was that they were arresting me to squeeze me to tell them where Patty was. They would assume he was hiding out somewhere in Jersey or New York. But Patty was out of reach, and I convinced myself that what was happening to me was no big deal.

On the way home I made a stop at a friend's and dropped off the money I was carrying, about $10,000. Then I rushed home, expecting to find the cops ransacking it as they had the last time I was arrested. But when I walked through the front door, I found Ann and four guys sitting at the kitchen table drinking coffee.

The guy in charge politely introduced himself as New Jersey State Police Detective Sergeant Ed Quirk. He said he was there to arrest me based on a warrant charging me with racketeering, conspiracy, usury, usury as a business, and promoting gambling. I asked who else they had warrants for, and he said Patty, Slicker, Nick Cifelli, Jimmy Santoriello, and Stephen Blum.

Still very politely, Quirk said they had a warrant to search the house, and I could save them a lot of time and myself and my wife a lot of grief if I told them if and where I had any gambling records or the like. I said I had none in the house. By this time the kids were up and getting ready to go to school. The four cops just sat quietly in the kitchen while the kids got dressed and my sister-in-law took them for breakfast at McDonald's and then to school. When my oldest son asked them who they were, they said they were my insurance agents.

After the kids left, Quirk read me my rights. Then they started to search the house. If you can search a place and be neat about it, they were. Ann went with them, and they let her open drawers and lift stuff out. At one point they opened my closet and went through the suits I had hanging there. In the inside pocket of one suit they found my emergency money, $1,000. Ann spoke up and said it was hers. Most cops would have said, "Yeah, right," and confiscated it as fruits of a criminal enterprise. Ed Quirk handed the money to Ann. "Put it someplace safe," he said.

They finished up and found nothing because there was nothing to find. They said they had to take me in and book me, but they didn't handcuff me as we were leaving. That impressed me, too. They seemed like decent guys doing a job. But what I will never forget that morning was the look on Ann's face as I was being led out the door. She said after I came home from Rahway that she had lived through my going to prison once but never again. Her look that morning, a combination of sadness and anger, told me clearly that she meant it.

6

CONFIDENTIAL SOURCE

I was back home in time for dinner. Ann took the five thousand the state police had missed when they searched and the ten grand I had stashed on the way home from the monte game, and together it was enough both to pay my lawyer a retainer and to pay a bail bondsman to put up my bail. During what was a very long day, first at the police station and then at the courthouse, the cops told me surprisingly little. I figured that was because I was really not the guy they wanted, and they hoped the arrests might flush Patty out of hiding. I later learned that had been the case.

I was still puzzled, though. When Quirk read me my rights, he indicated they were arresting me on charges of racketeering, conspiracy, usury, usury as a business, and promoting gambling. I was absolutely at a loss to explain how one or two taped conversations in Turk Cifelli's car could possibly be enough evidence to allow a grand jury to return such a wide-ranging indictment. All I thought of was that we had been talking about the shy business in the car, and that could have led to the usury charges. I would have been surprised if they had taped a conversation in which we didn't talk about gambling. But it must have been very nonspecific for them to charge me only with "promoting" gambling. I knew enough about the law to realize that under New Jersey statutes if more than three guys discuss anything illegal, it is considered a conspiracy and can be called racketeering. I thought it might have been possible for a grand jury to return the indictment they did based on one or two conversations, but the state's willingness to release me, technically a three-time loser, on such relatively low bail made me believe they had a weak case against me.

As soon as I could get to a safe phone, I called Patty in Argentina. After listening to him sing several choruses of "I told you so," I gave him my theory that he was the main target and I had been swept up either as an afterthought or to pressure me into giving him up. He was not worried about me, though. His main concern was himself. He said I should call his lawyer in the morning and have him talk with the cops and the Attorney General's Office to see what the charges against him were. "Looks like I ain't coming back for a very long time, George, but let's see what I'm up against."

If he expected the worst, that's exactly what he got. The lawyer found out that Patty was being charged with the same crimes as I was and also as a leader of organized crime. If found guilty, he was likely to get a minimum of twenty-five years. We had no idea how strong the evidence was, but from what we were hearing on the street, what the cops had told me, and what Patty's lawyer found out, things looked pretty bleak. Patty would have to remain a fugitive.

Patty and I talked four or five times over the next few days. I played messenger boy, taking several messages to Patty's wife and to Scoops and Slicker, and also letting Cousin Anthony know that Patty had screwed and was not likely to be back for quite a while. Anthony said he wanted to talk directly with Pat. I passed along the message, and Pat called him. Anthony then called me back and said he wanted to see me, Scoops, and Slicker in Philadelphia right away. I was to drive them down the next morning.

The meeting took place in a conference room at Donald Manno's office; he was Cousin Anthony's lawyer. As long as I knew him, Anthony had been more than a little paranoid about being bugged, and given what had just happened to us, who could blame him? As he had it figured, the cops could never get a warrant to bug a lawyer's office, so it was safe to talk business there. I guess over the years I sat in on half a dozen meetings in Manno's office. He was never there, and he did not appear to want any part in what was being discussed. If asked, he was just making a conference room available for a good client to conduct some business; it was not his concern what that business was.

On the day in March that Patty left for Argentina, Scoops, Slicker, and I met with him at the house he was hiding out in. He did not know if he was leaving for a week, a month, or forever, so he said the three of us should run things jointly. "The three of you handle anything that comes up," he said, adding that we should talk among ourselves and come to day-to-day decisions jointly. If we had a major decision or could not agree, I was to call him, and he would make the decision. Now with the indictments in, we knew that Pat was going to have to stay away for an extended period. Thus Anthony wanted to formalize the arrangement that Patty had made the day he left.

"Pat's going to be away for some time, so we have to get you guys reorganized" was the way Anthony started the meeting. He said he thought, and Pat agreed, that the way things had been left was too informal a way for the family to operate. So now he was going to change things around slightly.

He said that he and Patty had decided Pat would remain the captain even though he was not going to be back anytime soon. By this Anthony meant that Pat would still be responsible for making major decisions. Since it was best for as few people as possible to know where Pat was, I was to be the only person who would communicate with him.

"Joseph," Anthony said, looking at Scoops, "just as it has been, if you need to get in touch with Patty, do so through George. If Pat needs to get a message to you, he will do so through George. If something cannot wait, then you can always call me directly. But George has my confidence and Pat's. You can be sure if he tells you something, it's coming directly from Pat."

What Anthony didn't realize was that I knew exactly what he was going to say that morning because Patty and I had had long conversations about it over the past few days. When Patty had first spoken to Cousin Anthony, he said he wanted me put in direct control by making me the acting captain while he was away. Anthony said that was impossible because I had never been straightened out, and he would not put an unmade guy in charge of made guys. Patty had countered that that was a perfect reason to straighten me out immediately. Anthony replied that was also impossible, repeating what he had said at Patty's Christmas party: Nicky saw the making of any new guys while he was in jail as an admission that he was no longer in charge. Anthony had told Patty that if he straightened me out, Nicky just might feel he had to have me killed to make the point that he was still the boss.

What Anthony was telling Scoops that day was that he and Pat had agreed on a kind of unusual compromise. Scoops, as the oldest made guy around Patty, while not being officially named acting captain, would be designated as first among equals. Patty would retain control, and I would be the only contact between the family and Patty. If Patty wanted to give me authority to do things on my own in his name, that would be between Patty and me. As far as Anthony was concerned, if I said something was coming directly from Patty, it would be.

You could see that Scoops was pleased. After all those years of hanging around first Tony Bananas and then Patty, he would finally have some power and authority. He made the obligatory statements about how proud he was and how hard he would work, and he promised that as long as Patty had to be on the run, he would help him out while continuing to make good on all his obligations to Anthony and to Atlantic City. If Scoops hadn't been lying through his teeth, things might have worked out just fine.

Over the next week or so I received several calls and a visit from Ed Quirk. He was a big guy—he looked like the football player he was in college. My first impression of him the morning he arrested me was that he was a nice guy. It was also clear that he was very sharp and went about his job in a professional way. As I suspected he would, he began to pressure me to cooperate with him and give up Patty. I told him "no way," that he was wasting his time. Then he told me quite a bit more about my arrest and the evidence against me. "Our confidential source has been Steve Blum," he announced.

It was as if he had dropped a bombshell. As he related what had happened, I listened with both a growing rage and a sinking feeling. I had been done in once again by a gambler in trouble, turning in his bookie; only in this case it had gone one step further. The cops had picked up a guy on drug charges. To make a deal, this small-time drug dealer started giving up everyone the cops would be even mildly interested in. One of the guys he gave up was his bookie, Steve Blum. The cops knew Stevie was around some wiseguy, but they were not sure who, so they decided to get into Stevie more deeply. The drug guy the cops had on the hook introduced Quirk to

Stevie as the owner of a limo company. Quirk started to bet with Blum. When he lost, he paid up. When he won, he collected his money. All was carefully documented and often recorded. Quirk and Stevie became friends. The cops had even acquired a limo, and Quirk and other state cops playing the company's drivers actually drove guys to Atlantic City in arrangements made through Blum. What they were hoping for was to get wiseguys into the limo to see where they went, who they met with, and what they talked about during the ride. I think I was in their phony limo once when Blum and I went down to Atlantic City for a night of blackjack.

By this time Quirk knew that Blum was around Patty, so they were patient and waited. Then after Nicky Sr. went to jail and they heard that Patty had been approached to become acting boss, they sharply upgraded Patty as a target and decided it was time to reel in Stevie. By then they had their hooks so deep into Stevie that when they arrested him, he had almost no choice but to cooperate. He was not a very strong personality and did not want to go to jail. When the cops squeezed him and then made him an offer—get us Pat Martirano, and you can walk—he jumped at the chance and went right to work.

Stevie told the cops that Patty was being driven around in Turk Cifelli's car, and he became the "confidential informant" who gave the cops the affidavit that got the judge to approve the planting of the bug. What I was hearing annoyed me, but it didn't worry me much because I figured I had been in the car only a few times. I was about to say "so what" when Quirk dropped an even bigger bombshell: "Blum wore a wire," he said.

Then he went on to tell me exactly how deep I was in. My indictments were not based on conversations recorded in Turk's car; they were based on conversations I had had with Stevie and with others while Stevie was present and wired. The cops had the whole thing on tape. "Really clear, really good quality," Quirk said.

He was very specific about one meeting that took place on April 13 in the parking lot of a McDonald's on McCarter Highway in Newark. Stevie Blum owed us a lot of money. Almost all bookmakers need working capital from time to time, and Blum was no different. He had borrowed $38,000 from us and some other money directly from Scoops. He was paying two percent interest per week, $760 on the loan. He also was paying us another $750 a week in street tax, both for protection and as a commission for the players we had sent him. But he was having trouble making his payments. Quirk told me that at least three of the conversations recorded in Turk's car were about Blum's debts. Patty had said he was sure Stevie was doing a lot better than he was letting on. In one conversation he told Turk that we might have to hurt Stevie if he didn't start repaying some of the principal on the loan and his street tax every week. What was not on tape was Patty telling me that since I knew book-making and I knew Stevie, I should examine his whole operation and try to figure out whether he was really having hard times or if he was scamming us. Patty said if I thought his troubles were real, I could make some adjustments in his pay-back schedule.

That's what the McDonald's parking lot meeting had been all about. I was there to collect Blum's weekly interest and street tax payment, and to go over his books to try to find out why he was so broke. And when I remembered that, I also remembered that when Steve paid, he had practically counted out the money dollar by dollar. It hadn't registered at the time what he was doing. And when he gave me the money, he had been very careful to say, this is for the interest on the loan, this is for the street tax. He was setting things up for the recording. That meeting was a day or two after we had found the bug in Turk's car. I had warned Turk about it and told him that there might be more bugs, to be careful what he said and where he said it. Quirk said the cops had a good laugh when they played that part of the conversation back.

Quirk didn't play the conversation for me or give me a transcript, but I believed him. I remembered the meeting very well. I had tried to be a nice guy. I had told Stevie that we were willing to give him the benefit of the doubt. I negotiated with him to cut his interest rate in half, from two points a week to a single point as long as he made his payments on time and without the recent hassles. That would have dropped his weekly interest payment from $760 to $380. I also told him that his alternative was to keep paying late and risk getting hurt. Now I realized where the two usury charges and the promotion of gambling charge came from. The cops probably had me pretty tight just from this one meeting.

If they had this conversation between Blum and me recorded, then what others between us might they have? I racked my brain trying to remember every conversation I had had with Steve Blum over the past couple of months and every conversation I had had in his presence. All I could figure was that there had been quite a few. In retrospect I could see that Stevie had been hanging around Patty much more than usual, but we simply had not noticed it at the time.

It was really impossible to figure out what else the cops might have recorded. It could be that they had me cold. Or their case might be very marginal. I had no way of knowing.

Although it was now clear that my situation was more serious than I had first suspected, I still told Quirk I had no interest in cooperating and would not even consider giving up Patty. The news didn't seem to faze him. He didn't try to get tough, and he didn't threaten. He just said he would get back to me with some more information that I might find of interest.

Patty went nuts when I told him it was Stevie Blum who had screwed on him. "That fucking piece of shit, after all we did for him," he exploded after I told him what Quirk had told me. "There's no honor left in this thing, George, no honor left at all."

Over the course of several phone calls, Patty was able to remember several of what he now considered strange conversations with Stevie Blum, who had obviously been setting him up to get him on tape admitting various things. Patty figured they had him dead to rights.

Patty was not all that happy in Argentina. He was safe but didn't particularly like the place. His son-in-law's relatives were there and his own aunt and uncle, but he didn't speak Spanish and was not about to learn. Then, too, he was feeling ill and couldn't get the level of health care services he wanted. He and I talked at length about whether I thought it might be safe for him to sneak back into the United States and maybe try to hide out in Florida or California. But he worried that he would be picked up when coming in. We figured the cops had a warrant out for him. We discussed the possibility of sneaking him back in by car, either through Canada or Mexico. We thought it would be safe, but there was some risk and Pat figured he had too much to lose. Finally, after about a week of calls, Pat told me what he had decided to do: he would go back to the old country, he would simply disappear into the Calabria region of Italy, probably in his father's town of Reggio. He had friends and relatives there, and clout through the Mafia. And he was sure he could be comfortable there for as long as it took to make this New Jersey indictment go away.

Patty still worried that he would be caught as he entered Italy. He was worried that New Jersey had issued an international fugitive warrant on him through Interpol. If so, he might be stopped going through the Rome airport, or if he got to Reggio, the Italian police might come looking for him. He practically begged me to find a way that would allow him to get to Italy.

The way was both simple and very difficult. Ed Quirk had been promising me all kinds of things if I would turn snitch. He promised to make my case go away, get me money, get me into a Witness Protection Program. But the bottom line to any deal that he wanted to make was that I would have to give up Patty, and that was the one thing I was unwilling even to discuss.

His promises got me thinking, though. Instead of giving him Patty, maybe I could get the cops to be Patty's protectors. Quirk sounded surprised when I called him. Later on I found out that he had been very surprised. With my prison record, he thought I would be the easiest of the group to turn. When I stonewalled him, he wrote me off as a hard case and was about to move on to Turk to see if he could squeeze him. I called him on a Friday, and we tried to figure where we could meet unseen the next day. He actually lived well south of Newark, and we finally agreed to meet first thing in the morning at a Toys "R" Us store in the Blue Star Shopping Center in Mountainside.

We walked the aisles of that store for more than two hours, just talking. It ended up being a big day for my kids and his, too. We both bought all kinds of stuff to make our being there for so long look legit. He thought I wanted to make a deal to save myself, and our conversation quickly took a turn that clearly surprised him again. He was visibly taken aback when I said I was there to make a deal for Patty. He was surprised, but he was willing to listen.

"What I want is simple," I told him. "I can guarantee you that Patty Specs [I used his street nickname] is not in this country, that he has no intention of coming back, and that he will never set foot again in the State of New Jersey. From your point of view, it's the same as if you had put him in jail. I'm willing to cooperate with you in some manner if you can absolutely guarantee that you will not issue any kind of international warrant for Patty and that you will not actively try to track him down."

We spent a great deal of time talking about what I would do for him. I said right off that I would not wear a wire, I would not rat out any of my friends, and, above all, I would never appear as a witness in court against anyone. If there was still a way beyond all this that I could help him, then I would if he could guarantee Patty's free movement outside the country. It became a kind of bidding situation. Will you do this, will you do that, he wanted to know. What we finally agreed on was that I would become a "confidential source" for him. I would not have to volunteer any information, but if he came to me with information he had obtained elsewhere or had heard on the street, I would confirm it if I could. In exchange he would get the Attorney General to agree not to pursue Patty or to issue any warrant to either the Feds or through them to Interpol. I thought I had worked out a pretty good deal. I would be giving up very little, and Patty could go to Italy without any worries.

Quirk had his requirements, too. "Let me warn you about two things, Fresolone," he said ominously. "Never lie to me. If you don't know something, just say you don't know. If you know but don't want to tell me, then say that. But don't ever lie, or this deal will be off. And if I ever find that Patty Specs is back in the state, I'll come down on you as hard as I can."

During the whole two hours of our conversation, we talked only about Patty and said little about my own case. A couple of days later Quirk called to say his bosses had approved the deal. I would become his secret source, and in exchange the State of New Jersey would kind of forget that Pat Martirano existed—unless he gave them some reason to remember, like setting foot back in the state. Then he threw me a surprise bonus. As long as I was cooperating with him, he said, my own case would start to move in slow motion. It would be too obvious if the charges were dismissed, but there would be continuances and postponements so that it might take years before much happened. By then, he said, "if things work out," maybe the indictment would simply disappear. So I was helping myself while I was helping Patty.

I was stumped about what I would say to Patty. There was no way I could tell him I was cooperating with the police to get them off his back. I honestly think he would have come back and turned himself in before allowing me to become a fink. So when I called him that night in Buenos Aires, I launched into this complex explanation. I told him that my lawyer had found out that since the case against him was based on a wire worn by an informant, that was enough to bring charges against him in New Jersey but wasn't sufficient to allow the courts to issue an international fugitive warrant. Thus he was free to leave for Italy without worrying that he would be stopped by Italian immigration or that the Italian cops would come after him.

I could hear the relief in his voice.

. . .

Mafia wives are meant to bear and raise children, cook dinner on Sundays, go to weddings (but not funerals), and be shown off occasionally at a party or on some vacation. A good Mafia guy never tells his wife anything about his business. I guess I was never a good Mafia guy in this regard because I always told Ann everything that was going on. This time was no different. As soon as I had cut my deal with Ed Quirk, I told her.

She didn't quite know how to take the news. Her initial reaction was to be happy that my case was going to be put on a back burner by the state. I knew she was terrified that I was going back to jail, but now this deal gave her a new thing to worry about. I was trusting my life to some guy on the state police she had met for a couple of hours the morning he came to arrest me. The equation was very simple, and she understood it perfectly. If word ever leaked out that I was cooperating with the police, I was a dead man. I wouldn't be given a chance to explain that I was doing it for Patty or that I wasn't really giving up vital information. If they found out, I would be whacked immediately.

I had thought about that. I knew from firsthand experience that the Luccheses had a source high enough in the Attorney General's Office that he heard about the bug only a couple of weeks after it had been planted. I knew of at least two or three other leaks in the state's anti–organized crime effort. I had only Ed Quirk's assurance that he, and only he, would know my identity. I would be his source, and I would be known to others only by an identification number. I was taking a risk, but I thought it was a manageable risk. More important, given what was at stake for Patty, it was a risk I was willing to take.

Ann was smarter than I was about many things. I had jumped into this deal as a quick way of helping Patty out of an immediate problem. I had not done it as part of any long-range plan. I did it without taking much time to think through the ramifications. Maybe I thought I could just walk away from the arrangement when I no longer needed it, but Ann knew immediately that the decision would alter the course of our lives. She knew instinctively that I was starting down a road from which there would be no turning back.

"George," she said, "they'll never let you walk away from this. At best you're going to be tied to this guy Quirk until you can't do him any more good, and then he'll throw you to the dogs. Every time you give him information, he'll be able to use the fact that you're helping him to blackmail you. You may be helping Patty and you may be helping yourself, but you're going to be digging a deeper hole for yourself every day. Why can't you just tell them what you know, and then we'll walk away from this whole thing?"

"I can't just walk away," I tried to explain. "I can't walk away from Patty. The family is certainly not going to let me walk away, and now the state isn't going to let me walk away from this indictment. I have to start doing this now. I know we have a problem, and I'll come up with a solution—but it might take time."

Within a few days Ed Quirk set up a meeting, the first of many. And over the next months our pattern was that he would page me, and I would call him back. We would agree to meet at some random place—usually the parking lot of a store or shopping mall or at a rest area on the parkway or an exit of the turnpike. He would then get in my car, and we would drive around and talk. Even though his car was unmarked, I hesitated getting into it. Someone might recognize it and see me in it. We were always careful where we drove. It was never around Down Neck or even Newark.

That first time, Quirk wanted to give me what amounted to a test. And in doing so we established a method of operation that now seems mostly silly even to me, but at the time it was very important.

I was doing what I was doing only with the greatest reluctance and only because of Patty. It was absolutely necessary for me to believe I was doing only the absolute minimum I had to do in order to help Patty. I had told Quirk I would confirm information that he might have, but I wouldn't volunteer anything. As a result, we began to play word games as if we were contestants on the game show "Jeopardy." For example, if Quirk asked, "Who is your family's acting boss?", I would refuse to answer. But if he said, "I hear with Nicky in jail, Cousin Anthony has been made acting boss, is that right?", I would say it was correct.

The first time we met, we struggled for quite a while to establish these ground rules. He asked me a couple of questions for which I knew he knew the answers. So when I told him something was correct or it wasn't, he knew I was being truthful. He kept pushing for more, but my truthfulness in what I confirmed seemed to give him confidence that the relationship was going to be beneficial for him.

A couple of days later we met again, and this time the session was more serious. I was not Quirk's only informant. Nicky Crow—Nick Caramandi—the made family member involved in the attempt to extort Willard Rouse the developer had flipped. And he was just one of several of our family members who had become government informants and witnesses. Another who had flipped was Tommy Del-Giorno, a captain who had been arrested in 1986 on multiple charges. Quirk had recently interviewed both the Crow and Tommy Del at great length. They had both told him a lot, and now he needed help sorting it out, confirming some information and reconciling some seeming contradictions.

I was amazed at what I heard from Quirk that afternoon. When you're in organized crime, you sort of assume the enemy is all knowing and just one step behind you. That's especially true in New Jersey where the state police operate the most extensive and best financed anti–organized crime effort of any state in the country. Many guys who were then serving time or who had served time in the past in Jersey believed that if they had lived and operated elsewhere—New York City, say—they would not even have been bothered by the local cops for what they were hunted down and prosecuted for in New Jersey. So if you were a mob guy in Jersey, you just assumed your enemy—the state police or the Organized Crime Task Force—knew all about you and what you were doing. But in that conversation with Ed Quirk, I discovered how little they really did know. And I suddenly realized why my being Quirk's confidential source would be of such great help to them, even given my strange "I only confirm, I don't volunteer information" restriction.

It became clear that day that the police were totally confused about how the Bruno-Scarfo family was organized now with Nicky Sr. in jail. Tommy Del had been out of circulation since 1986, so his knowledge of the family still had Nicky Sr. on top and Philip Leonetti as underboss. The Crow's information was somewhat more recent, but he, too, wasn't exactly sure where things stood. So Quirk and I fenced back and forth, but eventually I was able to confirm that Cousin Anthony was the acting boss, generally what the current chain of command was, what the chain of command in our northern faction was, and how money flowed from Newark to Philly and Atlantic City.

By the time the session was over, Quirk was thrilled with what I had given him. Technically, I guess I had volunteered some things, especially when I updated or straightened out incorrect or outdated information he had received from the Crow. But I was satisfied that I had stayed close enough to my self-imposed guidelines to establish our relationship on my terms. I think we both left the meeting feeling good about how things were going.

. . . .

I could understand why the police were confused about our family's organization. With so many guys whacked or arrested, and now with Nicky Sr. in jail, even guys in our family were confused. For a long time the so-called northern faction of our family had been split in two, divided after Tony Bananas' death between those who were tied to Blackie Napoli and those who were around Patty. We—that is, those of us around Patty—had been very close to what was going on in Philadelphia after Nicky Sr. went to jail because Patty was asked to take over the family and because he was very close personally to Cousin Anthony. Those who had been around Blackie really didn't know what was going on beyond rumors they heard or things they were told unofficially by us.

After Patty screwed to South America, I got a call one day from a made guy who had been around Blackie. He was demanding to know if our family was being disbanded and given to one of the New York families. Rumors were flying around that the Commission—the heads of the five New York families—thought the Bruno-Scarfo family was in such a state of disorganization that it should be disbanded and its members divided between the Gambinos, the Genoveses, and the Luccheses. Actually, the rumors were even more explicit: The Gambinos would get the portion of the family in Philadelphia and with them control of Philadelphia; the Genoveses would get us in the northern faction; the Luccheses would get the few of our guys, such as John Praino, who were active in New York City; and those guys left in Atlantic City would be divided up in some yet unspecified way.

The rumor was nonsense, of course. I almost wished it had been true. Those of us in Newark weren't real close to Philadelphia. About the only thing I really knew about Philly was where to get a decent plate of pasta. On the other hand, because of the monte games, I was very close to a number of important guys in the Genoveses. If we had gone with them, I probably would have been straightened out within six months and made a captain within a year. But even if the rumor was nonsense, we still had to do something immediately to put it to rest.

I called Cousin Anthony in Philadelphia and told him about the confusion and the rumors. He told me to get everyone together, and he would come up and set everyone straight. So I arranged a dinner in a private dining room at the Seven Hills Restaurant in Bloomfield. All the made guys in the northern faction would be there.

Cousin Anthony and Nicky Jr. came up, and I drove them to the dinner from the Holiday Inn in Kenilworth. On the way over, Anthony told me that he had been communicating with Nicky Sr. through Nicky Jr. about these rumors, and Nicky's answer was for him to be more open about his leadership and to get more involved with us in the north, especially with the guys who had been around Blackie. This was the message Anthony was delivering that night.

Nicky Jr. and I were the only unmade guys there that evening, so we had to wait in the bar while Cousin Anthony was formally introduced to all the guys by Scoops, the acting boss. This was all more mob protocol. Once that was out of the way, Nicky Jr. and I were able to join the group. Cousin Anthony told everyone that he had been named the acting boss with the full knowledge of all the New York families and that our family was going to stay intact and would start to grow again. "The rumors of a breakup are bullshit," he told us, "and you can tell any guy from another family that I am in charge, and it's business as usual."

He was asked about Patty and responded that while Patty was away he would remain the captain. He again stopped short of calling Scoops and Slicker acting captains but repeated that they would be the ones making day-to-day decisions. He also said that I was in constant touch with Patty and would continue to communicate orders from him. If anyone needed to reach Patty, Cousin Anthony said, they should do so through me. Moreover, if I said some order came from Patty, they should trust that it had. What had been sort of unofficial before was now out in the open and official. From the looks some of the guys gave me later and from their comments, they knew Scoops and Slicker might appear to have the authority but I had the real power because I could countermand anything they did or said, and do so in Patty's name. That gave me the actual power.

The arrangement was all so official, in fact, that it got back to the state police with surprising speed. A couple of days after the dinner I was paged with a number I now knew was Ed Quirk. He said he had an urgent reason to see me, and so we set a meeting up for the next day. He got in my car in a liquor store parking lot, and we drove up Route 22. "I'm told there was a major mob sitdown the other night," he said as soon as we got the pleasantries out of the way.

I was about to tell him I knew nothing about it when I realized he was talking about our meeting. I kind of thought of it as a bunch of friends socializing and having drinks and dinner; I just didn't think of it in terms of a "major mob sitdown." So Quirk's question put me in a bit of a quandary. He was really asking me to do more than simply confirm information he already had since his information was so sketchy. Yet he already knew everything that had been discussed at the meeting since I had told him previously how the family was now organized in Nicky Sr.'s absence. After pondering what I should do for a few moments, I told him the major mob sitdown he had heard about was nothing more than Cousin Anthony being formally introduced to our guys as the acting boss, officially placing Scoops and Slicker in charge of the day-to-day, and telling everyone I was the only point of contact with Patty who continued as captain.

This news left Quirk with an interesting expression on his face. He probably had visions of the Commission meeting in his backyard to plan all sorts of new mob activity. I guess he was relieved that had not happened but disappointed that the only business transacted at the meeting was stuff he already knew. But over the long run this meeting with Quirk was significant for another reason: I had started, ever so slowly, to volunteer information about stuff he did not know.

Life returned to a strange version of normal that summer. Patty went from Buenos Aires to Reggio in Italy without incident, and he was sounding much more upbeat in our phone conversations. His wife and kids went to visit him, and I sent along another $10,000. The money was all mine. I had gone to Scoops and Slicker and asked them to contribute to the cause; what I got was more of the same: They were too broke to help out now. I knew they were lying, and my blood was beginning to boil.

I continued to go to one of the card games, four and sometimes five nights a week, and one night a week I went to Atlantic City to play blackjack. I was making the kind of money I had been earning before I went to jail, and I was doing it without bookmaking.

I also spent extra time with my kids, including starting to coach my oldest son's Little League baseball team afternoons and weekends. It was no big deal. I love baseball, I always have. I played it as a kid, and what's more natural than wanting to help your son learn to play and love the game? Coaching was something I really enjoyed doing. I found that I worked well with kids, and the fact their parents were model citizens never entered into it. In fact, Ann and I began that summer to spend more and more time socializing with friends from her job and with some of the parents of our kids' friends, all of whom would probably have gone into shock if they found out what I did for a living and that I had been in jail. Now, as I look back on that summer and my first experience coaching, I realize that I could be comfortable in the straight world with people far removed from the mob. At the time it didn't register—only the vague notion that maybe I could live without the company of wiseguys.

Around Memorial Day several things happened at once. Patty had not been feeling well; the constant pain in his stomach was worse, and the doctors in Italy were not much better than the doctors in Argentina. They couldn't figure out what his problem was. He was obviously worried when he called me one night with a question: "Do you think it would be safe for me to try to come back to get some decent doctors to look at me?"

I could not very well tell him that I would ask the Attorney General's Office, so I said I would poke around and try to come up with an answer. I had a previously scheduled meeting with Ed Quirk the next day, and I thought I could get the answers I needed there. After I had confirmed some information Quirk had about a labor racketeering scheme in northern Jersey involving several of the New York families in cooperation with the DeCavalcantes, I brought up the subject in an offhand way.

"Ed, I've been meaning to ask, has the Attorney General's Office issued any kind of warrant or detainer on Patty?"

"No, absolutely not," he said. "That was our deal, and as long as you cooperate, we won't."

It was obvious from his tone that he was more than a little curious, so I hastened to reassure him. "Patty has no intention of visiting the Garden State," I said, "but to be honest, he is considering going from place to place a distance from here and wants to know if it's safe to move."

"As far as the State of New Jersey is concerned, it is."

That night I called Patty and told him that a contact we had developed with the state had checked, and there was no warrant issued for him. So we made plans. In about a week Patty would fly from Rome to Chicago and then would take the train to Florida where he would stay in John Praino's winter home. He said he was planning to stay only as long as it took to see a couple of doctors. He would then reverse his route and fly back to Italy. In some ways the trip would be a test. If things went well, maybe he would consider alternating between Italy and Florida. That would not be a bad retirement for him.

At about the same time Slicker went into the hospital and had part of a lung removed. He came through the surgery fine but would need a long recovery period. And on top of that, about two days later I got a call from Cousin Anthony. He told me Scoops had been complaining about me, about having to go through me to get to Patty and about there being no captain on the scene day to day. Anthony said he agreed it was a problem, and he wanted to talk to Patty about the situation. I said I had something to tell him but that I had better do it in person. So we agreed to meet for lunch the next day halfway between Philly and Newark.

When we sat down, I told him that Patty was ill and was on his way to Florida via Chicago. I said I wouldn't know where he was for several days, but I would put the two of them together by phone as soon as I heard from Patty. Anthony was concerned that Patty was taking a risk by coming back to the States. I told him we thought there would be no problem. Then he said that he would officially name Scoops acting captain but wanted to assure me that it wouldn't cause me a problem. "Scoops is not happy with you, George, but I'm making sure he knows that both Nicky and I are very happy with what you have been doing. There won't be no trouble."

Late that week Patty and Cousin Anthony talked. Patty then called and told me to reach out for Scoops. Scoops was surprised to hear that Patty was in Florida. He flew down, and Patty officially made him acting captain. But he also said he would not be in Florida long and that Scoops and everyone else should continue to communicate through me. Scoops said he understood. Patty told me later that he wasn't sure if Scoops really did understand, and if there was ever any problem between Scoops and me, he and Cousin Anthony had already agreed, I should call Anthony immediately.

I asked Patty if he wanted me to come down, but he said Anna Marie was coming down and then he was going back to Reggio within a week. He said not to worry, the doctors had given him a clean bill of health. They gave him some pills and told him to come back in February.

Scoops quickly proved that he wasn't all that comfortable with leadership and authority. Around Christmas it appeared that we suddenly had developed a major problem with John Gotti's crew.

The Gambinos under Gotti had this elderly captain who over the years had given some players to John Praino. Every Christmas season John made up a "package" of a couple of thousand dollars to give to the Gotti captain as a thank-you. This was not really required of John, but it was considered good mob etiquette. And it was good for business because the guy would send more players John's way from time to time.

Over the past year this guy had finally gotten too old, so Gotti had sent him into quiet retirement in Florida. So when it came time for the package, John Praino naturally took it to this guy's replacement, Louie Brajoile, and received a very rude reception. Instead of a thank-you, John received a "Welcome. I'm your new partner. From now on I get half."

Patty had known Louie Brajoile for years, and I had met him a number of times. But I really don't think he knew John Praino or knew that he was around Patty. John told him, and this probably puzzled Louie because he knew Patty, and Patty had probably never mentioned John. So Louie stepped back and called his boss, Frankie Loc—Frank Locascio. He was John Gotti's underboss and became the Gambino consigliere after trading jobs with "Sammy the Bull" Gravano.

At the time Frankie Loc was partners with Joey Sodano, the guy who had pissed away many of my bettors when I was in jail and who was with our crew in a whole bunch of stuff. Frankie called Joey and asked if this guy John Praino was around us. Joey didn't know him and said he would find out. He called Scoops and said the Gambinos were looking to take over some New York City–based bookie named John Praino who said he was around us. Was he, Joey asked.

Now Scoops knew John very well and also knew he was very close to Patty. But once he heard the names John Gotti and Frankie Loc, he became scared. What Scoops should have done was pick up the phone, call Frankie Loc, and say, "Yes, Frankie. John Praino is with us." But suddenly he started to see all kinds of dark motives in what Louie was doing. If Louie didn't know that John was around us and had made an understandable, innocent mistake, the whole thing could easily be settled in a phone call or at worst a short meeting with a few friendly drinks afterward. It would be no harm—no foul. But Scoops worried that all this might mean that Gotti was beginning to move on our operations in New York City. It could be the opening act of a very serious drama. If that were the case, things would have to be dealt with at a level much higher than Scoops, and he was petrified that if he did or said the wrong thing, it would make John Gotti or Frankie Loc unhappy. And that would definitely not be good for Scoops's health.

So Scoops didn't know what to do. He told Joey Sodano he would have to check, and then he called me and asked what I thought he should do. I said he should call Frankie Loc and tell him John Praino belonged to us. "Maybe they want him, George. Maybe we should give him up to them," Scoops whined. He said he didn't want to have to make the decision. He just wanted to hand the problem off to someone else. He called Cousin Anthony.

Anthony in turn called me to ask if I could get Patty's read on what was going on. I told him I had already talked with Patty, who thought it was not a major thing. Anthony said that was what he figured, but he was concerned that if he dealt with it—if he called either John Gotti or Frankie Loc directly, it would blow it up into something too important. When he paused, I said I would take care of it.

"I don't know, George, you not being a made guy and all."

"Don't worry," I said. "I know a lot of the Gambinos, and I can at least find out what's going on. If it's serious, I'll call you."

That night I was with a Gambino captain at the monte game and said I needed to talk with Frankie Loc about a problem that Louie Brajoile was having with one of our guys. The next night the guy gave me a phone number, and the next day I called Frankie Loc, who had no problem at all with the fact that John was around us. He asked me to call Louie and gave me another number. Louie could not have been nicer. He hadn't known John Praino from Adam, so when he showed up with the package, Louie assumed he was a freelancer without a connection who had been paying the old guy a very, very light street tax. That's why he had made a move on him. There were apologies all around, and Louie asked me to extend his best regards and a Merry Christmas to Patty. I later found out that Louie had called John to thank him for the package.

Scoops could have achieved the same result with a phone call, but the whole idea of dealing with the Gambinos frightened him to the point that he was willing to consider giving up our old friend rather than possibly having to stand up for him. This certainly did not bode well for his career as our family's captain. And I started to have more second thoughts about Scoops.

The winter and spring seemed to just fly by. I fell into almost a regular schedule, not quite nine to five but as regular a schedule as a wiseguy could expect. I would basically work all night, sleep into the afternoon, spend some time with Ann and the kids, hang out a little with the guys, eat a late dinner, then go back to one of the card games and start all over again.

But it did become a progressively more lucrative life. I was attending the card games both as a player and as part of the bank. In the two largest games we were partners with other crews, so every week the net take, which ranged anywhere from $10,000 to $20,000, was usually split two or three ways. Our part—and I say "our" as opposed to mine since the take was officially the family's—would come to $5,000 if the net was $10,000 to $15,000 in a given week. I would keep $2,000 and give the rest to Scoops. He would keep a thousand and send the rest to Philadelphia. On those weeks when our take was greater, Scoops might also give a taste to some of the other guys around him.

Most weeks I made considerably more playing in the games than I did running them. I guess in the winter and spring of 1989 I probably averaged about $5,000 a week in winnings from the monte game and a like amount the one night a week I went to Atlantic City to play blackjack. Thus in a normal week I might be making $10,000 to $12,000. One week I vividly remember winning more then $40,000 at the monte game. But that was one week. On a couple of others I lost, one time about $10,000. But on average I won and generally ended up taking about $10,000 to $12,000 a week.

But as fast as the money was coming in, it went back out. I felt as if I was on a treadmill running faster and faster and getting nowhere. I was earning big, but I was also supporting myself and my family, Patty in Italy, and Patty's wife and kids in Newark. I was also giving a thousand or two every couple of weeks to Anna Marie, Patty's girlfriend.

Patty had also developed something of a semi-regular schedule. He was bouncing back and forth between Italy and the United States. He would spend a couple of months in Reggio, a couple in Florida, and then a few weeks at John Praino's house in New York. His New York visits were a major secret. Only John and I knew when this happened because Patty came to spend time with Anna Marie and didn't want his wife or kids to know he was so close. In fact, he wanted his family to think he was in Italy so they wouldn't even try to track him down in Florida.

That winter I made a couple of trips to Florida when Patty was there. One was just business; I brought him some money and took back a number of messages for various guys. Another was a short vacation when I took Ann down for a little fun in the sun. And all during this period I was talking to Ed Quirk about once a week. We had developed a fairly easygoing relationship. He would ask me questions about stuff he or other state–organized crime guys were picking up on the street. I would corroborate what I could. If I didn't know, I would just say so. But on a couple of occasions when he said something was really important and I didn't already know the answer, I would quietly attempt to find out if I could in a non-obvious way.

One time Quirk came to me quite desperate to find out why a guy from another family had gotten whacked. The state police's fear was the guy had been killed by another family because he was trying to encroach on their business. If that was true, Quirk said, they were worried they might have a mob war on their hands.

This put me in a quandary. I remembered Patty's very old advice from the time Bananas was whacked: Don't ask questions about a hit because you never know if the guy you're asking is the one who did the hit or ordered it, and he might think you were being too nosy. "Just keep your ears open, and you'll hear what you need to know," Patty said. But Quirk was pushing me very hard to find out quickly on this one.

Luckily, wiseguys tend to gossip like old ladies, and the guy who got whacked was in the same crew with some of the guys with us in one of the card games. Killings were not all that common. They were events which shook everyone up, especially those who were around the guy who got whacked. And this hit was topic number one that night at the game. From the discussion that was going on all around me—I didn't even have to ask a question—it was clear that the guy had been killed because of a dispute within his own crew. He had apparently been holding out, or at least that was the word that was circulating, and he had been ordered hit to make an example of him.

When I reported this to Ed, he seemed relieved. "No war, that's good," he said. But it occurred to me that he seemed almost too relieved, and this got me thinking. What if the guy who got whacked was another of the state police's "confidential sources," and Ed was concerned not because the hit might portend a mob war but there might be a leak in his organization? Now that was something for me to worry about. But the people I had talked to seemed pretty sure the guy had been whacked for holding out. If he had been a snitch who had been found out, they wouldn't have hidden that fact. It would have been trumpeted. The fact that it wasn't led me to believe this was not the situation. So I kind of let this new worry slide.

Over this period Ed began to push me gently into giving him more and more. It was constant pressure, but he applied it subtly. Even though he tried not to be obvious, I understood what he was doing. In some cases I did give him additional stuff, and other times I didn't. He seemed satisfied, and in my mind I still felt I was upholding my end of the bargain without really compromising my own ethics or giving up any of my friends.

"My friends"—now that's an interesting choice of words. As the weeks passed I was getting progressively more disgusted with "my friends." Money and Patty: That is what was at the root of the problem. Patty would need some more cash—or his wife would or Anna Marie would—and I would go to Scoops or Slicker, and neither gave a shit. All I got was excuses. "I'm broke this week." "Guys ain't paying me." "Things are really bad now." You name the excuse, I heard it. Patty was their captain. They had a family obligation to give what they could to help him. It was exactly the same as when I was in jail. Exactly. They were obligated to help my family then, but they had copped out. Now they were obligated to help Patty and his family, and they were again shirking their responsibility. Once or twice when I really started to scream, and once when I called Cousin Anthony, they came up with a thousand or two and then were pissed that I had gone over their heads.

So I went along paying almost everything out of my own pocket and getting madder and madder each time I went to Scoops and he stiffed Patty. Then I would look around and see him driving a new car, flashing money, buying stuff for his wife and his girlfriend, living high. Finally, I just said fuck it and stopped asking.

I kept expressing my frustrations to Ann. She knew how much I was sending to Patty, and she never raised the issue that it was money that should have remained in our own family. But she did start to push me to do something if I was so unhappy. "Let's get out," she said one morning when I was bitching about Scoops again. "Let's just pack the car and go somewhere far away and start all over again. We can survive, and we would all be a lot happier."

It was an attractive idea, but again it raised all the impossible questions: What would I do for a living? How would I get away from the family? How would I get out from under the pending New Jersey indictment? A life on the lam was no better than the life I was leading. But I started to think seriously for the first time of finding a way to give it all up and to start all over again.

. . .

Everything seemed to cave in at the same time that spring. The sequence started with Patty deciding to leave John Praino's house in New York and go back to Italy for the summer. He needed money for the trip, and he told me to put together $10,000 for him. The request came at exactly the wrong moment. I had just paid my bills and was in the middle of an unusual two-week losing streak at the card games. And I had actually lost a few thousand that week in Atlantic City, one of the very few times I had ever come away from a blackjack table a loser.

So for the first time in a while I went to Scoops to ask him for money for Patty. The result was the same as in the past: excuses on top of excuses. I was reduced to begging, and with a show of great generosity, Scoops finally came up with a couple of grand. This was not an act of charity on his part. Patty was Scoops's boss, and he should have been giving Patty half of his earnings. He was giving him nothing, and now when pressed, Scoops was making a big deal out of a couple of thousand. And that was when my feelings for these guys—all of them: Scoops, Slicker, Turk, the whole lot of them—turned from disgust to white-hot anger.

At the same time Ed Quirk renewed pushing me to do more, but again with subtlety. Part of it was my doing because I had begun to volunteer some stuff, most of it about guys with other crews. Some of it I just found interesting and passed it along to Ed for his general information, stuff such as who was up and who was down in a particular crew at the moment. On one occasion I think I saved a guy's life. I heard that some guys on one crew were not very happy with this freelance bookie, and they were about to hurt him very badly. I told Ed, and I later heard the guy had dropped out of sight. I subsequently learned he was cooperating with the state police in exchange for relocation. I had met the guy once, and he seemed pretty decent. So I was glad I had helped him.

I had also started to use Ed to settle a few of my own scores. A guy owed me some money from one of the card games. He was not paying up and seemed to have little interest in doing so. In one of my conversations with Ed, I indicated that he might be interested in looking at a company the guy owned and some of its not-so-public activities.

Right after Patty left for Italy I had a meeting with Ed that really got my dander up. He brought along a tape and played it for me. It was a bugged conversation between some of my "good friends," Turk and Slicker and a couple of other guys. I was the subject of the conversation. "Who the fuck does he think he is?" Slicker said at one point. "He ain't straightened out. In fact, he ain't shit. It's time we put him in his place."

That was the general tenor of the conversation. I was getting too big a head and had to be taken down. Who the hell were these guys? I was helping to support half of them through the money I was giving Scoops. I had known some of them all my life. I listened to the conversation in disbelief. Ed wouldn't tell me where it had been made or when, and it was only much later that I realized it could have come from the bug in Turk's car months before. But all I knew then was that what I heard left me speechless.

"Think about this, George. Think about what it means," Ed said as we parted. I knew what he was saying. He thought I was on the verge of getting killed. I didn't think it was that serious. Between Patty and Cousin Anthony, those assholes couldn't really touch me. But this was nothing less than my family turning on me, and the level of hurt was deep.

A few days later another incident gave me a big jolt. I had dropped a dime with Ed on one guy who owed me money, but he wasn't the only one. A couple of guys owed me quite a bit, and I went to Scoops, as our captain, to get his help in collecting. His response basically was that I was a big boy and it was my problem. Actually, it wasn't just my problem; it was our crew's problem. If word got out that we could be stiffed, everyone would start doing it. But Scoops never could see the big picture, so he just turned his back on me.

Then I discovered that he was also holding out on me. The financial arrangements in some of the games we were running were complex. I was collecting our share of the monte game, and I gave Scoops his share and also Philadelphia's share. I was always dead honest. Maybe under the circumstances that was stupid, but I always made the cut exactly where it should have been. I didn't try to pocket a cent that wasn't mine.

But the money from the baccarat games we were running ourselves and from the shy business went directly to Scoops. I guess I was slow, but it took me quite a while to realize that he was shorting me. Scoops was pocketing some that belonged to me and some that should have gone to Patty. Learning that almost sent me over the edge.

But the final straw I learned in a meeting with Nicky Jr. on the boardwalk at Seaside Heights, a New Jersey shore resort where he had a place. I had brought him some money and the moment I saw him I knew something was wrong. He looked distraught. At first he didn't want to talk about what was bothering him, but finally he looked down at the boardwalk and said softly, "We think Philip has flipped." About the only thing he could have said that would have shocked me more was to say his father had decided to become a government witness. I immediately pressed him for details.

"Philip has flipped," Nicky said more loudly. And then he added, "And the fucking Feds have stolen a million dollars of my father's money."

Philip was, of course, Philip Leonetti, our underboss, who was Nicky Sr.'s nephew and Nicky Jr.'s cousin. And he possessed this amazing record for beating convictions. In September 1984 the Feds had indicted him for extortion and conspiracy but couldn't make the charges stick and had to dismiss them. Then Philip was indicted by the State of New Jersey, along with Nicky Sr. and a bunch of other guys, in November 1986 for a whole collection of crimes. Those charges were later dropped. Then the whole group was again indicted by New Jersey in April 1987. The same month, Pennsylvania indicted him for conspiracy in the murder of Salvy Testa. He was guilty, of course, but they couldn't prove the case and he walked. Then two months later the Feds arrested him again, this time on a bunch of narcotics charges. He beat this rap, too.

It all seemed pretty amazing, and Philip was starting to feel invincible. I remember one time he bragged to me, "These assholes will never get me." But he was wrong. He was arrested again in January 1988, again by the Feds, and this time he was charged with ten murders, five attempted murders, and a catalog of other crimes. The arrest had been a year and a half ago, but the trial was now finally over. Philip had been found guilty and sentenced to forty-five years.

Now Nicky was telling me that Philip the invincible, Crazy Phil who was called crazy because he loved to kill, was going to roll over on the rest of the family in order to win a reduced sentence. And if that wasn't startling enough, the Kid went on to tell me that the Feds had helped Philip steal almost a $1.5 million from his father. Philip was being bought and paid for with Nicky Sr.'s money.

It was a complicated story, but Nicky told me that when Philip flipped, his family went into hiding as protected government witnesses at the same time. Philip's mother, Nancy, was Nicky Sr.'s sister. Nicky Sr. owned a large four-family flat, one of those old, solidly built brick buildings that were so much a part of old Atlantic City. Nicky had combined the two apartments on the ground floor into one very large apartment for himself. His mother, Catherine, and his sister Nancy lived in one of the two apartments upstairs. The other was always kept vacant as a kind of safe house. When Nicky went to jail and the bottom flat became empty, his sister moved downstairs.

The previous weekend, Nicky Jr. had gone to see his father. He often dropped by his father's place to see his grandmother Catherine or his aunt Nancy, so having him out of town was probably what the Feds had been waiting for. When he got back, he found his grandmother absolutely beside herself with anger and grief. Catherine had last seen Nancy shortly after eight the previous evening when she went to bed. The older woman was very hard of hearing, and when she took her hearing aid off, that was it. She would have slept through a major explosion. Apparently she almost did. The next morning when she went downstairs to go to church with Nancy, she found the apartment almost destroyed. She was shocked to find all of Nancy's clothes and personal possessions gone, some pieces of furniture gone, and the safe gone.

As Nicky Jr. described it to me, the safe was a cast-iron job that weighed more than two hundred pounds empty and that had been set in cement, four feet into a brick wall, halfway up a set of interior stairs between the lower flat and the always empty upstairs flat. Nancy did not know the combination, and the safe was said to be pick proof; and it had lived up to its billing. The Feds didn't just peel it open and take the money. They virtually had to tear down the wall, yank out the entire safe, and haul it away.

"A million four, George," Nicky Jr. moaned. "The goddamn safe had a million four in cash in it. That was the money we were living on and the money that was going to pay for Dad's appeal. What the fuck are we supposed to do now? Shit, I had ten thousand in a drawer up in the empty apartment, and the bitch took that, too."

To say Nicky was not too pleased with his aunt Nancy would have been a grand understatement. In fact, the family quickly came to the conclusion that they wanted her dead. Catherine had first feared that what had happened was some kind of weird mob hit and that Nancy might be dead or taken. But that afternoon Nancy called her mother to tell her not to worry, that she was gone because Philip had flipped and that she was now a federally protected witness. She also said she had taken the money "for my new life."

Nicky said his grandmother had been very blunt to her daughter: "Don't ever call here again." His father had been even more blunt when Nicky got the word to him about what had happened. "They're both dead," he said of his sister and her son. "I don't care how long it takes, they're both dead."

All this left my head spinning. As I drove home that night from Seaside, all I could think about was that there was no honor left in this family. Philip's flipping was simply beyond belief. And what about our system? Turn stoolie and your government is willing to forgive a dozen murders and will reward you with a new life in the sun somewhere. It will allow you to keep a couple of million dollars you made from the rackets and had salted away. Then it will steal another million and a half dollars in order to make you more comfortable. How could all this be, I kept asking myself. How could this be?

I didn't sleep for what was left of that night. I don't know that I ever consciously came to a decision, it was just that suddenly I knew it was all over. My friends had become my enemies. The life I had been brought up in had no meaning. I knew for certain now that I had to get out, and I knew that the only way that was likely to happen was through the New Jersey State Police. Ed Quirk wanted me to do more. Well, goddammit, I would do more for him than he ever dreamed possible. I would get out, and I would settle a few scores in the process. The kids were just getting out of bed when I picked up the phone and dialed Ed at home.

7

WIRED

One of the worst of my many bad habits is that I'm an unreformed Cher fan, or at least I was a few years ago. From her days with Sonny Bono, whenever Cher made a personal appearance in the New York metropolitan area, I had to be there. Ann humored me in this and would go with gritted teeth. But I was hooked, and Cher was going to be at the Garden State Arts Center. That's why at 7:00 A.M. on a Saturday morning I found myself on line waiting for the box office to open. I had come straight from the monte game. It was a perfect place to meet with Ed. Not many wiseguys stand on line to be among the first to get Cher tickets.

The box office opened at 9:00. Ed got there in a van about 8:30, and after I bought my tickets—fifth row center; I was thrilled—we drove to a deserted area near the beach and began what was probably the most fateful conversation of my life. "I've had it, Ed," I blurted out. "I've had it with these guys, with this life. I want out. I want to bring these guys down, and I want out. You get me out, and I'll give you the whole bunch. I'll do whatever you want, but I have to get out."

Ed was a great poker player because he had one of those faces you just can't read. You can never tell what he's thinking. That morning in the van as I was making him the most extraordinary offer I had ever made anyone or would ever make anyone, he wasn't reacting in the way I had expected. He had been pushing me and pushing me to do more. Now I was telling him I was willing to do anything he wanted, and he just sat there quietly asking question after question.

I had assumed he would be excited at the possibilities I was offering him. If he was, he sure didn't show it. Later, when we talked about this meeting, I learned that he simply didn't trust any wiseguy and figured I was scamming him to get out from under my indictments. It was only after he realized how really angry I was that he began to see the potential in what I was offering.

What could I give him, he kept asking. What did I want in return —a pardon, money? To be perfectly honest, I had reached this decision only twenty-four hours earlier and hadn't really thought the whole thing out. I knew I wanted a new life and I wanted to see guys like Scoops brought down, but I hadn't begun to consider the details. I guess I knew that I would need a new identity if I was to start a new life. It was clear that something would have to happen to the indictment I was still facing. But I didn't know anything at all about the New Jersey Witness Protection Program, or anything about how the state might deal with someone who starts cooperating with them.

We talked for several hours about the various possibilities. Over and over Ed kept coming back to the same thing: Would I be willing to wear a wire, to record conversations I had with various wiseguys? Actually, up until that moment, I hadn't really considered the matter. But I was resolved to do what I had to do to get out of there with my family and my life intact, and, equally important, to bring Scoops and the rest of these guys down. Yes, I said. I was willing to wear a wire. And when he asked me the same question again and again, the answer remained yes.

When we finished our conversation, Ed said he had to talk with his superiors. I said I had to think more precisely about what I wanted. We agreed to talk again on Monday.

I went home and told Ann what I had done. Her face was not hard to read: She was both thrilled and frightened. She let loose with a torrent of questions: Where would we go? How would I support myself? What would it mean for the kids? How soon would it all happen? Those were good questions, and I had no answers. I admitted I hadn't really thought that much about anything she was asking, so we talked about what we wanted and when we might want things to happen. Together we reached some decisions that would become the framework for my relationship with the state.

I was still very confused in my own mind. As Ann and I talked and as I began to sort things out over that weekend, I realized I had several different priorities. I wanted out, and I wanted to be able to start over. That couldn't happen in New Jersey or New York, which meant relocating a considerable distance. I also wanted to get back at those who had turned their backs on Patty and on Ann and me when I was in jail. Almost above all, I didn't want to hurt Patty; I would never do anything to hurt him. If the state wanted me to target Patty, I would just say no. But I also didn't want to be simply a snitch. I wanted to be more than that. I somehow wanted to be in control. I would bring these guys down but in the way I wanted and when I wanted. The deal I was going to offer the state would be very unusual and very complicated.

Ed and I talked on Monday, and he wanted to know if I was willing to start immediately. I said yes. He asked if I had anything important set up, and I told him that Nicky Jr. was coming down for a meeting the next day. Would I wear a wire to it, Ed wanted to know. Yeah, I said, "if it can be done safely." "Okay," Ed said, "we'll get this thing started tomorrow." He told me to meet him early in a Toms River motel room.

At the motel the next morning I met three new faces. One was Detective Sergeant William Newsome, "Billy," of the State Police Organized Crime Bureau. The second was Sergeant Richie Gallo, Ed's superior in the intelligence division, who I later learned had spent the morning in a car outside the Toys "R" Us store where a year earlier I had agreed to become Ed's confidential source in exchange for protecting Patty. Ed had brought him for backup in case the meeting was a setup. The third new face was Jimmy Mulholland, another officer and a wiring expert.

It was obvious they were all suspicious of me. Before they went any further, before they agreed to anything, they wanted to test me. And this was to be that test—to wear a wire to a meeting. I guess they figured that once they had me on tape, they could hold it over my head if I decided to back out later. What the hell, I thought. I was ready. I said sure, I would wear the wire to the meeting I had scheduled that morning. Let's get it on, I said.

They put a Nagra recorder on me, and I set out for the meeting at a company called U. S. Video in Mount Holly, a company run by Tyrone DiNittis, a guy who had long been around Nicky Sr. but a guy we didn't trust much. Those of us who were close to Patty thought that Tyrone was an FBI informant. We dealt with him, but very carefully. That day Nicky Jr. and I were to meet with two guys who were around John Gotti. Joey Sodano was doing some business with them in New York, and he had set up the meeting so these two guys could discuss something they wanted to do in Philadelphia. The location had been chosen because these Gotti guys also wanted to see a video jukebox that U. S. Video was making.

Nicky Jr. had come up to do a little business with these two Gotti guys, but he had also come to deliver a message to me from Cousin Anthony. We were having trouble collecting money from Joey Sodano, who was not paying his monthly tribute to Philadelphia, and this was really angering Nicky Sr. in Marion.

Joey had grown up in the neighborhood and had always been around Patty. But he had drifted over to New York and was involved in running a major bookmaking operation (or "office," as we called it), a shy operation, and a bunch of other scams. He was in very tight with the powers in the Gambino family and with the Luccheses, and he seemed to know everyone who was important in New York. He had the reputation of a mega-earner, and he was a very mysterious kind of guy. Early on, he had acquired a place in Florida. At first he would spend some time there in the winter, then gradually he spent more time, until he was spending half a year in Florida and half a year in New York. Finally, by the late 1980s, he was living mainly in Florida and would come up once a month, maybe for a few days, maybe for a week, and then would disappear again. He often wore disguises, had no assets in his own name, and had no permanent address in New York or New Jersey. He would stay with various people, and you could never find him unless he wanted to be found. To top it all off, he had a reputation for violence, and he was surrounded by a small group of guys who owed their loyalty to him. In many ways he was a throwback to Tony Bananas in the old days.

But he was still around Patty, and he still owed his loyalty and his monthly tribute to Philadelphia. He had stopped paying, and Nicky Sr. was getting very mad. "I want you to bring him down to meet with us in Philly," the Kid told me. "We need to get this straightened out immediately. My father's angry, and if this doesn't get taken care of right away, bad things could happen."

He didn't need to elaborate on what he meant by "bad things." Too many bodies had been left around by Nicky to miss the meaning.

We talked at length about the various other matters that the two Gambino guys—Richie Martino and Zeff Mustaffa—wanted to discuss. When the meeting was over, I hung with Nicky for a few minutes more, and then I went back to the motel room where I had started my day. Ed and Billy had watched the meeting. They were there partially out of curiosity and partially to protect me. Their operating rules were simple: Anytime anyone was out wearing a wire, he was under constant surveillance, so if anything went wrong, he could be rescued. By the time I got back to the motel, Ed, Billy, and Gallo had been joined by a couple of others: David Brody, the Supervising Deputy Attorney General in charge of the Organized Crime Bureau of the state's Division of Justice, and Major Lindy Tezza, the number three man in the New Jersey State Police.

When I entered that motel room, I was so charged up I could barely contain myself. I knew what I wanted, and I guess I came across to Brody and Major Tezza—neither of whom had ever met me at that point—as both brash and boastful. I found out later they all thought I was some kind of small-time punk trying to inflate my importance when I told them I could get them made guys, captains even, in four separate families.

Brody opened the conversation by saying he understood I would be "willing to help bring down guys in the Scarfo family." Absolutely, I replied, and I could do a lot more. "I regularly deal with guys in the Gambinos, the Colombos, the Luccheses, and the Genoveses," I boasted. "I can help you in all four of the families."

But what really set them off was when I said I could get them John Riggi, the boss of the DeCavalcante family. John had been a major target of the State of New Jersey for a decade, and he had always been able to stay a step or two ahead of the cops at every turn. Now here I was, in their eyes some unmade punk willing to make a deal, telling them I could do for them something they had tried unsuccessfully for years to accomplish. I think it is safe to say they were skeptical.

I told them what I wanted: "I want a new life, and I want your help in setting it up. I want a new identity and everything that goes with it. I want to be able to forget the indictment you now have on me, even though I don't think you can make it stick. I want to make absolutely sure you bring down certain guys I have a beef with. You do this for me, and I'll give you more than Riggi, I'll give you more than anyone has ever given you at one time."

We talked back and forth for the better part of several hours, and the question always came back to how I could best help them make cases against guys. Various avenues were explored, but finally we sort of mutually reached the conclusion that the most effective thing I could do was exactly what I had done that morning: record people talking about their crimes. If I could get people talking into a wire, they would end up convicting themselves. But this meant I would have to wear a wire for weeks or even months. Was I willing? Was I up to the challenge?

"Yeah," I said. "If that's what it takes, I'm ready."

Within a matter of days I had become one of the State of New Jersey's deepest secrets. The state police had some two thousand seven hundred employees, the Attorney General's Office hundreds more. Fewer than a dozen people would ever know my actual identity while the operation was under way. Others may have known of me in a general way or by a code number, but my life depended on my identity being known by as few as possible. I would be operating as an undercover agent, and those who knew were limited to a few in the state police and even fewer in the Attorney General's Office.

Ed Quirk, who had been running me as an informant for a year, was assigned to the state police's Intelligence Division. The way the state police divided up their functions, Intelligence was in charge of gathering information, but all operations against organized crime were handled by the Organized Crime Bureau. Once I moved from confidential source to operative, the OCB took over. Ed therefore was technically "lent" to OCB from the Intelligence Division for the duration of our operation. This also meant that except for Ed and his direct boss, Richie Gallo, most of those who knew my identity were in the OCB. There was Billy Newsome; he and Ed became my handlers on a day-to-day basis. There was Charley Crescenz, another OCB detective sergeant, who ran my elaborate backup operation.

I don't think in my lifetime I've met three more stand-up guys than Ed, Billy, and Charley. This was especially true of Charley. He was an old-timer, and this was to be his final assignment before retirement. He had been in the OCB since the days of my father and seemed to know every wiseguy who had lived in Jersey over the last twenty-five years. He knew which ones were good guys and which ones were stone killers. His instincts were always perfect. He knew just how far to push without going over the edge and saved my life on more than one occasion.

Ed, Billy, and Charley were the guys who would be out on the street with me. Another good guy, OCB Detective Sergeant Alan Drummond, was in charge of the day-to-day transcribing of the tapes I recorded. Then there were the officers. Major Tezza, who had been at the motel for the first meeting, ended up dealing with me often. His boss, Colonel Clinton Pagano, head of the state police, had to give the go-ahead for the operation to start. On the operational level, Captain Bobby Gaugler was the head of OCB and thus ultimately responsible for the operation. Then there was the guy who had direct charge, Lieutenant Barry Lardiere. I guess the most charitable thing you could say about the lieutenant was that he had been off the street and in the bureaucracy for so long that he had lost his instincts, if he ever had them. It seemed he was always more worried about his budget than what we might accomplish, and he would come as close as anyone to getting me killed. If there was a weak link in our operation, he was it.

There were also four people outside the state police who knew who I was and what I was doing: Assistant Attorney General Dave Brody, who supervised the operation; his boss, Michael Bozza, who headed the Organized Crime Section of the Attorney General's Office; Robert Winter, the director of the Criminal Justice Division; and their ultimate boss, State Attorney General Robert Del Tufo. My relationship with the state became so unusual that much of it had to be approved directly by the Attorney General.

Nothing had gone wrong that first day. Generally speaking, the recording was of good quality except when one of the video jukeboxes was blasting; then you had trouble hearing the conversation over the music. Some of the material was dynamite—stuff about the video poker business that the police had not known. And now that they knew I was willing to do the job, they indicated they were ready to deal. They were happy with the way the test recording had gone, but I wasn't.

There was no way I was going to wear a wire—a tape recorder strapped to my back or hidden in my groin with wires running to a mike in my sleeve—like the one I had worn to the U. S. Video meeting. Too much could go wrong, and it was too easy to be discovered. Somebody pats you on the back or gives you a hug, and it's all over. During the meeting it had felt as if the recorder weighed a ton, and the wires ran everywhere. I felt that any second the damn recorder would fall out of my shirt or one of the wires would come poking out and be noticed. There was no way I was going to expose myself to that much risk again. "If you want to wire me okay," I told Ed, "but find another way because this way is not going to work."

He did. He set the state police electronics experts to work, and they came up with a positively ingenious solution. For years I had worn a pager, and anyone who knew me knew that I was beeped all the time. So what they did was build a transmitter into a standard pager. It was a self-contained unit with both the microphone and the transmitter, and it had a range of about a quarter of a mile. That meant someone would have to sit in a van or truck within that quarter-mile radius to record what the transmitter was sending. Short of some absolutely incredible foul-up, the system was virtually undetectable, but it remained to be seen just how good the transmissions would be. We couldn't nail these guys if we couldn't hear what they were saying.

It took three weeks of rather intensive work to accomplish all that had to be done before we could formally begin what became known as "Operation Broadsword." First, I had to sit down with Major Tessa and negotiate a complex employment contract, one with some very unusual twists and turns. I was not just some snitch collecting a few bucks for information. I effectively became a contract employee of the State of New Jersey, paid a weekly salary based on what a detective sergeant could expect, with benefits such as health and accident insurance. During the operational phase, which we orally agreed would be no more than one year, I would be paid $900 a week in salary to cover my expenses, plus the state would give me $10,000 to purchase a new car. The car would also be wired so that the transmission power of my pager was amplified, and transmissions of what was being said in the car could be picked up and recorded in another moving car or van following behind. (We later discovered that the transmitter was so powerful that on a clear night my pager transmissions could be heard forty miles away in Trenton.)

We also agreed, Major Tessa and I, that once the operational phase had ended, the state would pay for my relocation to a mutually-agreed-upon location. He and I shook hands on the deal, and he promised that I would get a written contract filling in all the details. It would take them three months to draw up the document, but when they finally produced it, it stipulated that the state would provide Ann, the kids, and me with new identities, new Social Security numbers, and new birth certificates. For security reasons all of us would be walking away with only the clothes on our backs, so the state agreed to buy my existing home furnishings and furniture for $5,000 in order to give me money to buy new things. In addition, I would get $30,000 to buy two new cars, since we would be walking away from the old ones.

For an eighteen-month period, until I could get established, I was to get $3,000 a month for living expenses in my new location. Finally, for eighteen months after I relocated, I would continue on the state's payroll at $3,800 a month because it was assumed I would be working full-time for that long getting ready for trials and appearing as a witness.

But the deal came with a great number of obligations on my part. I had to agree to tell the state anything and everything I was asked about organized crime, including things having to do with Patty. He was now quite ill, and I rationalized that by the time this thing finished, he would either be dead or too sick to ever stand trial. I had to agree to take lie detector tests when and where required by the state, and I was told to expect them often. If I ever lied or withheld any information, the contract would be void. I had to agree to record any and all of my conversations, and I had to agree to appear and testify at any subsequent court proceedings. I was not allowed to commit any crimes without the direct knowledge and permission of the state. Any crimes I committed could be undertaken only in the furtherance of the investigation, and I had to turn over to the state any money I earned from any criminal enterprise. Finally, if I kept my side of the bargain completely, the state would allow me to plead guilty to one count on the indictment I was facing, and I would be sentenced to probation. And as long as I was cooperating, I would not be the subject of any other criminal investigation.

It all sounded like a pretty rich deal: $900 a week, then $3,800 a month plus $3,000 in expenses, money for cars, and money for furniture. But let me tell you, I would earn every penny. First of all, since I was effectively an undercover agent, I was expected to maintain a wiseguy's life-style while not keeping the profits I might earn from any criminal enterprises. I knew what it cost to hang out. If the state had been able to use one of its own officers in a situation like mine, it would have had to pay his salary and benefits plus all his wiseguy life-style expenses. If they had been able to accomplish this, which was doubtful, it would have been a much more costly proposition. And most important, in the final analysis, the state would make quite a profit from me. I figured that what the state would end up with in fines and confiscations from cases I made would exceed all they had spent on me by several hundred thousand dollars. At twice what they were paying me, I would be a good investment—that is, of course, if we could pull this operation off.

While Major Tessa, Dave Brody, and I dickered over the

agreement, Ed, Billy, and Charley worked out the elaborate backup scheme that was going to be necessary to support me. Given my lifestyle I might be recording at almost any time of the day or night, so they had to be prepared to follow and record me around the clock. And because they couldn't have the same car seen around me too often, they had to be prepared to change vehicles continually. We ended up using cars, vans, trucks, and occasionally limousines with uniformed drivers. Then they also had to set up a combined operational headquarters and safe house for me. It was an apartment where we could meet, where I could get and give orders, and a place where I could run or my family could flee if things fell apart.

I had no illusions about what I was doing. One slipup and I would be dead. I thought I could control things on my end, but what I worried about was a leak on their end. That fear would be my constant companion. I knew what an information sieve New Jersey law enforcement was—how many guys were on the pad. I often talked about this fear with Billy, Ed, and Charley. They would always insist that only a handful knew my identity, and no one would ever talk, even to other law enforcement agencies. I hoped they were right. My life was riding on it.

We figured it was going to take about a month to get everything ready so we could start recording on a regular, everyday basis. We set a tentative start date for after the Labor Day holiday. In the meantime, I got asked a whole bunch of questions, and I had to volunteer a lot more information than I had in the past. But then near the end of August an opportunity came along that we all felt was too good to pass up. The meeting that Cousin Anthony had requested with Joey Sodano had been set up in Philly, and Scoops and I were going to drive him down. It would be a perfect test of how the recording equipment worked, especially while my car was in motion.

It turned out to be quite a production. The car the state was going to give me money to buy wasn't ready yet, so I told Scoops I had an idea. Everyone around us was still pretty spooked about the bug that had been placed in Turk's car. They were paranoid enough to believe that somehow the cops had gotten their hands on their cars and had bugged them, too, which meant that no one said much about anything in cars, even in their own cars. I told Scoops I had decided to have some guy I knew rent me a car. That way it would be a clean car, not in my name. The cops would not know about it, and we could use it to drive around, safe from being bugged. Scoops thought it was a terrific idea, so the state police rented a car using a cover name and wired it with both a retransmitter for my pager transmitter and a separate Nagra recorder.

When we set out for Philly, we were actually part of a four-car caravan. We were in the lead, followed by two recording cars—one a limo that stayed directly behind us and the other a van that ran parallel to us in the truck lanes of the New Jersey Turnpike. Finally, a command car brought up the rear to supervise the whole thing and to provide security if necessary.

On the way down we had some very interesting conversation. Joey told us that times were hard even for a mega-earner like him. He said he was taking care of Big Don's and Vinny's families—Don Hingos and Vinny Russo—while they were in jail. He said that a lot of his bookmakers were into him for big dollars; one guy, named Klein, owed him $180,000. He complained that he just didn't have the money to pay right now.

Since this was the first day we were really recording, I got Scoops and Joey to talk generally about the organization and their places in it. We had a long conversation about friends of ours who were doing time in various joints. It was kind of a stretch, but it got some of the basics down on tape if the cops needed the information in someone else's voice rather than mine.

There was just one hitch: The laws are such that I could only record conversations that took place in New Jersey and across the river in New York City. In order for us to record in Pennsylvania, we needed a court order, and that would have meant informing the U.S. Attorney's office. In turn, they would have told the FBI, which would then have been aware of our operation. The New Jersey State Police had been burned bad once by the FBI, and they were not about to let it happen again. In November 1986, New Jersey had indicted Nicky Sr., Philip, and a bunch of other guys as a result of a year-long operation called "Tigershark." But after the state indicted, the Feds moved in and took over the case. They had the New Jersey indictments dismissed and filed superseding federal indictments. When the trial took place, all the state's evidence was used, and the state's bugs and wiretaps, but the State of New Jersey received no credit. The Feds hogged the limelight entirely. That really pissed the New Jersey state cops off big time. In fact, most of the state cops I met hated the Feds and would do nothing to help them under any circumstances. While Broadsword was going on, I think it was a higher priority to keep the Feds from learning about it than keeping it from the wiseguys.

So on this first excursion into Pennsylvania, the guys turned off the recorder as we crossed the bridge into Philly. They could still listen to what was being said, but it was not recorded and could not later be introduced into evidence. What they then ended up eavesdropping on was me chatting generally about nothing with Nicky Jr. as Scoops, Cousin Anthony, and Joey met in a McDonald's on Front Street. Cousin Anthony was a mobster of the old school. Since Joey was a made guy and Scoops was theoretically his captain, Anthony would not allow the conversation to take place in front of anyone who was not yet straightened out—which meant Nicky Jr. and me. We had to sit at another table and make small talk for the better part of an hour while the three of them discussed business.

On the way back to Newark, with the recorder turned on, Joey continued bitching about how tough times were. Then he launched into a tirade that would make this tape just about the state police's favorite of the four hundred or so we recorded. Joey began to complain bitterly about how hard it was to be a crook in New Jersey because of the state police. "I wish we were all born and lived in New York," he said. "We'd have plenty of money and a much better shot to keep going."

"Yeah," Scoops agreed.

"Here you're a stickout," Joey continued. "You're just fucking dead. There's no place in this country that has the state police like New Jersey. . . . Here the state police are everywhere."

"Yeah," Scoops agreed again.

Then I threw some of my newfound knowledge into the conversation. "They got more different squads, Organized Crime, Intelligence," I said. "They got this, got that."

"For many, many years in New York their view of gambling was nothing, absolutely nothing," said Joey. "You could have maybe a hundred and fifty pinches, then on the hundred and fifty-first you get a three-hundred-dollar fine. And they almost apologize. We gotta do it, if you keep getting fifty-dollar fines. We gotta do three hundred dollars now."

Then the conversation turned back to the family and all that had happened over the past decade. "This guy gotta be sick, too," Joey said about Cousin Anthony. "I guess he thinks about everything that happened. And now with Philip. It's got to take a toll on you."

"Yeah, oh yeah," Scoops agreed softly.

"Sometimes I'm driving by myself, I don't give a fuck where I am," Joey continued. "In North Carolina, in Florida, wherever. I get tears in my eyes just thinking about all the things that have happened since Tony and Angelo—all the fucking garbage that's happened and all the guys that got killed. Not one fucking stool pigeon got killed. And all the guys who got killed were good guys: Tony, Freddie, Keys, Sindone. Crazy. Fucking madness!"

The conversation then moved to Tommy DelGiorno, who had been the first major made guy in our family to roll over and become a snitch after he had been arrested for murder—one of Nicky's many hits.

"Tommy Del," Joey said with a sad shake of his head. "If they had only left him where he should have been."

"Bookmaker," said Scoops.

"Bookmaker and a restaurateur, period," Joey agreed. "They didn't have to make him something that he wasn't made out to be or cut out to be. Send him on missions that weren't for his stomach. Nicky got impatient. I guess he figured at his age, where he should be and what he should have. He would have got there, nice and easy. He would have lived his life out on the street, not where he is now."

Later, after we had dropped Joey off, Scoops gave me a blow-by-blow of how the meeting went in Philly. We were still sitting in the car, and every word was recorded. Cousin Anthony had leaned hard on Joey for money, telling him, "Joe, we're in need here. If you can't do a whole loaf, do like half a loaf. Do something." But Scoops said Joey had resisted. He told Anthony that if and when his gambling business became profitable, once again he would resume his tribute payments. But in the meantime, he would pay nothing and would not make up payments he had missed.

"He's not going to make up nothing?" I asked.

"Nothing!" Scoops said.

Scoops had another worry. Joey was no ordinary bookie. He had friends in very high places and was in business on several levels in New York with a couple of families, including the Gambinos. He was close to the Gambinos and to John Gotti. He brought us business through these contacts, and they would not look too kindly on us leaning too hard. Even though he was a made member of our family, we didn't have the power to keep Joey from doing most of his business in the future with the Gambinos if they wanted him.

"You know you don't want to jeopardize him neither, you know what I mean," Scoops said. ". . . Let's try to keep low-keyed, of course. . . . God forbid we got a beef with New York. I don't know what else to say to you."

Scoops said that Anthony had asked him to find out if Joey's gambling business had really gone bad. He passed the assignment on to me, and before he left, he gave me $2,000 to pass along to Nicky Jr. for his father. I guess I hadn't realized how much the meeting had shaken him. He also said that Cousin Anthony had told him Patty was getting something from Philadelphia, and this was to explain why Scoops was giving up the two dimes to Nicky and not to Patty. But I knew the real reason was that Scoops was scared of what might happen to Joey for not paying, and if it went down and he was also behind in his payments to Nicky, he might be included for good measure.

This meeting with Joey Sodano in Philly did not end it, of course. What Scoops did not tell me about the conversation between Joey and Cousin Anthony I learned that night in a phone call from Anthony. Joey had said that he was never under any formal obligation to pay Patty or our family anything. It was not any kind of formal arrangement, and he had only paid in the past out of generosity and respect for Patty. Anthony wanted me to reach out to Patty and find out exactly what the truth was. He also asked me directly to find out if Joey's business was operating at a deficit. It was clear from his tone that this matter was far from closed.

Things had gone almost perfectly on the trip to Philly and afterward in Newark. We ended up with eight tapes of material that everyone in the state police was thrilled to get. Things went so well, in fact, that we decided to move up the schedule for starting full-time. We decided our next target would be Nicky Jr.

By this time I was meeting Nicky almost every week, usually to give him tribute either from Scoops and me, or from one of the other guys. I met him in Atlantic City to pass along the $2,000 that Scoops had given me. We talked about recording that meeting, but Ed thought we were not ready to try it in Atlantic City. "Too many eyes around," he said. We would really have to get everything down pat before we tried it in a casino, which was where I usually met Nicky. But this week Nicky was coming north. We were going over to look at some video poker machines and talk a little business. We decided to meet at the Forked River rest area on the Garden State Parkway to do our business, before continuing on to our meeting. Ed thought that would be a perfect place to record, so our little traveling troop mounted up and drove out to make a most unusual encounter.

I met Nicky in the rest area. He got out of his car and climbed into mine. I gave him our weekly tribute, $1,200 this time, and we got down to business. What Nicky wanted to talk about was Joey Sodano. Joey had told Cousin Anthony that among his problems was that he had $300,000 tied up in video poker machines that were not yet producing. "The meeting didn't go as well as I thought," Nicky said. "Is it true with this guy ... about losing the three hundred thousand dollars and not doing any more work with us? My cousin Anthony is relying on Scoops."

I told him my advice for now was to let it go, let it go at least until football season, which is when all bookies make most of their money. "Let's see what happens in a couple of months with the football," I said.

Nicky wasn't sure. "What am I going to do with this guy?" he wondered out loud. "I'm sure that this guy is still dealing with what he's dealing with and not bullshitting. 'Cause if he's bullshitting, then he's gonna be hurt, hurt bad, you know what I mean?"

Then he repeated that Anthony wanted Scoops to check up on Joey. "Because if this guy's bullshitting, he wants to call him back in. He wants to call him back in."

As this was going on, I knew that Ed was there in a van to record the conversation. And I knew that Charley was there in another car to act as backup for both me and Ed. But what I didn't know was that a third car was also interested in Nicky and me. Almost immediately Charley spotted the nondescript car with the Pennsylvania plates and two guys in it. He sized them up with one look. Feds. The FBI was tailing Nicky.

There were some frantic conversations between him and Ed. Had I walked into a bust? It didn't look like it because there was just a single car. Could Nicky have been wired? No, it didn't appear the Feds had recording equipment, although that was a possibility to be considered further later. No, it looked like simple surveillance. But if the Feds followed us to our next meeting, then they would likely know of our connection to the video poker machine business and might also become aware of our little roadshow. Both had to be avoided, but how? Ed and Charley talked about warning me, but that could blow the whole operation. They talked about crashing Charley's car into mine, a fender bender that would keep me from going. Finally, it was Charley who came up with a brilliant ploy.

Nicky and I got in our cars, and as we pulled out, the Feds started to follow us. But before they could get out of the parking space they had pulled into, a car directly behind them—driven by Charley, of course—suddenly stalled almost on their bumper. Cursing and apologizing all in the same breath, Charley took almost two minutes to get his car started again. By this time Nicky and I, and Ed in the recording van, were long gone. So much for law enforcement cooperation.

The next few weeks passed quickly. At the state's request I went back into the bookmaking business. The idea was that if I was bookmaking again, I might be able to record some of the players, and, more important, it would give me a chance to lay off action with other books or with other guys higher up in the chain. It was kind of funny. My book was about five guys, two of whom were Billy and Ed who were playing with the state's money just to give me some action.

On September 6 I got into a taped conversation with Scoops about this new gambling business of mine and whose "office" I might run it through. If you run it through someone bigger, then you don't have to finance it, and you're not exposed if the players hit a lucky streak. I suggested that I run my business through Michael Perna, a Lucchese guy I had been partners with before in the monte game and some other stuff. Since Michael was with another family, I had to get Scoops's permission because he was the acting captain. He didn't care as long as he wasn't exposed for any losses.

"Yeah, sure, whatever you want to do," Scoops said. "We'll take fifty percent with him. Let them hold the money, or else all he'll want to give us is quarters."

Scoops and I met six days later with Michael and Bobby "Spags" Spagnola, the Lucchese family's bookmaking "bank," to make the deal. Michael and Spags were happy to take the business. Spags had one question: "Are they straight players, George, or wiseguys? I don't care, just so I know how to deal with them."

I assured them that none of the guys I was sending was a wiseguy, and I promised in the future that if I sent them a wiseguy, I'd let them know before he started playing.

And as Scoops feared, Michael was going to play hardball on the split. He said he would give us twenty-five percent of the profit he made from the guys I was giving him. But he promised, "As business goes up, it'll do better for you, George. Listen, you won't be disappointed at the end of the year. That I promise you, you know."

Actually I did give him some more players, and eventually he did give me a better cut. At the end of the year I was not unhappy. The state police also were not unhappy. This business arrangement, starting with only five players, two of whom were plants, was more than enough for the state to get solid indictments against both Michael and Spags.

My undercover career almost came to an abrupt end just as it was getting under way. About a month after I started wearing the wire, I was beeped one night at the monte game, and when I called the number, it was the same Lucchese guy who had warned me earlier that a bug was planted in Turk's car. Their undercover network was still in operation, and their plant on the New Jersey State Parole Board had heard from his friend in the Attorney General's Organized Crime Task Force office that someone close to us was now working for the cops. He said his guy did not know who it was, but he was trying to find out.

Talk about scared. Here I was being told I was about to be uncovered. Early the next morning I went to Billy and Ed, and screamed bloody murder, but they assured me over and over that I had already met everyone who knew my identity and they were not talking to anyone. Anyone else who had knowledge of the operation—and there were only a few—knew me only by the code name "Freddy." They promised they would go to extraordinary lengths to find the leak, and a few weeks later they said they were pretty sure they had identified him. But they couldn't be sure, so they couldn't arrest or even fire the guy. They swore they had made sure that he would never get any information about Broadsword, let alone the key fact of who "Freddy" was. But this fear of a leak remained my most constant worry every day I was out there wearing the wire.

I racked my brain about any leaks or potential leaks I might know in the criminal justice apparatus. There was the guy who had lent us the bug detector, who also did work for the state police. I mentioned him to Ed, but he was so far out of the loop that we all agreed he did not pose a threat.

My biggest worry was another guy who was one of the chief investigators in the Attorney General's Office. I had known the guy years ago when he worked as a county investigator. He hung around us, and Patty told me he was on the pad. I had never personally handed the guy a cent, but there was no reason for Pat to tell me the guy was on the take if he wasn't. In those days it was just an accepted fact by all of us. So when Ed, Billy, and I started talking about possible leaks, I brought this guy's name up. Ed said he would look into it. The Attorney General's Office went berserk.

Apparently this guy was beloved by one and all there. I had absolutely no idea if he was honest or crooked at that moment. All I knew was that he was dirty when he worked for Essex County. The people in the Attorney General's Office simply would not believe it. They accused me of lying. They accused Billy and Ed of putting me up to saying it—an intramural rivalry thing between the state police and the Attorney General's Office.

One day some investigators from the Attorney General's Office brought me into a room and plunked down on a table about sixty photos. Pick the guy out, they demanded. I did so without any hesitation. That shook them, but they came right back and said that only proved I knew the guy. They accused me of having some kind of vendetta against the guy from my arrest in 1983, even though he had had nothing to do with it. To me this was all very illogical. Everything else I had told them or would ever tell them, proved to be completely true. I passed lie detector test after lie detector test. But on this one thing, about this one guy, they just wouldn't believe me. Billy, Ed, and the state police believed me, and they started treating the guy differently, careful of what they told him or talked about around him. But his own people in the Attorney General's Office protected him, and he was even given a major promotion. Now it was their problem, but for the year I was wearing the wire, I worried every day that the problem was mine.

All during the fall I continued doing what I had been doing on a day-to-day basis, with the exception that everything I did was watched by the state police and every word I said or that was said around me was faithfully recorded and later transcribed, ready to be introduced into evidence. At this point I was running the card and crap games at night, and during the day I helped out on some of the collecting from our loan-sharking business. In a one-week period in September we recorded conversations of me collecting interest from guys on the street who owed us and then turning that money over to Slicker, both at the East Side Social Club and one time at his house. In another recorded conversation Scoops gave his permission to lend five grand to Richie Sagotta, a neighborhood lounge singer, and to show that he had heart, he told me to charge Richie only two and a half percent a week instead of the usual three percent. In the best conversation I got on tape, I brought Scoops the news that a guy named Mario wanted to start up his own shy business. Scoops told me to give him permission and to say we would protect him. In return we would get a piece of his action, but we would put up no money. I later told Slicker that Mario was his to run.

It was in September that John Riggi reached out for me. He was concerned about his "Christmas money," the annual amounts that wiseguys pay to those higher up in the chain to whom they don't owe direct tribute, or amounts paid by guys outside the organization as a thank-you or in the hope of getting future favors. Mike Salimbene, the owner of Tectonic Construction, was paying Christmas money to John Riggi and the DeCavalcante family for labor peace. This had been going on for years. It had started at about $2,000 a year, got up to $15,000 a year, and now it had become a problem. The year before, Mike had been broke in December. It had taken him until March to pay up, and then he could raise only half, $7,500. Now John Riggi had financial problems. This year he wanted the full amount to be there, on time, or even early if possible. He told me to see Mike Salimbene and make sure.

On September 25, Billy, Ed, and I, along with our tape recorders, paid a visit to Mike. He was not happy to see me. I told him that John was noticing that he was "living very, very, very well."

"What does the way I live have to do with him?" Salimbene wanted to know.

I said the way he was living meant he couldn't cry poor. His response was that Riggi and I should stay away from him.

"What do you mean stay away from you?" I asked.

"Stay away . . . get the fuck out of here," he responded in an angry voice.

Then I told him what John had told me to tell him, that because he had paid only half last year, this year he must at least make that up plus the new payment.

"I don't give a fuck what he's looking for," Salimbene responded. "I don't ask him for nothing."

"But what do I tell him, Mike? What do I tell him?" I asked.

"You tell him anything you want to tell him," he replied. Then he got angry again. "Let me tell you something, George. I've been playing this game for too many fucking years."

I assured him I was only the messenger and that none of this money went into my pocket. That was a lie, of course. We always took half. I told him that Riggi sat behind the scenes, and while he may not ask anything directly, he made sure no strikes hit Salimbene's jobs. But from his look I knew he had no intention of giving up $22,500 in December.

I reported the conversation to Scoops, who was not happy. I asked him what I should tell Salimbene when I saw him again the following week.

"Say, 'Listen, if I mind my fucking business, they're going to knock your fucking head off,' " Scoops said, almost shouting. "Tell him just like that. You're going to get a fucking beating."

I went back the following week to see Salimbene again and to pass on Scoops's threats. It did little good. So on October 6 I met with John Riggi and told him Mr. Tectonic had started crying the blues to me again.

"He's a liar," Riggi said. "Motherfucker. He's lying."

Riggi wasn't impressed when I told him what Scoops had told me to tell Salimbene. "I'm going to tell you something, Georgie," he said angrily. ". . . I want this guy harassed every day. Every fucking day! You tell him, 'You know you can bullshit me, but don't bullshit him. . . . Now if you want that man to go out and give you a headache, just say it right now, and you'll get such a fucking headache, you won't know what hit you. People are in trouble. You're a man. Do what's right here. . . . Who are you fucking bullshitting?' "

"Yeah, okay," I responded. "And you want it before Christmas."

"Yes. I want it way before Christmas."

We got every word on tape. A month earlier, guys like Dave Brody and Major Tessa didn't believe I even knew a boss like John Riggi, let alone was able to get him on tape incriminating himself. Yet there it was, enough on tape from this one conversation to bring him down for extortion and conspiracy. There would be other tapes of Riggi in the future, including a videotape of him eventually getting the payoff from Salimbene. But this one tape was enough to send the credibility of the whole operation soaring. Suddenly we were the most valuable anti–organized crime operation that the State of New Jersey had launched in two decades.

I met Salimbene about two weeks later and started the conversation in what I thought was an appropriate manner considering the circumstances. "They nailed Harry this morning, you know," I said.

"Who?"

"Harry Serio. Two behind the head. Two behind the head, in his office. This morning. I can't get over it."

Harry Serio was a Teamsters Union official who was about to run for president of the local. For years he had gotten jobs, real and no-show, for guys from any of the families. He was also addicted to gambling, and when I was running my book in the early 1980s, Harry had been my biggest customer. In fact, very indirectly he was the reason I went to jail. The cops originally got onto me when my then-partner Don Hingos called me from his house because he didn't want to go out into the rain and call from a pay phone, and the cops had his home phone bugged. Don was calling me to see how Harry had done that day. At that point Harry was up about $60,000 for the season, and this was making Don crazy because Harry always lost. I had always liked Harry, and I was genuinely upset when he got whacked. But now I was using it to throw a scare into Salimbene.

It didn't do any good on that visit. Salimbene still said he wasn't going to give up one red cent. I knew that if I brought this answer back to Riggi, at the very least Salimbene would get some bones broken. I didn't think Riggi would have him whacked because dead men don't pay off in the future, but I had no doubt he would get a very serious beating. And this was something I wanted to avoid having on my conscience because I thought Salimbene was right in not paying off if Riggi wasn't doing anything for him. So I worked on him a bit more and finally got a promise from him that he would at least think about it. Now I could report back that we had started to make some progress.

All hell broke loose on Halloween night. I stayed home that night from the monte game in order to take my kids out trick-or-treating. About nine the phone rang. It was Charley Crescenz saying that Nicky Jr. had just been shot in a restaurant in Philly, and he didn't know if Nicky was dead or alive. As I was digesting this news, Phil McFillin called from Philly with the same news but had a few more details. The Kid had been eating dinner with his cousin John Parisi at Dante Luigi's when a guy walked in with a silenced Uzi and emptied the magazine into Nicky. He had been hit eleven times but amazingly was still alive. Phil was calling me from the hospital where they had taken the Kid into surgery. He told me to tell the other guys in Newark.

I made a bunch of calls. After talking with Scoops and Slicker, it was decided that we should meet at the Italian-American Club on Clifford Street, the place we called the "Am-Vets," to try to figure out what was going on. "Bring some guns, George," Scoops had said to me. We didn't know if the shooting might be some kind of move against the family, so Scoops wanted protection.

By the time I reached Ed Quirk, he had heard about Nicky Jr. I told him I was on my way over to Slicker's to pick him up and then we were going to the Am-Vets to meet Scoops. Ed asked me to stall until he, Billy, and Charley could get in position to record what would be said. I waited as long as I could, and on the way over to meet Slicker at his house, I picked up a couple of pieces from a guy I knew in the underground gun business. By the time we got to the club, Scoops had worked himself into a lather.

At that point I had two ideas about who might have done the shooting, which obviously was a professional job. After Philip Leonetti flipped, Nicky told me that his father had given him the order to have him killed. He said his father felt it might take some time, but at some point Philip would have to show himself and could be hit. Money was no object, Nicky Sr. had said. Whatever it cost, it cost.

"My father says . . . this one is definitely my responsibility," the Kid had told me in a conversation we recorded. "He can't rest. I told him, I says, I ain't resting till it's fucking done. I ain't resting till it's done. . . . It's eating at me, George, eating at me, you know? Especially him being so close to me. You know what I'm saying? You don't know how it feels."

I wondered if Philip had managed to reach out from jail or federal protective custody and hit the Kid first. I doubted it, but it was something to consider. I felt it was much more likely the shooter was either Joey Merlino or someone hired by him. Nicky Sr. had had Joey's father Chuckie whacked, and Joey still took it very hard. Only a little while ago I had asked the Kid if he was having any kind of beef with Joey Merlino. I had heard rumors that Joey was telling people he was going to kill the Kid. But Nicky said he almost never saw Joey and that he didn't think he had a problem with him.

Scoops had another explanation entirely. By the time Slicker and I got to the Am-Vets, he was sure, absolutely sure, that the Kid's getting whacked was all part of a takeover plot that was actually aimed at him. He figured that Joey Sodano was behind it because he was pissed at us, and to get out from under what he owed and maybe just to take over. He might have figured that things were in such turmoil with Patty gone and Nicky Sr. in jail that no one would stop him.

And Scoops was sure it was more than just Joey involved. He had it all figured out. There was a conspiracy going on. A whole bunch of other guys were ready to take us over, and in order to do it, they had to whack him. "What the fuck's going on here?" Scoops demanded. "Come on, what are we, crazy? I don't want to get caught here with our pants down because some of these cocksuckers might be scheming. Let me tell you something. I got a wire a few months ago. The 'Nodder' told somebody they wanted to make him a captain."

The "Nodder" was a nickname for Joey Sodano. A "wire" in this context was a message from some guy.

"The Nodder?" Slicker asked in surprise.

"Yeah," Scoops said. "Listen to me. I'm not sleeping. I'm way ahead of all of them. Will you listen to me?"

Scoops then reminded us that in the car on the way to Philadelphia and the meeting with Cousin Anthony, he asked Joey if he had been talking recently with a certain guy, and Joey said yeah. Now I realized this guy must have been the one who told Scoops about Joey bragging he was going to be a captain. To add to this, Scoops had heard about a recent meeting between Joey and Mickey Ricciardi, Pete the Crumb Caprio, and "Shotzie"—Salvatore Sparacio—all old made guys from our crew who had been straightened out by Blackie Napoli in the Tony Bananas era. Scoops had never forgotten or forgiven Blackie for the way he had abused him. He believed that Blackie, who was semi-retired, still wanted to take over the family, the whole family, and to install Shotzie as the captain in northern Jersey. Who knows what these guys had gotten together about? Shotzie was a major bookmaker, so it was probably just some business. It could even have been social. But to Scoops the meeting was a signal they were scheming. He was sure that Shotzie wanted to take over and that he, Scoops, was all that was standing in the way.

If this was not enough, we had started to have yet another potentially major problem with Joey just the week before. Before I went to jail, I had a guy by the name of Carmen Albanese working for me collecting bets. When I went away and my guys were divided up, Carmen was given to Joey. Now Carmen was starting to have problems with Ray Springer, the guy who actually ran Joey's betting office. So Carmen had gone to Scoops, as the acting captain, and asked to be placed with someone else. Scoops and I talked it over, and we decided to give Carmen to Michael Perna.

As usual, Joey was nowhere to be found, so I left word in a couple of places that I needed to talk with him. Days passed and suddenly out of the blue I get paged. When I called the number, it was Joey saying he would meet me in an hour at the Pacific Cleaners on Pacific Street, which was owned by a guy who was close to him. I got there and explained the problem Carmen was having with Raymond, the fact that he had gone to Scoops, and the decision to give him to Michael. It was obvious that Joey was really pissed, but I had the impression at the time that Carmen was simply not a big enough producer to make a big deal over. So I told Scoops that Joey was angry but said he didn't give a damn what Carmen did. Now Scoops thought pulling Carmen away from Joey might have been enough to trigger a revolt. And he was ready to fight.

"He's up to— They're all motherfuckers," Scoops said. "Him, Mickey, they're all mother— And we're going to give them the same thing back. But I'm going to be prepared for them. They think they're going to come with a new boss down there, and Nodder is going to become captain or whatever. Fuck them. We'll kill them."

Oh, Christ, I thought, this is nuts. Somebody shoots the Kid in Philly, and Scoops is going paranoid and threatening to start a war because he somehow sees himself as the target. He's saying stuff like "It's them or us" and "We'll stick it in their ass" and "Let's go and clip a couple of them" and "I've got two guns and plenty of ammo in my car trunk." I figured if I didn't defuse this quickly, the way Scoops was working himself up, he was just liable to order us to go looking for Joey Sodano.

To calm him down a bit, I said we had better get hold of Cousin Anthony before we did anything too rash. And then Scoops realized he didn't have the slightest idea how to contact Anthony. As crazy at it sounded, Scoops was the captain but he had no way of reaching the boss. Anthony always figured he was being followed everywhere he went and that every phone he even stepped near was bugged. So the only way we could reach him was through the Kid. Anthony would call us directly, but if we needed him, we had to reach out through Nicky Jr. I figured that Patty in Italy probably had a phone number for Anthony, and if things got more out of control, I would have to get him involved. But things cooled down a little when Scoops decided that he would wait until the morning and reach out for Anthony.

Things actually calmed down a lot when we learned the next day that the Kid had survived the shooting. The doctors said half an inch here, half an inch there, and he would have died instantly. He took eleven bullets at point-blank range, yet none of them struck anything vital. It was as close as I have come in my lifetime to seeing a miracle. When Scoops finally talked to Anthony, he was told to cool it. Anthony said this was something that had to do with the Kid or with Nicky Sr., and nothing to do with him. So Scoops let things get back to normal. But the whole thing was another sign to me that he was not handling the pressure of leadership very well.

8

BABY-SITTER

I don't know who was more amazed, me to get the call or Billy and Ed when I told them about it afterward. The call came from Phil McFillin a couple of days after Nicky Jr. was shot. The Kid was still in the hospital, but it was now certain he would not only survive but would probably show few long-term effects. A couple of bullets would probably have to remain inside him forever, but he was going to be out of the hospital within a week to ten days. His father and Cousin Anthony feared that whoever had done this was going to be very annoyed he had failed; thus a repeat performance sometime in the near future was almost assured. That's what Phil wanted to talk to me about.

"George," Phil said after he had given me an update on Nicky's condition, "he's gonna get out in a week or two, and we're worried. He can't stay here in Philly because he'll be just a walking target. Besides, we don't know who we can trust here and who we can't. Little Nicky and the Kid both trust Pat, and they both trust you. Little Nicky and Cousin Anthony want you to hide the Kid while he heals and until we're sure we know what's going on down here."

We talked back and forth for a few minutes, and it became clear that what they had in mind was relatively long term. They wanted the Kid out of Philly and out of Atlantic City for at least six months, and more likely for a year or longer. I was about to become a baby-sitter.

Billy and Ed saw it as a stroke of unbelievably good fortune. The Kid had already been up on enough visits to Marion for us to know that he was the main conduit for orders from his father as he tried to retain his hold on the family. Now, if I was going to be with the Kid constantly, I would be a party to everything that was going down on a day-to-day basis.

There were a couple of drawbacks to this new "opportunity," however. The first was simply the danger. Cousin Anthony was not getting the Kid out of town for nothing. They suspected that whoever had made the try would try again. The danger was that when they found out the Kid had been sent north, they would come looking. If they found him and I was standing next to him, that would be a decidedly unhealthy place to be. Then, too, there was the cost. Although Phil didn't come right out and say it, I was not only going to be the Kid's baby-sitter but I was also going to be his host. I would have to put him up somewhere, feed him, clothe him, and entertain him—perhaps for as long as I remained in New Jersey. That was going to cost, and I would have to come up with the money from somewhere. Under my deal with the state, I was not supposed to be profiting from any criminal enterprise, so I would have to use a couple of grand a month of the expense money the state was providing to the operation for the care and feeding of Nicky Scarfo, Jr. I assumed the higher-ups would have no problem with that.

When Nicky got out of the hospital, he spent the first night at Phil McFillin's house on Twenty-sixth Street in Philly. The next morning, November 14, I drove to Philly to pick him up. I didn't know what kind of shape he would be in—I mean, eleven bullets and all—so I had made plans for him to stay at my house initially where someone would be with him at all times. But he was in amazingly good shape. He was weak and tired, but what would you expect? He was already strong enough so that on the way back to Newark we stopped at two places to conduct some quick business and pick up some money owed us.

Nicky ended up staying at my house only a few days. He saw a doctor we knew who said he was doing fine, so he moved into a room at the Sheraton Newark, by the airport—a room rented under an assumed name, of course. He stayed there a couple of weeks, and then, for security reasons, we moved him to the Sheraton Woodbridge, again under a different name. Finally, after about six weeks, he ended up in an apartment I rented for him in Belleville, fairly near me. I saw him every day. At times I thought I had acquired a shadow, and as Billy and Ed suspected, I soon became privy to the orders his father was passing out of Marion.

It was hard but far from impossible for Nicky Sr. to run the family from a maximum security cell. He received information and sent orders out when he talked with or saw his visitors, including Nicky Jr. Whenever the Kid went out to Marion, he would update his father on what was going on and bring back orders.

Nicky also had a third way of communicating his orders that was very ingenious. In addition to calls to his attorneys, he was allowed two calls of twenty minutes each to approved direct family members, so he had developed a routine. Once a month he would call the Kid and once a month his cousin Johnny Parisi in Margate. What they did when Nicky Sr. needed to talk with someone else was conference him in. Before he was sentenced, while he was still in a Philadelphia jail and seeing his son and Bobby Simone daily, Nicky had worked out a simple but effective code with them. A weather report the Kid gave his father might tell him how business was going and who they were having problems with. Words had a different meaning. For instance, a dinner invitation was not what it seemed. If Nicky Sr. told either the Kid or Johnny Parisi that someone should be taken out to dinner, he was not being sociable. Far from it. Taking someone out to dinner was Nicky's code for whacking him. On more than one occasion Nicky ordered a murder from his cell in Marion, just as he had ordered me to kill Long John Martorano, which I hadn't been able to carry out because Long John was in a secure federal lockup.

I learned all about the way Nicky Sr. was communicating shortly after the Kid came north, and I was present when Johnny Parisi dialed someone into a call with Nicky. I was recording at the time, and Billy and Ed heard what was going on. Within a few days they had a wiretap established on Johnny Parisi's phone, and over the next few months they heard some interesting discussions in Nicky's calls from Marion.

November proved to be very eventful. Phil McFillin's call asking me to baby-sit the Kid was only one of a number of things that occurred that month. To start, we finally nailed John Riggi, first on the extortion beef we had been working on and then for good measure on a witness-tampering conspiracy that he was thoughtful enough to dump in our laps.

For weeks, ever since my last visit to Mike Salimbene at Tectonic, Riggi had been pressuring me to get him the money he believed Salimbene owed him. I went to a meeting with Riggi, his underboss Jack D'Amico, and Cousin Anthony, which I helped set up so that John and Cousin Anthony could formally meet. After the formalities were over, all John wanted to talk about was Salimbene. Scoops was going nuts. He was the captain, and by not collecting from Salimbene, he was not coming through as a powerful boss. This was making him look bad, and his only way of saving face was either to get Mike to pay up or to put him in the hospital for a long stay.

I had called Mike and told him this as clearly as I could. He thought it over and finally saw the wisdom of what I was saying. He called me back and said he would pay $10,000 but not a cent more. I called John who said to pick it up quick.

On November 6 I went to Tectonic to get the money. I told Mike that John would take the $10,000 but that he wasn't happy about it.

"He can scream all he wants," Salimbene said.

"That's all he's getting?" I asked.

"That's it."

"All right, Michael" was all I could say.

We then made some small talk, and the whole meeting took less than fifteen minutes before I was back out in the parking lot. Billy and Ed had recorded the conversation, and they followed me to a spot down the road where I gave them the $10,000, all in hundred-dollar bills. They took the envelope to the state police crime lab where the sealed envelope was photographed and fingerprinted. It was then opened, the money counted, and each bill photographed. Then they took out $2,000, which they exchanged at a bank for $2,000 in new bills with sequential serial numbers so that the stash would be easier to identify.

John was out of town, so he and I agreed to meet at noon on the fifteenth at the Lido Diner on Route 22. Billy and Ed were there to tape what was said via my transmitter, and they had a camera set up in the camper they were using to try to get the exchange on video tape.

John was on time, we sat down, and I got right to business. "I have an envelope here for you. Ten thousand dollars. Believe me, I wish he could do more. He can't. I didn't touch it, John. I didn't even count it."

I handed him the sealed envelope, and he looked unhappy. First he was annoyed because I hadn't already removed our share, $5,000. But Billy and Ed were hoping to get some video of John actually handling the money. I knew he would never insult me by sitting there and counting it. I figured the only way was to leave the whole thing intact so he would have to count out our half. But this was not the kind of thing a boss did very often, and John was clearly annoyed. Then, too, he was still unhappy with the amount. He had demanded $25,000, and Mike was coming across with only $10,000. John had said to take it because he knew that $10,000 was better than nothing, but he still wanted it all.

"Tell him my advice," John said with some menace in his voice. "He went this far, now go the rest of the way."

Then came the split.

"George, he gets half of it," John said, referring to Patty. "And George, you know that."

I apologized again for not opening the envelope, but I said that since it was less than he had wanted, maybe he should take it all.

"Ah, shit, you're supposed to get half," John replied, but he obviously didn't want to sit in the diner counting out five grand in hundreds.

"Let's go in the bathroom," I suggested.

"No. That looks too obvious. Follow me down the road."

So he got up and left, and a few seconds later I followed. We went across the parking lot to a spot outside Dunkin' Donuts, and John took out the envelope. As luck would have it, in leaving the diner he had walked almost directly in the direction of the camper. Now he was making the split right in front of the camera. Even better, Billy and Ed had the camera right next to the machine that was recording the audio from my transmitter. So we ended up getting John Riggi, the boss of the DeCavalcantes, counting out his extortion take live on video with good sound. We could not have done much better if John had come into a studio to do it. There was no way he could beat this rap.

Then he dug himself an even deeper hole. He was under a federal indictment for labor racketeering and was sure the Feds were looking into a $15,000 payment he had received years before from a guy he barely remembered, a guy who at the time was building some condos in Scotch Plains. He wanted me to find out the guy's name.

"I talked to him about two to three minutes," John explained, "and he mentioned he had a job on Staten Island. And I don't remember the kid's name or the company's name. Hell, I spoke to him ten years ago. Now I got to have this guy's name and the company name."

What he did remember about this kid was that he said he was

Santo Idone's nephew. In fact, as John remembered it, Santo had introduced them. An old Philadelphia captain in our family, Santo had been a power in the Angelo Bruno days. John wanted us to talk to Santo to get him the information he needed. He had talked with Scoops about it a few weeks earlier, but in his usual fashion, Scoops had come up empty. So now John was bypassing Scoops and wanted me to reach out for Cousin Anthony to find out who this kid was. What's more, he wanted the kid to lie about how the two of them had met and what the money was for.

I called Anthony, and he agreed to meet the next morning, as usual in his lawyer Donald Manno's office. Then I called Scoops to tell him I was going down, and he demanded to be included. He was the captain, he said, and he wasn't going to have one of "his men" meeting the acting boss without being there himself. I let the reference to me as his man drop and simply told him I would pick him up the next morning on the way.

We got to Manno's office in Cherry Hill the next day about 10:30 A.M. Cousin Anthony was not the most punctual guy around; he kept us waiting for almost ninety minutes. When he finally arrived, I told him about John Riggi's problem. John needed the name of Santo's nephew so he could get the word to him that, if the Feds came calling, the kid should say he met John through some union guys and not through Santo.

But it was all kind of complicated. Santo was in jail at the time with a racketeering trial about to start in Chester, Pennsylvania. We had heard that Philip was going to be the government's star witness, which had left Santo not exactly happy with the family. So getting a conversation with him about something as unimportant as John Riggi's problem with his supposed nephew was going to take some arranging. Anthony said he would handle it.

It ended up taking about a month. On December 16, a Saturday, Anthony called us to another meeting at Manno's office. By this time Nicky Jr. had recovered enough to travel, so he, Scoops, and I went down to Cherry Hill and met with Anthony. He gave me a business card from Dominic Pillari, owner of the Just Development Company in Brick Town, New Jersey. Dominic was Santo's nephew and he remembered well the payment he had made in 1981 to John. He had been talked to by his uncle and was willing to say whatever John wanted him to say. Anthony gave me the card and told me to tell John to call Pillari and set up a meet.

When I talked with John, he asked me to set up the meeting. So I drove down to Brick Town and met with Pillari on December 20. I told him John wanted a meet, and he readily agreed, saying he would tell the police whatever John wanted him to. We arranged to meet with John at the Holiday Inn in Kenilworth, a couple of days after Christmas. But John and I got stood up.

Pillari called me at the last minute and said some business matters had come up, and he would have to reschedule. It was too late to reach John, so I had to go to the hotel and tell him. He was pissed that the guy had not shown, but he did tell me more about what had happened ten years earlier. Pillari was just starting out and had done some work for a guy named Newman who was not paying up. He told his uncle, and Santo himself had called John to ask if he could help collect. John knew Newman, and what he did was collect the money the kid was owed plus $15,000 for himself. Now apparently Newman was talking with the prosecutors, and John wanted Pillari to say they had met through some union guys, not through Santo, and that the entire amount, including the $15,000, had actually been owed Pillari. John and I finally met with Pillari on January 2. He and John got their stories straight, and Pillari ended up telling investigators exactly what John wanted them to hear. Unfortunately for John, they also heard a lot more. Based on tapes of these meetings, they were able to indict him for witness tampering, Cousin Anthony for his role in the matter, and Pillari for conspiracy. Pillari later worked out a deal with the state and ended up testifying against John on both the original extortion charge and the witness-tampering charge.

Scoops was still running scared, and it turned out that he had insisted on coming along to the original meeting with Cousin Anthony because he had his own agenda in mind. He was not there to help out John Riggi but to get Anthony's help in putting down the imaginary coup he thought Blackie Napoli and Shotzie Spallichio were involved in.

After we got the Riggi business out of the way, the four of us— Scoops, Manno, Cousin Anthony, and I—went to lunch at the Golden Dawn Diner in Moorestown. While Don and I went in, Scoops kept Anthony outside talking about this problem. The conversation stopped while we had lunch but continued in the parking lot of Manno's office when we got back. I wasn't a made guy, and this matter was between Scoops, as captain, and Anthony, as acting boss.

They didn't talk in front of me or the state police recorder, but Scoops gave me a play-by-play on our drive back to Newark.

Scoops was right in one thing: Our family was drifting. Anthony was only acting boss, with Nicky Sr. still trying to hold on to control from jail. It wasn't working. Unless Anthony began to act with some amount of independence from Nicky, began to actually assert himself like a boss and to back up his words with some strong actions, our family was going to weaken to the point that one day we would find ourselves being run by one of the New York families. To Scoops the place where Anthony had to start was by naming an underboss with some authority and by reigning in Blackie and Shotzie.

"I told him, George, 'Nip it in the bud, and you'll solve everything,' " Scoops said, recounting his conversation with Anthony. "Am I right, George? We must nip it in the bud."

Then, referring to Blackie, Scoops said he told Anthony: "He's dangerous. You know what I mean? If you can't put everything back together again, he's putting you out. I'm sure they must be maneuvering something."

But Anthony had been noncommittal at best. Scoops thought he was chicken. "You can see that this poor bastard, he don't want no part of this. . . . What's going to happen is that New York is going to get involved, and we'll wind up out there," he said, complaining bitterly. "Whoever's left down here will wind up with Russ Buffullino or somebody, or everybody will be under New York. And then what will it be? They'll bust your balls and want you out there every week. You know what I'm trying to say?"

I knew exactly what he was trying to say. He wanted permission for us to whack Blackie. That wasn't something that was going to happen anytime soon, but I thought it would be interesting if I was wearing a wire if and when Cousin Anthony ordered us to make the hit.

In 1987, while I was still in jail, my aunt and uncle invested $25,000 with Jeff Kleinbaum, who was then a broker at Prudential Bache. Every month for a couple of years thereafter they would get a Pru Bache check for $250. Thus, as far as they were concerned, they had an investment that was returning them in excess of ten percent. Then one day Kleinbaum got himself fired, and suddenly the monthly checks stopped coming. So my uncle called Pru Bache and was shocked to learn there was no record of any investment account in his name or of the $25,000. Kleinbaum had simply pocketed the money and had been paying my uncle $250 a month so he wouldn't know.

My uncle turned to me for help, and for over a year I worked with Kleinbaum trying to get their money back. He gave me a few hundred here, $750 there, a thousand one time. In all I guess I ended up getting them about $12,000 of the $25,000 they had originally given him. To prove what a tough guy I was, at one point when he was really broke, Kleinbaum asked me to lend him $1,000. I got the money from Slicker's shy operation and had to charge Kleinbaum three points—that is, three percent, or $30 a week. I collected $120 from him once a week.

On November 3 I was due for my monthly meeting with Kleinbaum. Billy, Ed, and I had fallen into the habit of getting together every Monday morning to go over the meetings I was going to be having the coming week. That way we could plan ahead about what we wanted to record, and they could see what nights and how much overtime they might have to work. So this week I told them I was meeting Kleinbaum on Friday around lunchtime.

On Wednesday I got beeped from the safe house and went there to meet Billy and Ed. Billy had a kind of strange smile on his face. "Your meeting on Friday with Kleinbaum, he's going to be wired," he told me. "The criminal justice division of the Attorney General's Office is running an operation on you."

He went on to explain that he had been in the Organized Crime Bureau's offices the day before and just happened to overhear Kleinbaum's name being mentioned in a conversation between two officers. He kept his ears open, asked a few questions, and learned that Kleinbaum had been picked up on a drug possession beef by the local Millburn, New Jersey, cops, who had then turned him over to the state police. The hope had been that he could lead them to major drug dealers, but it seemed the only guy he really knew was the two-bit operator who was selling him a little coke. They asked him who else he knew that might interest them, and my name was put at the head of the list. Billy told me the guys Kleinbaum was working with had made me a specific target, and they were trying to get me on a shylocking charge. Kleinbaum would be wearing a wire, and they were hoping to get enough on me from the Friday meeting to send a case against me to the Attorney General's Office and get an indictment for loan-sharking.

It was spy versus spy, and it would have been kind of funny except that Billy and Ed couldn't quite figure out how innocent it may or may not have been. On the one hand, so few people knew what I was doing that it might well have been possible for this thing to go as far as it had without bumping up against anyone who knew I was working as an agent. On the other hand, anytime an informant is wired, there has to be approval at several levels, and at these higher levels there were people who knew my identity but who might not have been told I was a target of Kleinbaum's. It was likely that the people who knew about me had not been made aware that Kleinbaum was going to troll for whatever he could get to make his deal on the possession charge.

But this incident came just at the time I was going around and around with the Attorney General's Office about their high-level investigator, whom I had known when he was still a local guy on our pad. Ed was afraid that this guy knew what I had been alleging about him and that he and his friends were trying to set me up through Kleinbaum. If that was the case, we might have even bigger problems down the road. But the immediate problem was what to do about Kleinbaum and the wire.

Kleinbaum and I met midday at the Route 22 Diner in Union. It started in a way that was typical of our past meetings, with us shooting the breeze a bit about what he was doing and how he was getting back on his feet. Then he did something I would never have expected if I hadn't known the real reason for the meeting. First he gave me a couple of hundred for my uncle, and then he paid off the entire amount of what he owed Slicker. More than just paying it off, he counted out the money—$1,000 for principal, and then he said, "Here's the one hundred and twenty dollars, George, for the three-percent-a-week interest you were charging me."

If I had taken the money and thanked him, which I normally would have done, that would have been all she wrote. That action alone would likely have been enough to get me indicted for loan-sharking. But I threw a monkey wrench into their carefully laid plans. "Interest, Jeff? What do you mean, interest?" I said with all the surprise I could muster in my voice. "I'm hurt. You thought I was going to charge a friend interest? Nonsense. Although I appreciate your offer to pay interest. But no, it was just a loan between friends."

Kleinbaum looked stunned. I guess about nineteen different thoughts must have been running through his mind, not the least of which was that somehow I had learned he had become a snitch and was wired. And if I knew that, I guess he thought I would come after him, and his life was in danger. But I simply smiled, thanked him for repaying the loan, and told him I would see him next month to get some more of what he owed my uncle. As I walked away, I left him with his mouth hanging open.

Billy and Ed thought it was about the funniest thing they had ever seen. They had watched from a very safe distance in the parking lot, which they said looked like the parking lot at headquarters with so many undercover cars all over the place. After I left, there was another frantic meeting between Kleinbaum and a couple of the cops and another frantic scene back at headquarters. They knew I had been charging three points for the loan and didn't believe for a second that Kleinbaum had made up the story. But the fact that I went out of my way to deny it had to mean I knew something was wrong with the meeting. They just couldn't figure out how I knew.

Obviously, the tape was worthless to them, so they dropped me as an investigatory target. Billy later talked with Captain Gaugler, and the matter was put completely to rest. But the incident got me to worrying that there might be guys in the state police who were not on my side and that someone could drop the dime on me anytime to anyone in the five different families we were dealing with. That would be a death warrant.

Actually, I was already on somebody's hit list. A couple of weeks earlier, soon after Nicky Jr. had come north for me to baby-sit, I was beeped by Ed. He beeped again a few seconds later, and again a few seconds after that. It was obviously important.

"George, you came very close last night" was the first thing he said when I got to the safe house. He went on to explain that the Intelligence Division had heard from an informant in south Jersey that a couple of hit men were on their way to Newark to make another attempt on Nicky Jr. The information was deemed solid, and Ed and Billy believed these guys would probably come looking for me since they didn't know where Nicky was stashed. But at the last minute the two of them decided to deal with it without telling me, both to keep me from getting too spooked and out of fear that I might do something to blow my cover.

The informant had apparently been very precise, and what followed was several hours of cat and mouse. Billy and Ed told the state police's elite anti-drug detail that a couple of major drug couriers were coming in by train. So every train into Newark from the south was met, and everyone matching the general descriptions of the two guys was stopped and questioned. Finally, the right two were detained as they got off the train. The only thing they could be held on was a weapons charge, since they were both armed, but it was enough to stop them. The way the whole thing went down, the two guys never knew that the police knew where they were headed and why. They thought they were just unlucky to be picked up as possible drug dealers, and this protected the informant.

I later saw their mug shots, and neither guy was known to me as someone in our family or around anyone in our family. It appeared that both were outside guys who had been hired to do a job. But I couldn't very well tell Nicky or anyone else in the family what had happened because how would I explain how I had found out? Even more troubling was the fact that even after we got these two, we couldn't tell who had sent them. Again, we all assumed it was Joey Merlino, but even the informant didn't know. He apparently knew one of the hitters and found out where he was heading and who he was after, but not who was footing the bill.

Perhaps our suspicions that it was Joey Merlino were confirmed because there was no repeat performance. Shortly after these two guys were stopped at the Newark train station, Merlino went to jail. I could only assume that when he went away, he just decided to wait until he got out and then do the job himself. But the whole episode left me even more on pins and needles. I was baby-sitting a target, and I had to worry that either they would try to get to Nicky through me or else I would be with him when it finally went down.

My agreement with the state was that I was on salary like any other police officer and that I could not profit personally from any illegal activities I was engaged in. But I did cheat a little, without Ed and Billy's knowledge.

It took me the better part of two months to get Nicky Jr. permanently set up. Michael Perna gave me the use of an apartment for him, and I spent a couple of thousand furnishing it with basics. In mid-December he quietly settled in for what we now knew was going to be a long stay. That money the state police knew about. What they didn't know was that I was also holding back money to send to Patty. I guess over the spring and summer of 1989 I sent him about $15,000—money to support him and to get him from Florida back to

Italy. I also gave money to his wife, Lee, to help support her and the kids, and a couple of thousand to Anna Marie to enable her to take some time off to spend with Patty in Italy.

As usual, I was doing this all on my own. Whenever I asked Scoops to contribute, he would complain that he was having a tough enough time scraping together the money he was sending to Cousin Anthony every week and the few hundred he was now giving Nicky Jr. He said this, and then would go home to his million-dollar house. But in a way it was good that he continued to act that way because every time he did, he only made me more certain that I was doing the right thing and more resolved than ever to bring them all down.

A few days before Thanksgiving 1989, I got a call from John Praino. He asked me to meet him that night for dinner at Gino's on Lexington Avenue and Sixty-first Street in the city. He said it was very important, that he needed to talk with me. When I walked in, I was stunned. Patty was sitting there.

I had not seen him since the previous May when he left to go to Italy. He had spent the summer in Reggio, and I knew that two weeks earlier he had traveled what was now his usual route—a plane from Rome directly to Chicago and then the train to Fort Lauderdale. Anna Marie had been with him in Italy and made the trip, too. I had sent him money for the tickets and to get reestablished in Florida.

"What are you doing here?" I managed to stammer as I hugged him. He said that Anna Marie had to come back to work, so he decided to come up with her. He would stay in John's apartment in the Bronx, and he planned on being there through the holidays. He would then spend the rest of the winter in Florida.

The dinner was social. Anna Marie arrived a few minutes later, and when the surprise of seeing Patty passed, it struck me how ill he looked. Despite the summer in Italy and then the couple of weeks in Florida, he was pale and thin. He had lost enough weight over the summer that it was really noticeable. He looked sick, and he was.

"This damn stomach, Georgie," he said during dinner when I commented on how lightly he was eating. "I have pain all the time now, and those doctors in Italy were no help. All they would give me were antacids. I'm going to go to a stomach specialist next week while I'm here."

I had talked to Patty only a few days earlier and had brought him up to date on everything. He had been in transit when Nicky Jr. was shot, and I was only able to tell him about it when he arrived in

Florida. Immediately after Phil McFillin called to ask me to hide Nicky Jr., I called Patty in Florida to get his input on what I should do. He thought it would be good for me because it would put me in the center of the family's business, and Nicky Sr. would owe me a big favor. He was still determined that I be straightened out as soon as possible and that I take over running the family in Jersey. He, too, was getting very tired of Scoops.

Actually, Patty had slipped into a kind of semi-retirement. The fiction still existed that he was the captain who was making the decisions and that I passed orders back and forth from him, but the truth of the matter was that Patty had pretty much accepted the fact that he was never going to be able to come back to Jersey and resume the life he had led before we were indicted. The very best he could hope for was to be able to live openly in New York and resume some of his past activities. But even that might be only a pipe dream. Patty just seemed to have lost much of his interest in what was happening day-to-day, and after Scoops was named acting captain, he pretty much left all the minor decisions to him. Over that spring and summer I still talked to Patty several times a week, first in Florida and then in Italy, keeping him up to date on what was going on. But for the most part, if I was told to pass something on to him for a decision, I made the decision myself and told him about it later. He said whatever I decided was fine with him.

But, interestingly, he was still very concerned with the big picture —the future of our family as a whole. Here he agreed with Scoops that unless Cousin Anthony started asserting himself and stopped depending on orders coming out of Marion, our family would get weaker and weaker until one morning we would wake up with a new boss installed by the Gambinos or the Genoveses or the Luccheses. That would be the end of the Bruno-Scarfo family. From that point on we would be a wholly owned subsidiary of some other family until eventually we would simply be absorbed.

Patty being in New York caused me some major problems. He wanted to see me a lot—and for that matter I wanted to see him— but I couldn't let on to Billy and Ed and the rest of them from the state that he was back in the area. Given what our deal was concerning Patty, I didn't think they would go after Patty, but it would cause complications and would perhaps put Billy and Ed in the middle. So I had to find a way to see Patty without alerting them to what was going on.

I was helped by the fact that by now Ed, Billy, and I had settled into a very businesslike five-day-a-week, nine-to-five schedule. When we first started, I wore my transmitting beeper day and night, and we set out to get whatever we could get. But now that we knew how well everything was working, we chose specific targets and specific situations. I could usually schedule meetings during the day where we could get incriminating evidence on tape. So except for the unusual situation or a dinner meeting now and then, my nights and weekends were my own. This made Billy and Ed's superiors happy because it meant much less overtime, and the budget's bottom line was always critical to them. And it made me happy because I could sneak over to New York almost every night to see Patty.

During December I usually had dinner with Patty in the evenings. I would get done with Billy and Ed in the afternoon, spend an hour or two with Ann and the kids, maybe taking my oldest son to basketball practice, and then go over and meet Patty for dinner, and move on to one of the card games around eleven. It was a schedule that allowed me to get in everything except sleep. I would come home at four or five in the morning and would have to be up and out doing the state's work by ten or so. I couldn't even catch up on my sleep on the weekends because it was football season. My weekends were taken up making book again, an activity I had resumed at the state's urging to allow us to get our hooks on both players and other bookies. I was almost glad when Patty left for Florida on January 2.

The six weeks in the Bronx had been good for him. He put on a few pounds and got some of his color and appetite back. The doctor he saw in New York put him through a battery of tests that had been essentially negative. He gave Patty some pain medicine that was more effective and referred him to another specialist in Miami for the winter. By the time he left for Florida, Patty was even feeling optimistic that his health problems would go away.

I had finally signed my contract with the state—they called it a "memorandum of understanding"—the first week in November. It was really a simple contract, reducing to writing what I had agreed to in September. For weeks I had been asking almost daily what was holding up this process. I got all kinds of answers—everything from it had to be approved by people all the way up to the Attorney General, to the fact that it was a first-of-its-kind contract. The state had never before hired a wiseguy to function as what was effectively a criminal law enforcement officer, and they had to make sure every possible contingency was covered. Yeah, right. The real reason for the delay was for them to be sure I could deliver what I had promised. By October I already had enough on tape to indict two bosses—Cousin Anthony and John Riggi—and a half-dozen other guys. So I guess they finally felt comfortable enough with what we were doing to put everything in writing.

But as always I was so caught up in the day-to-day that I never really stopped to consider the longer term. Thank goodness Ann did. From the moment I started working with the police, she began to think about where we would go and what we would do once we got there. She and I had agreed, and I had gotten Billy and Ed to agree, that at the outside this would be a one-year-long operation. In our minds we put the end date around perhaps the first week in August 1990. We wanted to be moved into our new location and into our new lives before the kids started school, which we assumed would be either right before or right after Labor Day, depending on where we ended up. So we figured we would have to decide where we were going by April or May in order to have everything ready to actually leave in August.

Just after I signed the contract with the state, Ann and I started to meet with two New Jersey State Police officers who were in charge of the state's protection and relocation program. Probably of necessity, New Jersey's program is the nation's most sophisticated. I had a choice of going into the federal program run by the U.S. Marshal's Service, but I believed New Jersey's program was superior to the Feds'. The first time we met they outlined the program for us. The state would provide us with new identities, including birth certificates and New Jersey driver's licenses so we could immediately get new licenses in the state where we ended up. We would also be provided Social Security cards in our new names with numbers that tied back into our old numbers, a link that would be buried deep inside Social Security's computer, in a secure file, along with those in the federal program and other state programs. That way, when we retired, we would have available the contributions we had previously made under our old names.

The state would also see to it that our kids' school records were reissued in our new names and that even our dental records were changed. Finally, we would be provided with a range of credit cards in our new name. We would be required to pay the bills, but the cards would help us establish credit immediately.

They told us we were not really free to go wherever we wanted. He had a list of what he called "hot spots," places where, for our own protection, it was not safe for us to relocate. In this matter the state was actually more thoughtful than the federal government. Basically, the federal government let its witnesses relocate wherever they wanted to and were prepared to move them again if necessary.

I know, for instance, from talking to Nick Caramandi, what happened to him after he went into the federal program. For some insane reason they let him relocate to Ocean City, Maryland, on the theory, I guess, that Philadelphia hoods only vacation on the Jersey shore. All was fine until one day at the height of the summer vacation season Nick looked up and saw coming down the street the wife of one of the guys he was testifying against. He quickly crossed the street, but it was obvious from the shocked look on her face that she had recognized him. The marshals had him packed up and out of town under heavy guard within a matter of hours. Now he was in a place much more removed but still too vulnerable, I believed. New Jersey would be willing to move me again if my cover was broken, but it wanted to lower the odds on that ever happening, so parts of the country were put off-limits.

We could not resettle anywhere in the tri-state area—New York, New Jersey, or Connecticut. Because of the mob family I belonged to, the eastern half of Pennsylvania and the State of Delaware were also ruled out. It was also likely that I might be spotted in south Florida by one of my former associates, so everything south of Orlando was put out of bounds. Thrown in on top of this was Vegas, for obvious reasons, and Chicago because the mob was so strong there. Other than that, the rest of the United States was at our feet.

But settling on a new place was more involved than deciding whether we wanted to be near snow skiing or water skiing, and how good the local school system was for the kids. We had to go someplace where both Ann and I could find work. Ann had gotten several promotions on her job in New Jersey and now had readily marketable skills as long as the area we picked had jobs requiring those skills. Filling out a job application would be somewhat difficult because she couldn't very well list her current employer as a reference, but the state promised that when the time came and she needed references, they would provide them either by saying she had worked for the state or through "friendly" companies the state knew.

With me it was a different story. In a way it was a shame that Vegas was out of the question. I mean, after all, what was I trained to do? I was a big-league bookmaker, and I knew how to run card games. These skills made me eminently employable in gambling centers such as Vegas and Reno, except that with my criminal record I could never get licensed. And there was no way the state could provide me with a new identity that would withstand a Nevada licensing check. Besides, if I lived in Vegas—or Reno, for that matter —it would not be a case of "if" I was ever spotted by my old friends, it would be "when."

Ann and I talked it over at some length. As we understood matters, I would probably have to travel back and forth from New Jersey to testify in trials for some time after we relocated. For that reason I would still be on the state's payroll. So we decided that our top priority after moving would be to get the kids started in new schools and then establish our new home and begin adjusting to what surely would be a very different life-style. Our second priority would be to get Ann established in a new job, equal, we hoped, to the one she was leaving. If that happened, between what the state was paying me and what she would be making, we ought to be all right financially. We also decided that I would have great difficulty ever working for any employer and would be much better off running my own business. So once we got settled, I would concentrate on finding a business opportunity I might be able to buy or buy into. With that as our game plan, we got down to picking where to go.

We were trying to cover all the bases, and this was not a relaxed decision-making process. The unspoken fear constantly with us was that the whole plan would suddenly blow up in our faces—a mole in the state government would learn my identity or some enemy of mine would leak it, or something might go wrong with our recording system and I would be found out. So while we planned to be ready to pull up stakes in July or early August, almost a year away, we also had to have a backup plan if we had to bail out within a matter of hours. Unknown to the kids, we had a set of emergency bags packed and ready to grab. All our important papers and personal remembrances were gathered together so that if the fateful call ever came, we could walk out the door within minutes and never look back.

But we hoped to have the full year to make the decision about where to go. And around mid-November Ann started to send away to various chambers of commerce and tourist bureaus for information on their areas. We set certain parameters as to the size of the community we felt we would be comfortable in, the quality of the school district, and the kind of life-style we might like to live. In one way it was all very exciting. How many people at that stage in their lives have the freedom to start all over again without the burden of their pasts? Depending on how we felt about it at any given moment, it was both a problem and an opportunity. If we were lucky, we would be able to lead completely new lives. If we weren't, our lives would be over.

One day in September, early in our operation, Billy, Ed, and I sat down to try to figure out what major players from other families we should target and what we needed to do to get them on tape. In the two and a half years since I had gotten out of jail, I had been running card games at various times with guys from the Gambino, Genovese, Colombo, and Lucchese families. There were still several big monte games going on, most of them in New York City, but the major game in the Newark area—run by the Genoveses—had recently shut down. So I had a bright idea. I would suggest to the Gambinos that we join together to start a game in Jersey, one big enough to entice the players who might now be going over to New York. My idea was to record the entire process of setting up this game and then continue to record various meetings throughout the life of the game. By the time we were finished, I argued, we should have all these guys dead to rights.

On September 22 I met with "Joe Rackets," Joseph Casiere, a Gambino guy I had worked games with in the past. At the time he was acting as Robert "Cabert" Bisaccia's driver. Cabert was a Gambino captain who ran all of John Gotti's interests in New Jersey. I laid my plan out for Rackets, and he thought it was a great idea. He called me a couple of days later and said that Cabert and Charles "Blackie" Luciano, a major Gambino guy in Jersey, wanted to meet with me to talk further. We agreed to meet that night at the Roseville Avenue Social Club, the main Gambino club in Newark.

When I got to the club, Rackets and Blackie were waiting for me. Blackie apologized that Cabert was tied up in New York at a dinner and probably wouldn't make it, but he was very enthusiastic about starting the game. "George," he said, "Cabert has spoken to John about this, and we have gotten his permission to start a game with you all. The split will be fifty-fifty, and each of us will put up half the money to get this started."

Then he added something that annoyed me greatly. "George, one thing is that ten percent off the top will have to go directly to John. That's his thing, and we have no control over it."

He was saying that each of us had to give John Gotti five percent of our cut off the top. That was, of course, manifestly unfair. If this was a share-and-share-alike partnership, then Nicky should also get ten percent off the top, the same as John, or both of them should take five percent each. What Blackie was proposing was actually a 55–45 split in favor of the Gambinos.

If I had been in this for the money, I would probably have walked away. Even if I had wanted to stay in, the honor of our family would have required at the very least that I clear the split favoring Gotti with Nicky in Marion. But I was not in this for the money, and what did I care about the honor of our family? I was in this to put Cabert and Blackie and the guys around them in jail. So I said sure. "Ten percent for John is okay with me, Blackie."

Later that same night I ran into "Fat Ronnie," Ronald Catrambone—a Genovese family associate who was around "Joe Z," Joseph Zarra, the man in charge of the Genovese interests in Jersey. Fat Ronnie had been involved in a number of games with me over the years, and he had been running the Genovese game that just shut down. He was very interested in the fact that I was starting a game with the Gambinos, and he said he would talk with Joe Z about whether it wouldn't make more sense for the Genoveses to join with us in forming a very big game rather than restarting their own game in competition with us.

We were recording my meetings that night, and Ed and Billy were very excited at the prospect of involving the Genoveses in this game. As they saw it, and I agreed, the more involved—and on tape—the better. But given mob protocol, I couldn't at this point go to the Gambinos and suggest we now let the Genoveses in. I would have to bide my time and kind of let nature take its course.

The game started as planned at the Roseville Avenue club. And after the first three nights or so, it was apparent that we were not getting the number or the quality of players we wanted. I made some calls and found that some guys we thought we would attract were waiting to see if the Genoveses were going to restart their game. In the meantime, they were going over to New York to play. I broached with Blackie the subject of my conversation with Fat Ronnie, and somewhat to my surprise he readily agreed to invite the Genoveses in. We would approach Joe Z to see if the Genoveses were willing to come in with us. The only catch would continue to be that John still got his ten percent off the top before any further splits.

We held a big meeting at the Cage, a large social club that Joe Z owned. There was general agreement that all three families would operate the game together, with Cabert, Blackie, and Casiere as partners from the Gambino family, Joe Z, Fat Ronnie, Anthony "Babe" DeVino, and Phil DeNoia as partners from the Genoveses, while Scoops, Slicker, I, and another of our guys—Jerry Fussela —as the representatives of the Bruno-Scarfo family. Gotti would continue to get his cut off the top, and we would split the rest of the profits three ways. The game would be held at the Cage because it was considerably larger than the Roseville Avenue club. The game started that night, October 10, and within three weeks was running smoothly and profitably.

Ed and his superiors, both in the state police and the Attorney General's Office, were absolutely thrilled. Cabert, Blackie, and Joe Z were three of the biggest mob figures in north Jersey. To have all three on the string in the same operation was unprecedented. Tying up these guys became a major priority for us.

Every night those of us running the game took out some expense money—maybe a thousand a night split between us. The game built slowly, but by early December we had accumulated about $30,000 in profits ready to be split. A bunch of us met to discuss when the first cut should be made.

"Blackie wants to wait until after Christmas," Fat Ronnie said, explaining his boss's wishes.

Why wait, I wanted to know.

"I don't know," said Fat Ronnie. "Me, I don't give a fuck."

We didn't know what Joe Z wanted to do, but as far as the rest of us were concerned, we wanted our share before Christmas. When we got hold of him, Joe Z agreed on an immediate split. We got it all on tape.

The split was complicated. There were a lot of guys involved, and some of the seed money that had been put in, mainly by Blackie and Joe Z, had to be repaid. So when all was said and done, Scoops, Slicker, Jerry, and I from our family got only a little over a thousand each. Jerry had been getting money almost every night that he showed up at the game, but he was pissed that a bigger cut was going to the Gambinos and the Genoveses. Scoops, even though he had put up no money and did no work, was also pissed. What did I care? I was not in this for the money. But both Scoops and Jerry yelled like skinned rabbits.

Scoops took it further. Some months earlier Cabert had gotten himself arrested, and his bail had been set at $75,000. This meant, if he went to a bondsman, he would have to put up $7,500 cash. He didn't have the $7,500, and with his reputation of not paying his bills, no bondsman was going to front the $7,500 for him. The biggest bondsman in Newark was a guy around us, so Rackets had come to Scoops and me and begged us to get the bondsman to front the entire bond on the promise that Cabert would pay him off in installments. "George, I've talked with John," he said, meaning John Gotti, of course, "and John would consider it a personal favor if you would do this. If you have any trouble collecting from Cabert, John himself will make it good."

This was one of those offers you can't refuse. You do not say no to John Gotti over $7,500. You also do not try to collect such a small amount from John when the guy stiffs you, which is exactly what Cabert did, probably figuring he was too important a guy for us to make a beef about. So we went back to Rackets and told him that since he had made the arrangements, he owed the $7,500. He had paid it down to about $3,200, and we were now charging him three points in interest, about $100 a week, payable monthly. Come the holidays, Rackets was having some trouble making his required payment. And because Scoops was pissed over how little his first payoff from the monte game was, he wanted me to collect his interest payment from Rackets and lean on him for the full amount.

This was about the last thing I needed, Scoops's shy payment putting a wedge between me and Rackets and jeopardizing the way things were going with the monte game. I met with Rackets at a car wash he owned on McCarter Highway and allowed him to pay me a little light—less than the required amount. I put no pressure on him at all. I went back and gave it to Scoops, and convinced him that it was the best he was going to do for a few weeks. He wasn't happy, but he went along with it. So a crisis was averted, and when I spent Christmas with Ann and the kids, and New Year's Eve with Patty and Anna Marie in New York, I was very pleased at how 1989 was ending. So far, I said to myself, so good.

9

VIDEO GAMBLING

The first real notice I took of video gambling machines was when Jimmy Sinatra got whacked. That was his street nickname. His real name was Vincent Craparotta, and he was a Lucchese associate, an older guy in his mid-fifties who owned a small auto dealership in Toms River. I knew him slightly from some of the card games, and I knew he had some kind of business ties to our family through Joey Sodano.

Normally when you want to whack someone, you put a bullet behind his ear. Even in the modern era you followed some of the old rules. If it was just business, you tried to make it quick and clean, and above all you never killed a guy in front of his wife or kids. If you really wanted to make a statement, like when they whacked Tony Bananas, you pumped a lot of bullets into the guy—or cut him up, but after you killed him. If it was personal or if the guy was a snitch, then maybe things could get ugly.

By and large, killing was looked at as just a part of doing business. But no one could help noticing the way Sinatra died. He was found lying on the floor of his auto dealership in a pool of blood, beaten almost beyond recognition. Half the bones in his body had been broken, and his skull had been laid open. His death was so savage that at first most people, even the cops, assumed it was not a mob hit. But within a few days everyone was buzzing. I asked around, and some of the Lucchese guys told me Sinatra had been killed by his superiors in the Lucchese family. They told me they had heard the guy had been beaten to death with golf clubs, chosen because his killers were worried that baseball bats might break.

Patty later said that he had been told "Jimmy Sinatra" had enraged the Lucchese captain in northern Jersey, Anthony "Tumac" Accetturo, when he wouldn't give him a share of the profits that were coming out of a video poker machine company owned by Sinatra's two nephews. Apparently Craparotta was taking sizable sums out of the business, but he was keeping it all for himself and not sharing it with the Luccheses. We heard that Tumac ordered the hit to make a clear example of the guy. It was also an example of how profitable these video gambling machines were. Very big bucks were involved in the business, which was the reason Craparotta was so brutally whacked for holding out.

The subject of "electronic amusement games" and whether they are gambling "devices" or "paraphernalia" under New Jersey's very broad anti-gambling statutes is rather complicated. For instance, any two people could turn a Pac-Man game or one of the electronic trivia games into a gambling device simply by betting which of them will get a higher score; likewise an electronic poker or blackjack machine, the kind that are mainstays in the casinos in Las Vegas and Atlantic City. In the mid-1980s through at least 1990, you could hardly walk into a club, tavern, or convenience store in much of the Northeast without finding at least a couple of those machines. By law, except in casinos, they are supposed to be "for amusement only." They don't drop coins if you win a hand. Instead, you accumulate "points" on a counter. Using the blackjack machine as an example, two people could gamble by betting which would score the most points in a given number of hands.

But I'm not talking about using machines just for amusement. The way they are used to gamble is that you play to accumulate points, and then when you quit, your accumulated points are exchanged for cash by the bartender or someone working in the bar or club. So instead of getting payoffs directly from the machines, as you would in a legitimate casino, in bars and the like, the payoff comes under the table.

Under New Jersey law, Statute 2C-37-1(f), to be exact, made these machines "slot machines"—any machine that whether by luck or skill "may deliver or entitle the person playing or operating the machine to receive cash, or tokens to be exchanged for cash, whether the payoff is made automatically from the machine or in any other manner whatsoever." Under the companion section 2C-37-7, the use of such slot machines is illegal except in Atlantic City when licensed by the Casino Control Commission. Further, under section 2C-37-2, "manufacturing, selling, transporting, placing, or possessing such a machine can be prosecuted as promoting gambling" and can be punished in each instance by up to six months in jail and a $10,000 fine." For eighteen months I was involved in all of these offenses almost every day.

It is hard to overstate how profitable these machines were. The heart of this kind of video game is its "erasable programmable read-only memory chip" (EPROM). In Atlantic City the Casino Commission requires that all video gambling devices' EPROMs be programmed to pay out eighty-three percent of the monies put into them by gamblers. This means the house is limited to a maximum profit of seventeen percent per machine, and because of the competitive nature of the casino business, most advertise their games as "loose" and program an even higher payout ratio. Our machines were always programmed to pay out no more than fifty percent.

I would guess the average machine we had out at a good location was pulling in about $3,000 a week after all payouts. How we made our money was a little convoluted. In some cases we simply leased the machines to the bar or store owner, usually for about $1,500 per week. In other cases we split the net profit with the owner. Usually the split was 50–50, but in some cases, especially with unusually high earning machines, the split could be 60–40, with the larger share going to the bar owner. In some other cases the split was in favor of us. Then after we got our share, we in turn split it with the company that made and serviced the machines. But even after these divisions, we were still walking away with thousands a week.

It took us quite a while to get established in this business, but by 1989 video gambling machines were about our most lucrative source of income. We were making more off them than what we were making off bookmaking and loan-sharking. They were to us what crack was becoming to some other families.

And the state police knew little or nothing about the business and about organized crime's hold on it. Video gambling machines were becoming one of the major sources of illegal income for four of the seven families operating in New Jersey (us plus the Gambinos, Genoveses, and Luccheses), and the cops didn't know who the major players were, how the industry was run, where the money was coming from, or where it went. In the year I was Ed Quirk's confidential source, he asked me countless questions about video gambling. Some I answered and some I didn't, but by the time I agreed to become an operative for the state, he knew the extent to which I was involved in the business. That was one of the reasons both the state police and the Attorney General's Office were so excited when I went to them. I could finally get them inside the video gambling industry. It became a primary target of ours from that very first Toms River motel meeting.

Video gambling had grown into a big business for our family during the two years I was in jail. When I finally got to the halfway house in the spring of 1987, one of the very first people Patty introduced me to was Carmen Ricci, the owner of Grayhound Electronics in Toms River. Ricci was an old carnival guy who had started out on the carney circuit on the Jersey shore. He owned arcade games and branched out into placing the games into clubs, taverns, and stores. Eventually he started manufacturing the games himself, which led to the founding of Grayhound. Grayhound still made straight amusement games, but the real money was in making video gambling machines and refurbishing used machines it bought from the Atlantic City casinos. The company both sold the machines outright and placed them in bars, clubs, and convenience stores all over the country.

In New Jersey and Pennsylvania, Ricci worked with our family through a subsidiary of Grayhound, B&C Enterprises. Ricci was not a member of any organized crime family, but he was what was called "connected." He had an arrangement with us in Jersey and different arrangements with other families in other parts of the country. One time Patty and I were in Hollywood, Florida, and I walked into the bar at the hotel where we were staying and saw one of Carmen's machines.

"Jeez," I remember saying to Patty, "Carmen has his machines down here, too." Ricci later told me he had hundreds of machines working in Florida through A&G, a company he owned with his wife.

Ricci owned Grayhound along with his son-in-law, Brian Petaccio.

Alan Cifelli, who worked for him, was in charge of B&C. He ran the routes, and he and some guys he employed were in charge of collecting the money every week from each of the locations. Cifelli was around us; actually, Patty was his godfather. Patty had gotten him the job with Grayhound, and it was through Alan and Patty that Nicky Sr. was introduced to Carmen Ricci. At that point Ricci needed help, both in the form of protection and in establishing routes both in Jersey and Philly for his machines. Nicky gave him both, and by the time I got out of jail, Ricci was paying Nicky about $4,000 a week.

When Patty introduced me to Carmen right after I got out of Rahway, he told me he wanted me to learn the business, and before long I believe I knew the illegal video gambling business as few others did. I would hazard a guess that from that day I first met Carmen, I must have seen him on average three times a week for the next four years. I ended up as the Bruno-Scarfo representative to Grayhound and also became active in running the business. I introduced other families to Grayhound so they could buy machines (for which I got a commission), and I personally bought machines from Grayhound to resell to some families at a small markup. Later, for a while, I was the video poker machine supplier to the Gambinos and John Gotti.

By 1989, though, things had gone sharply downhill in the Scarfo family's relationship with Grayhound and Ricci. Nicky Sr. had sensed that Ricci and Grayhound had the potential of being very big earners for the family, so he partially cut Patty and our guys out of the loop. He started dealing directly with Ricci, and the money went straight from Carmen to him through Phil McFillin. But then Nicky went to jail, and the relationship began to tail off. By 1988, Carmen was down to paying about $1,000 a week, and this was starting to annoy Cousin Anthony who knew that Grayhound was actually doing better than ever.

A couple of months before I became an agent for the state, Cousin Anthony reached out for me to set up a meeting to see what was going on and what it would take to get Ricci's payments back up to their previous level. We met at McFillin's company in Philadelphia, Aqua Development, and then we went to dinner at Dante and Luigi's. At the meeting was McFillin, me, Carmen Ricci, Nicky Jr., Scoops, Slicker, Alan Cifelli, Tyrone DiNittis, and Joe Rocco, one of our guys in Philly who had helped Alan Cifelli establish the route. There was a lot of back-and-forth. Ricci said the $4,000 he had been paying was never an agreed-on figure but rather was based on the number of machines that were out and what Nicky was doing for him. Since Nicky went to jail, Ricci said, the number of machines had tailed off. What's more, he charged, some of our guys in Philly were starting to go into competition by putting out their own machines, buying them from SMS and other manufacturers.

Finally, I came up with a compromise that seemed agreeable to all. We would start again from scratch. On machines that we put out on routes, there would be a flat 50–50 split. It was agreed that Alan Cifelli would handle all the money and that he would pass our end of the split, along with an accounting, to me personally every week. I would be our family's sole point of contact with Grayhound.

The ways things went, if I hadn't been working for the state at this point, if I had actually been trying to maximize the family's earnings from Grayhound, I would have ended up killing Carmen. In a word, the man was robbing us blind. According to Nicky Sr., who sent word back from Marion, his deal with Carmen Ricci was to get a split out of every machine placed in New Jersey, Pennsylvania, and Delaware.

When he was getting the $4,000 a week, Nicky had been satisfied. He never stopped to consider that he was only getting the split off the one route that was being maintained by B&C. Gradually, as I began to understand the video gambling business generally, and Grayhound specifically, I came to realize that Carmen was making about $4,000 a week off just one route of ten locations and about twenty-five machines. I was never absolutely sure how many machines Carmen actually had out, but I estimated that it had to be two hundred stops, and possibly even three hundred. I used to go down to the Grayhound plant in Toms River every Tuesday to get our money. Often when I walked into Brian's office, his desk was piled high with money. Lord knows how much was there—certainly tens of thousands of dollars, probably more. At one point I sat down and tried to make a conservative estimate of how much money Carmen actually had coming in. I figured it to be somewhere between $100,000 and $125,000 a week. It was all cash; no taxes were paid unless Carmen wanted to declare something. And this was only from machines he placed out there. Grayhound sold many machines outright, and Carmen himself had numerous other interests.

By rights I should have said simply, "Carmen, starting next week it's going to be twenty thousand a week. Do the right thing, or I am not responsible for what will happen. What happened to Jimmy Sinatra could happen to you." If I had been a good wiseguy, that is exactly what I would have said. If he had balked, I would have spoken to some people, he would be gone, and I would have been running Grayhound. Then we would have gotten it all.

In short, Carmen was making the kind of money that guys are killed for. But by the time all this went down, I was working for the state, and they were more interested in who in the video gambling business we could get on tape than in the Bruno-Scarfo family maximizing its income from Grayhound. So I ignored Carmen's stealing. In fact, I liked him. I also knew that when all was said and done, he was not going to be able to enjoy his money. With what I was getting on tape almost daily, I was sure Carmen was destined to spend much of the rest of his productive years in some Jersey jail.

I thought I had seen just about every scam that was being run by the mob or by a mob-related "legitimate" business, but when I met Richie Martino and Zeff Mustaffa I learned a few new tricks. In May 1989, a couple of weeks before I started wearing my state police transmitter, I got a call from Joey Sodano. He asked me to meet with a couple of Gambino guys close to John Gotti who wanted our help in setting something up in Philadelphia. I met Richie and Zeff for lunch at a well-known Manhattan steak house. Their company was located nearby.

It turned out that Zeff, who obviously was not Italian, had grown up as kind of the adopted son of Frankie Loc, Frank Locascio, the Gambino underboss and one of the most powerful wiseguys in the city. I myself grew up around tough wiseguys. At age seventeen I was playing cards with Tony Bananas, who many regard as the worst mob killer in the last fifty years. I hung around any number of guys who made their reputations with a gun, including Philip Leonetti, the only guy I ever knew who seemed to really enjoy killing. In prison I hung with a dozen guys who were in for murder. But none of this ever bothered me. Zeff Mustaffa bothered me and even scared me a bit. He was the most menacing individual I can ever remember being around. We got along fine and even became friends, but he always had this air about him of being on the edge, of being almost out of control. I later learned he had a reputation around the city for violence. He had been in prison for manslaughter, and the whispers were that he had done any number of "jobs" for his stepfather. I sensed it the first five minutes I met him. In many ways he was a throwback to the wiseguys of the old days. He would have felt very comfortable, I'm sure, in Murder, Inc.

Richie, on the other hand, while a made member of the Gambinos, was a kind of laid-back businessman. He had more ideas for new stuff the mob could get into than any guy I have ever met. If there is such a thing as an entrepreneurial mobster, it was Richie Martino. We got along well from the very start.

During our meeting, to my initial shock, Richie explained that his and Zeff's company ran the Gambinos' 900 phone number business, the pay-per-call lines a person can dial for information on everything from the weather in another city to sports scores, horoscopes, and stock prices—or phone sex. It had become a billion-dollar industry, and the Gambinos had staked their claim early.

The company, Richie explained, ran a half-dozen different kinds of phone sex lines using recorded tapes, not sex talk with a live person; horoscope lines in both English and Spanish; a sports score line that was updated every five minutes during football season; a financial news wire line; lines that kids could call at Easter to hear the Easter Bunny and at Christmas to hear Santa; and lines you call to hear a recorded "personal" message from a favorite star.

"It's an unbelievable business, George," Richie said. "The phone company does all the billing. Ma Bell does all my collecting. I just sit back and every week they send me a check. It's even mostly legal."

I was blown away. I mean, the idea of John Gotti making a million dollars a year from phone sex and Santa just floored me. Richie said the company was grossing about $200,000 a month even after the phone company's deduction for providing the lines and collecting the money. Richie and Zeff were each pulling a hefty five figures a week out of the business, and more than a million annually was going to Gotti, Frankie Loc, and those close to them.

Actually, their biggest earning line was one that every night reported the illegal numbers for the day. Despite the presence of the legal state lottery, the illegal numbers industry still flourished. Hundreds of thousands a day were being bet in New York City alone, and the Gambinos controlled the industry. As soon as the day's numbers were arrived at, usually from the racetrack handle, the results would go onto the 976 line. On an average day, twenty thousand calls at a dollar each were made to this number. What Richie wanted to talk to the Bruno-Scarfo family about was duplicating this service in Philly for the illegal numbers there. We controlled the numbers in Philly.

I called Nicky Jr. and asked him to come up and meet with Richie and Zeff. It turned out to be the very first meeting I recorded, my "test" meeting that was held at U. S. Video on August 2. Actually, our conversation ranged over several subjects. Richie and Zeff were into various kinds of electronic amusement ventures. They had heard from Joey Sodano that U. S. Video had a new "jukebox" that played music videos. They thought they could place these all over the New York area if the money was good enough to make the effort. The problem was that the machines had never been tested in actual hard use, and it was still not clear that they would hold up to incessant play. Richie decided to wait and see.

Tyrone DiNittis was also at the meeting. Tyrone, from Philly, had grown up close to Nicky Sr. Nicky loved the guy like a brother. He lent him money, he hung with him, he confided in him. For years Patty believed that Tyrone was working with the FBI, so we had little to do with him and were always very, very careful about what we said around him. Tyrone had his fingers in a lot of things. He had a piece of U. S. Video, he was a talent agent representing entertainers, he booked acts into clubs all over the mid-Atlantic area, and he supposedly had high-level contacts in Hollywood.

Richie Martino wanted to use Tyrone's contacts. He had just started putting in "star lines," 900 numbers you could call for a buck or two to hear a personal message from some star. Richie wanted to know what stars Tyrone might be able to line up for a 900-number line. He had heard that Tyrone knew Sly Stallone, or his manager from when Stallone was in Philly making the Rocky movies. Could Tyrone help land Stallone for a 900 line? Tyrone said he would do what he could.

So at that meeting it was agreed that Richie was interested in the video jukeboxes if they proved durable enough, that Tyrone would see if he could get some entertainers for the 900 lines, and that Nicky Jr. would talk with his father about going in with them on a 900 line in Philly for the daily illegal numbers. Within a week Nicky sent back word from jail that it was fine with him as long as we got a cut. The numbers line was up and operating within weeks, but it was never the success the New York line was.

Another question that Richie raised during the meeting was whether U. S. Video made gambling machines. It did not. I told Richie I had several sources for them, and he said he would call me. He told me that he and Zeff had about a hundred machines on the street in New York, which he was currently getting from a manufacturer in New York. But, he added, he might need a new source soon. He would let me know.

He was on the phone within a couple of days. It seems that Zeff had developed some sort of bad feeling about their current supplier and had beaten the guy senseless. This caused the guy to have strong second thoughts about selling any more machines to them, and since the guy was connected, there was little they could do about it. Would I be interested in getting some machines for him? Absolutely, I said. I later asked Nicky Jr. to make sure the family had no objections. He said there were none as long as we could make a profit. Whenever the Kid thought about anything, dollar signs flashed in his eyes. I told him there was really not much money to be made, but it would help us get in with the Gambinos in video gambling. I ended up selling Richie about twenty-five machines, which I got from Grayhound at about $1,900 each and which I sold to Richie for about $2,200 each. It was not much profit, but the transactions made for some very interesting taped conversations.

When I met Nicky on August 29 in another of my early taped meetings, I gave him $500 as his share of a $1,000 profit I had made selling the initial five machines to Richie and Zeff. I also gave him $1,100 in tribute from Scoops. He was unhappy with the $500 on the machine sale; he thought we could have made more. I told him to cool it.

But he had also been thinking about Richie's proposal for getting more stars for his 900 lines. "Georgie," Nicky said, "you got to get hold of Richie for me and tell him I need four sets of proposals, saying what they're doing and how they're doing it. I got the Getter going to California, and he's gonna try to get Madonna. He's gonna try to get the Rolling Stones. He's gonna . . . yeah, and Michael Jackson, too."

The Getter was a friend of Nicky's by the name of Jerry Blavatt, who had contacts with a number of big agents in the business and who was also a friend of Jilly Rizzo, Frank Sinatra's good friend. Nicky said the Getter would also meet with Jilly to see if he knew any talent who might do a 900 line.

Nicky was also thinking about getting rich off the numbers line Richie was going to put in Philly. "I'm hoping, ya know what I'm hoping," he said, "three hundred thousand calls [a year]. Our end will be about fifty-five thousand. That is not fucking bad, that ain't bad, and I'm thinking of putting in my own sports line."

He told me all this at our meeting at the Garden State rest stop where Ed and Charley were taping our conversation and we were also being watched by the FBI. We were to go from there to Grayhound for a meeting with Carmen about the problems in Philly. It was because the state police didn't want the Feds nosing around Grayhound that Charley blocked their car and prevented them from tailing us.

Nicky also had another worry. Just after we started dealing with Grayhound, the company went public—it started trading its stock on the over-the-counter market. At the time I asked Carmen if I should buy some of the stock. He said no, that it was just going to sit for a while. He was right. It was issued and stayed at about a dollar a share for some time. Then one night at a card game Angelo Cifelli, Alan's father, came up to me and told me that I should buy immediately. I couldn't. I had been losing at cards and was kind of broke that day. But I quickly passed the word along to Nicky Jr. who bought a couple of thousand shares, to Michael Perna who bought shares, and to a couple of other guys who also bought.

Within a couple of days the stock went to three and a half. I figured that was about as high as it was going to get, so I didn't buy. But then the company announced it was going to begin marketing a new fireproof paint. The stock just took off, and within a month it was selling at nineteen.

This new "fireproof" paint was a wonderful example of how Carmen Ricci operated. Supposedly this stuff was going to revolutionize the paint industry and make everyone around it rich. Nicky Jr. thought so much about its potential that in the name of his father he demanded the exclusive distributorship for Philadelphia, eastern Pennsylvania, and Delaware. The key to the success of this paint was a certification by the Underwriters Laboratory as fireproof. All Carmen talked about for months was this UL certification and how close they were to getting it. In the end the UL certification never came through, and the paint was never marketed.

In hindsight the whole thing might well have been a scam. But if it was, it was neatly executed, and Carmen undoubtedly made millions. The talk alone had been enough to drive the stock up from $3 to $19. Nicky had sold out at the top of the market, and now his newest worry was that he would be found out by the SEC and charged with insider trading. "Think I got problems, George?" he wanted to know. "It was a sweet deal, a nice piece of change, and legal, too. But will the SEC notice? Do I have problems?"

I told him I didn't think so but that we could ask Carmen. There was no problem. The SEC apparently never took note.

At the meeting at Grayhound, which Ed and Charley recorded without the annoying presence of the Feds, I got a new price list from Carmen for different types of machines I might sell to Richie. Bill acceptors were the newest thing. If a player had to keep pumping coins into a machine, you were forever making change or limiting how much a person could play. Carmen was starting to equip his machines with electronic devices that accepted paper money and could tell the difference between $1, $5, $10, $20, $50, and $100 bills. A player could put in as much as $100 at a time, and the beauty of it was that the machine did not give change. So someone putting in a $100 bill had to play the entire hundred. Carmen estimated the take on an average machine would triple if it was equipped with a bill acceptor.

Carmen was also starting to make disguised machines, ones that looked and operated like a Pac-Man or video trivia machine, but by using something that looked like a TV remote-control device, it could be instantly changed into a poker machine. That meant that the machine would be in disguise when it was sitting unused. And if there was a raid, by the time the cops got through the door, all they would find was a bunch of guys playing video trivia.

Richie wanted prices on crane games, the ones where kids put in a quarter or fifty cents and tried to lift a small plush toy out of a pile with a crane and drop it down a chute. The mob had found these games very lucrative, and Carmen Ricci may have been the king of the cranes. Grayhound made the machines, and Carmen also imported the stuffed animal prizes from China or somewhere. He had machines all over Atlantic City and the Jersey shore. It was a constant source of amazement to us that he had his cranes in several major casinos. Given the fact that his relationship to us was widely known and given the New Jersey Casino Commission's paranoia and supposed diligence in ferreting out any mob-related businesses and keeping them out of Atlantic City, we could never figure out how he was licensed.

Carmen once told me that he was taking $60,000 a week out of these crane machines, and I believed him. Richie loved the idea and eventually started buying the machines from Carmen to put out in New York. Overall, our dealings with Carmen and Grayhound began to grow—and the tapes kept rolling.

Objectively, Scoops and Nicky Jr. were not the brightest guys ever to come down the road, but they were not completely stupid, nor were they blind. Carmen Ricci was what could only be called a conspicuous consumer. He owned a huge house and drove a new Rolls-Royce. Brian, his son-in-law, drove a new Mercedes. They either owned or leased a chauffeur-driven limo they used quite a bit. They dressed unusually well. It was clear that Carmen was rolling in the dough, and Nicky and Scoops realized one day that what Carmen was paying us must have been chump change to him. They decided they wanted more, but they never could decide on how much or how to get it.

At first Nicky came up with the idea that Carmen should give us a kind of advance on the money he was paying us weekly. He wanted me to hit Carmen up for $25,000, interest free, to be repaid by holding back $1,000 a week from his payment. Scoops thought this was a great idea and ordered me to make the demand. I didn't. I delayed and delayed, and finally I convinced them that such a request would only make us look broke and cheap, and would diminish us in Carmen's eyes. This got Nicky to back off for a couple of weeks, but he didn't drop it for long. Instead of a loan he decided he wanted Carmen to do the right thing by giving him some Christmas money. Twenty-five thousand dollars was still the figure he had in mind.

Again I stalled, but the Kid and Scoops got more and more insistent. Finally, I had to arrange a dinner at Casa Dante with all of us. I think Scoops had the idea that he would come down hard on Carmen at the dinner, and Carmen would whip out his checkbook and gladly hand over $25,000. What happened instead was that Carmen brought along a friend to the dinner, some guy we had never met before, and turned the whole thing into a post-Christmas social occasion. Carmen was no dummy. You really can't scam a scam artist. He knew what was up, and he also knew that I was pushing to expand our business relationship with him and not just trying to hold him up for more money. Bringing a stranger to dinner deflected the whole thing. It would likely be weeks before the subject came up again.

After dinner Scoops and Nicky Jr. were furious. I was, as usual, wired with my transmitter, and that night Billy and Ed were recording in a limo out in the restaurant's parking lot. It made for one of the more interesting tapes we recorded. Scoops, Nicky, and I walked out of the restaurant and stood talking in the parking lot. First Scoops looked around and tried to figure out which limo Carmen had come in. "I think that black one over there is his," he said with clear disgust in his voice. Actually, that was the one Billy and

Ed were sitting in, behind the heavily tinted glass, recording every word that was being said. Carmen owned the gray limo parked about two cars over from the state's car.

There was considerable ambivalence on Scoops's and Nicky's part. They still wanted to get some quick cash out of Carmen, but they didn't want to blow the longer term business relationship with him, either. In the next breath after Scoops said he thought he had a beef with Carmen, Nicky said his father wanted him to go to Pittsburgh, where his uncle ran things, to try to set up routes with Grayhound machines. "There is a strong business out there with the poker machines," the Kid told Scoops, implying that we could blow the whole thing by putting too much pressure on Carmen. "My father told me it was okay. And I'm going to reach out for—what's his name?— Michael Genovese; they have their own crew out there."

"Okay, do it," Scoops responded. "As long as your father tells you to go. . . . But I don't—you wanna know the truth—I don't trust him."

The more Scoops thought about it, the madder he got. But Nicky kept coming back to the argument that we might make more off Carmen by putting his machines out and selling the paint (Carmen was still waiting for the UL certification) and maybe even dabbling again in the stock that was back down to about $3 from its high of $19.

I kind of let them fight it out. The last thing I wanted to do was mess things up by getting into a major beef with Carmen Ricci. The way Scoops was starting to talk, he would end up wanting to whack Carmen if he didn't come through with the extra money. That was a complication I didn't need at this point, so I tried quietly to sell Nicky on the idea that we could make more money working with Carmen than beefing with him. I actually think I told him we shouldn't kill the goose that might still lay us a golden egg. Then I had to explain what that meant.

Nicky, bless him, took me seriously; he went to Pittsburgh and tried through his cousin there to get things going. Then he heard that some guys we knew up in New England—Al Bruno in Springfield, who was around the Genoveses, and a couple of Patriarca family members he knew—were interested in putting video poker machines in clubs they controlled in Springfield, Providence, and Boston.

"You get the locations, we got the equipment," Carmen Ricci told us.

Then Nicky got another bright idea. The Las Vegas–based criminal lawyer Oscar Goodman, one of the nation's best, had represented his cousin Philip for many years (but had withdrawn from that representation before Philip flipped). Oscar's wife worked at Caesars in Vegas, which was just announcing a major expansion, both of the hotel and of its casinos. They used a lot of video poker and blackjack machines, and Nicky thought maybe Oscar's wife could get Caesars to buy Grayhound machines. Carmen said he would give us a great price on five hundred machines. Nicky, with dollar signs in his eyes again, had it all figured out how we could make maybe $100,000 selling machines to Caesars. We could pay a $25,000 commission, he said, and split the rest. Then once we got Grayhound machines into one casino, we could hire clean guys to sell machines to other places.

So we decided to combine a business trip with a little holiday. We would go out to Vegas and talk with Oscar and his wife. A couple of the guys from Massachusetts said this sounded good to them, too, and they would meet us there to talk about video poker machines for New England. Billy and Ed also thought it would be an interesting trip. By law we could not record in Vegas, but they could follow me to make sure I stayed out of trouble and to observe what was going down. Actually, it would give them an excuse for a little working vacation around a craps table. The problem was how to get the state's permission for such an expensive trip. That okay had to come from the Attorney General's Office, so they put the question to Dave Brody. At first he said no, but then he too began to see the potential value of the trip. So he relented and said he would go along with the plan. Dave signed off on the expense voucher, and Billy and Ed were waiting in Vegas when we arrived.

It turned out that they weren't the only ones waiting for us. It was decided that we would go out to Vegas over President's Day weekend and that Nicky and Tyrone DiNittis would come home via Marion, where they would bring Nicky Sr. up to date on what we were doing. At one point shortly before we left Nicky told me that Bobby Simone would also be going with us. Simone wanted to see Nicky Sr. at Marion and do a little gambling and R&R on the way. He was also close to Oscar Goodman, and Nicky thought he might be able to help us in any negotiations to get machines into Caesars. At the last minute Tyrone backed out because of business, and Bobby Simone got tied up in court. Tyrone and possibly Bobby would meet Nicky in St. Louis on the return trip, and they would all go to Marion from there. Since I didn't like Tyrone, this did not bother me at all. It looked as though a great time was going to be had by all. But we hadn't counted on the FBI.

Greg Notti, my old gambling teacher, was a very big player at Caesars. He arranged for us to get a huge two-bedroom suite with everything to be comped—the suite, all the food, and even the shows. I figured that I would spend the weekend at the blackjack table, so I brought $30,000 along to gamble with. And at first everything seemed in perfect order. A hotel limo picked Nicky and me up at the airport. The front desk had our football-field-size suite all reserved and stocked with champagne. We settled in, but then I got a call to go back downstairs to see the guy at the front desk. He looked down at something attached to our reservation card and said, "I'm sorry, Mr. Fresolone. I cannot confirm your comp until you see the shift manager." He pointed me toward the casino.

The shift manager was both embarrassed and apologetic. "Mr. Fresolone, I know that we previously confirmed it, but we can't comp you."

"I don't understand," I said. "I'm about to deposit thirty thousand dollars in your cage."

"I'm sorry, sir. I can only tell you that no matter how much you deposit or how much you play here, we cannot offer you any hospitality. We must ask you to settle your account in full when you check out. The matter is out of our hands."

I was dumbfounded. I had been around casinos all my life and had never seen or heard anything like this. Obviously, something had happened, something was very wrong. I went back upstairs and got the Kid. We called Oscar, who said he would ask his wife to make some inquiries and try to have some answers by the time we got to his place. He sure did.

The long and short of it was that the Feds were still following Nicky. Two guys had been waiting for us when we arrived. They had even known where we were going to stay. Oscar's wife found out they had visited the hotel the day before and told them that we were a couple of organized crime guys. That instantly put the hotel in an impossible position. We were not on the so-called blacklist, persons barred by the Nevada Gaming Commission from entering a Nevada casino, so the hotel people had no basis on which to bar us from staying and gambling. But once they were put on notice that we were possibly organized crime figures, they immediately had to file a report with the Gaming Commission, and they were precluded by Commission regulations from extending us credit or from offering us any "inducements"—which meant they couldn't give us free room or free food or even drinks on the house.

It was typical of FBI arrogance. They had done this just to bust our balls and to show us who was boss. It was both stupid and totally gratuitous. If the Feds had wanted to use Caesars' security to help keep watch on us, they could have done so without revealing that we were organized crime figures. They had found out we were being comped, and they knew that by classifying us as organized crime persons the hotel would have to remove the comp. The incredible stupidity of this was that it instantly put us on notice that something was wrong. If it hadn't been for Oscar's help, we might not have found out so quickly that it was the FBI, but we would have known something was very amiss.

Let's say, for the sake of argument, that Nicky and I were in Vegas for some sort of major crime meeting, that we were there to meet with representatives of every crime family in America to plot the takeover of the Republican Party or something. Wouldn't it have made infinitely more sense for these two guys to do their jobs and keep us under surveillance to see who we were meeting and perhaps to find out why? But that would not be the FBI way. They loved to send messages to "bad guys." The message here was that they knew we were in town. And that was a guarantee that we wouldn't do any business in the open. I think as a citizen I was angry that my tax dollars were going to support this quality of law enforcement.

I also found out that the Feds had told the Las Vegas Police Department that I had arrived. Under Las Vegas law, since I was a convicted felon, if I was going to be in town for more than forty-eight hours, I had to go down to police headquarters and register. I planned on being there for three days, so Oscar went with me to sign in. It was no big deal, but it was annoying. That was the reason the Feds had done it, just to annoy me.

In the end it was no big thing for me. The bill for our three nights in the gonzo suite, with all meals, entertainment, and enough champagne to make any French importer happy, was $7,300. The first night I was there I took $6,900 away from the blackjack tables in about an hour. I figured that meant I had the weekend covered. Fuck this hotel, I thought. If they weren't going to comp me, I wasn't about to give them any of my money. So I really didn't gamble at all over the next three days. Thus, with the money I made in that first hour or so, the weekend ended up costing me only about $400.

I think it ended up costing the Feds a hell of a lot more. For making me pay a $7,300 hotel bill, they lost any hope of ever having me as a cooperative witness. I now know that they have spent hundreds of thousands of dollars to mount investigations to get the same information I could have given them for nothing if I had decided to cooperate with them. I told Billy and Ed point-blank that no matter what we got out of our operation, I would do nothing to help the Feds, nothing ever. I told them that if the State of New Jersey was stupid enough to give Broadsword over to the Feds, as they had other cases in the past, they could forget about me. No matter what, if the Feds were asking the questions, I would get a sudden case of amnesia.

As far as our business was concerned, we thought we made progress toward getting some of Grayhound's machines into Caesars. That turned out to be a long process. And as for the guys from New England, they never showed up. We later found out they had come into town, but when they called us, they were told by the hotel that we were not registered. Another little FBI joke, I guess. The Feds probably had the hotel pull us out of its computer so that calls would go to them or just to annoy us some more.

I met Billy and Ed late the first night in an out-of-the-way bar that was not on the strip, after I was sure I wasn't being followed. They had recognized one of the Feds watching Nicky as being from Philadelphia. Since they were waiting for us, obviously the Feds had known when we were going and where we were staying even before we left. We mulled this over for a moment and came to the only possible conclusion: Tyrone DiNittis. If I ever needed proof that Tyrone was an FBI watchdog, this was it. Nicky later told me that it was, in fact, Tyrone who had made the plane reservations and had gotten the tickets from "his" travel agent—probably FBI special agent someone or other. Because of the FBI presence, Billy and Ed agreed they would stay on a very loose watch so the Feds would not know anyone else was watching Nicky. It was a busted weekend for them as far as getting any real business done, but they had a nice time—a little February vacation in the sun on the state.

Several years later, long after we had shut down Broadsword, I was in an eastern city meeting with prosecutors preparing for a trial when I was told that the next day I had to meet with a couple of FBI agents who wanted to question me about some things connected with a federal case they were trying to make against Nicky's lawyer, Bobby Simone. We met in a Virginia hotel, and lo and behold, it was the same two guys who had been tailing Nicky in Vegas. They thought the whole thing had been hilarious. To show me how much they knew about Bruno-Scarfo family activities, they boasted that they had known about the trip in advance. When I brought up Tyrone's name, they only smiled. Then they readily admitted they had screwed up my comp at Caesars just to bust my balls. They thought it was a great laugh. Funny, I wasn't really able to help their case against Simone very much at all. What a shame.

Business was booming for Grayhound. In May I got into an interesting conversation with Carmen's son-in-law, Brian Petaccio, about various routes he had set up. "One machine I got, figure it out," he said. "It was taking five dollars in profit every eight minutes, around the clock. . . . I've got four hundred, see. I have four hundred in bars in a fifty-mile radius. But how long can it last?"

Over the previous few months Carmen and Brian had learned that if you put a machine in a bar or club, you almost certainly end up dealing with some wiseguy who wants a big share. But there were other locations that you could end up doing almost as well. "My idea is not to put them in a fucking bar," said Brian. "There has to be a thousand fucking laundromats or convenience stores around. That's what I'm saying to you. I mean, I don't have to go to bars. The other works just fine."

It may well have been that video gambling machines represented the opportunity of a lifetime for me in organized crime. If I had really been an upwardly mobile, nineties kind of wiseguy, I would have devoted all my energies to Grayhound and the video gambling machine business. Once I was straightened out and made a captain, I would have been a full partner in Grayhound, and I don't have a single doubt that those machines would have made me a millionaire several times over. I believe that today I would have been the head of a national operation that was not only selling machines to wiseguys and putting them out on routes but was also selling machines in the growing number of states, especially in the West, that have legalized video gambling machines.

South Dakota is an example. In 1989, in its wisdom, the South Dakota state legislature legalized electronic gaming machines as a tax revenue source. As is always the case, the state agency overseeing video gambling—in South Dakota it is the Lottery Commission —made a big deal out of ensuring that organized crime would be kept out of the state and the video gambling machine business. But

the simple truth is that there are only a limited number of companies involved in manufacturing these machines, and most of these
companies have some ties or alliances with organized crime families
or figures. So if a state is going to get machines, it almost *has* to deal
with companies that have some kind of ties to organized crime. It is
simple enough to "launder" machines you want to sell to legal state
operations or to legal casinos. In fact, Grayhound would soon be in
the process of setting up a number of clean front operations to sell or
place the machines in legal states. The first Grayhound machines
were already going into South Dakota.

When we went into Broadsword, it was with the general understanding that it would be a one-year operation because the longer
we stayed at it, the risks increased exponentially. Basically we had
set an agenda for that year, and that agenda meant I couldn't devote
more than a certain amount of attention to video gambling. By
around March 1990 it was clear that I had amassed more than
enough evidence to shut Grayhound down forever and send Carmen
Ricci and the others to jail. So it was decided I should begin concen-
trating my energies elsewhere. I did so reluctantly because I believed Grayhound could lead us high up into most of the New York
families and beyond. But in the final analysis, this was a New Jersey
operation to bring down New Jersey wiseguys, so my efforts were
now aimed in that direction.

10

DRUGS, GUNS, AND SWINDLES

The year 1990 started out with a bang for me. In its first week I was involved in planning to kill one of New Jersey's biggest drug dealers, and then before the week was out, I saved his life.

One of the first things Billy and Ed asked me when I started working for the state was whether I knew any wiseguys around Newark who were dealing drugs. I was acquainted with a few, mostly guys who played at one or another of the card games. But I did know one drug-dealing wiseguy very well. I had grown up with him, and he was the godfather of one of my kids: Anthony Dente— everyone just called him Dente—was heavy into drugs.

Patty had always warned me to stay the hell away from drugs. Don't use them. Don't sell them. It was one piece of advice that stuck. I grew up drinking and smoking too much, but I never used any kind of drugs, although almost anything you wanted was around us all the time. But Dente smoked pot as a kid, then started to sell it in small amounts to his classmates. By the time he was in his early twenties, he was involved with the Lucchese family, buying it by the ton from boats anchored off the Florida coast. They sold the pot in two-hundred-pound lots to wiseguys in Florida. Then whatever didn't sell, they put in the trunk of a car and drove it back upto Jersey. All during the 1970s, if you bought marijuana on the streets of northern Jersey, the chances were good that the dope had been owned by Dente at some point.

Probably more than any guy I knew, Dente was a party animal. He was a small, thin guy, about five feet six and probably no more than 160 pounds. His hair was slicked back and expensively cut. His clothes cost more money than any of us could afford. Because he was into the drug business, he was making money faster than any of us, but as fast as it came in, it went out again. I used to see him almost every day, and he would regale me with stories of all the money he was making and the fun he was having. He would beg me to come in with him, but I always said no.

By the early 1980s, Dente's drug business had switched completely to cocaine. Almost no one was buying pot anymore, and the Luccheses had stopped importing it. The money was in coke, and you could make more profit from a pound of cocaine than from tons of marijuana. Dente also owned a bookmaking operation that was run for him by Gene Wilson out of the East Side Social Club on Adams Street in Newark.

So when Billy and Ed started talking about drug dealers, I naturally thought of Dente. But I was not enthusiastic about the idea of bringing him down. I liked him a lot, and he was only on the periphery of our family. I described him in detail to Billy and Ed, and they got excited about the prospect of nailing him. But I kind of decided that I wouldn't go out of my way to rein him in. If he came to me, so to speak, I would have no choice. And that's exactly what he did when he asked me to get involved in killing a guy.

I only saw Dente from time to time during the fall of 1989, but we got him on tape one night in September at the East Side Social Club talking to me about the troubles he was having trying to find a supply of marijuana for a buyer who had suddenly appeared. He called the guy "the Jew" and was lamenting how difficult it was these days to find sources for marijuana. He said he had found a supply in the Bronx and was making a deal for it, but he couldn't afford to front the buy right then. The Jew was going to have to come up with the cash, which apparently was a problem.

At this same meeting Scoops gave Dente and Gene Wilson a bookmaking operation that had been run by Ted Panula, a guy we called Woody, who had been around Patty for years but was now in semi-retirement after being seriously ill for almost a year. All during that football season I spoke to Dente and Gene often about their bookmaking operation. I helped them set their pro football point spread and over-under line every week, and helped make changes in the line as Sunday approached. I also occasionally placed a bet or two with them. All this was no big deal and at worst would have exposed Dente and Gene to a third- or fourth-class gambling charge. They would have been first-time offenders, so they likely would have gotten probation.

That fall we never talked about drugs, never. Dente knew it wasn't my thing, so he kept that aspect of his business separate from the bookmaking. November was a busy month, so Billy and Ed put Dente on a back burner, and I was hoping I could get away with ignoring him. But then he came to me and started to dig a hole too deep to climb out of.

In early December we were talking about point spreads, and Dente told me he was having a problem. It was again about the Jew. He wanted to buy more marijuana, and again Dente was having difficulty finding it. He knew that I knew another drug dealer by the name of Michael Derrico from my card games. Derrico used to play about once a week, usually losing between $20,000 and $30,000, and would leave happy. That's what I meant about drug dealers having more cash than they knew what to do with.

Dente said he was having trouble getting enough coke to supply everyone he was selling to. He wanted me to put him in touch with Derrico, who he heard had a cocaine pipeline. I made some calls, and the next night I met with Dente again and told him that Derrico would be happy to talk with him. I would have been glad to leave it at that, but Dente just continued to dig that hole. He thought the Gambinos had coke sources, but he had never worked with anyone from that family. Could I introduce him to Blackie Luciano, he wanted to know, to see if the Gambinos could immediately supply him with a half key (a half kilogram). I made the call, and Dente made the connection.

Then just after the holidays Dente dug the hole so deep there was no way he was going to be able to climb out. He started talking about a major score, a stickup, and to do it he needed guns. He knew that I knew a guy with access to clean guns. Dente said he needed a couple of automatic weapons, preferably Uzis, and he needed them quickly.

He had found out that a drug dealer living in Summit, New Jersey, kept a large safe in his house containing a huge supply of drugs and more than $1 million in cash. They were going to hit this guy's house, take the safe, and probably whack him in the bargain. Right now, Dente told me, there were four of them involved: himself; Freddie Stewart, his drug business partner; Jerry Chilli, a Bonanno family member whose father was the Bonanno underboss; and Bobby Kapic. The latter two guys were going along as muscle. He wanted me to use my connections to get them a van and the clean, untraceable guns they needed. He also wanted me to go along on the heist and said I would be in for a full share. If the score was what he said it was, he was offering me perhaps a quarter of a million dollars. But we would probably have to kill this guy to get it.

We got all of this down on tape, of course, and it became another of those dilemmas for the state police. They now had prior knowledge of a crime and a possible murder. They couldn't very well let the event take place and the guy get whacked, but they had to give Dente and the others enough rope to hang themselves.

The robbery was to go down late the night of January 5. My source for guns was Babe DeVino, the Gambino guy I was involved with in card games. Babe had several junkyard and auto wrecking businesses, and he lived in a fortified warehouse on St. Francis Street so impregnable that we used to hold crap games there knowing that if the cops ever tried to break in, we would have more than enough time to destroy any evidence of a game in progress. Babe didn't have the Uzis that Dente wanted. All he could get on such short notice were some handguns, so Dente found his weapons someplace else.

I did get them a van, one equipped with a hydraulic tailgate. The plan was that they would bust in on the guy, and if he offered resistance, they would whack him and haul the safe away in the van. If he offered no resistance and opened the safe, they might let him live. If he refused, they would go back to plan one: kill him, and take the safe away intact, and open it later. So the question was how to stop them without exposing me since I was one of the very few they had let in on their plan and I had begged off being involved. "Not my thing, Dente," I had told him. "Just pay me for the van, that's good enough for me."

Billy and Ed and their superiors decided the best way to stop these guys would be to arrest them on their way to the job. They tipped the Springfield police, who stopped the van on Morris Avenue for a traffic violation. It was just a "coincidence" that a second car with two more officers happened by as the van was being stopped, so there were four officers present. They used some excuse to look in the van and found the guns, burglary tools, and ski masks. It was also coincidental that when they radioed for them, two state police cars were there within less than three minutes. All the four could be charged with was possession of illegal weapons, possession of burglary tools, and conspiracy to commit burglary. But it was enough since those were felonies. The murder had been avoided, and I was not exposed.

We all thought it was a good night's work, but the whole thing moved Anthony Dente to a front burner in our operation. He had made himself a primary target. To get him good on drug charges, I would have to buy drugs from him or set him up with an undercover drug agent, and the drugs would have to be in sufficient quantity to qualify as a first-class felony. With cocaine that meant at least five ounces, which is an amount for more than personal use.

The night after the abortive robbery I met Dente at the East Side Social Club. He had chalked up what happened the night before to just plain bad luck. He believed the van had been stopped because they ran a yellow light, and it was unlucky that the guns and tools had been in relatively plain sight. He just shook his head and mumbled something about trying again later.

The question was how I was going to get him to sell me drugs when he knew I didn't use them and in fact had an aversion to them. So I invented a nephew who wanted to start in the drug business and could end up being a regular customer for Dente. I said the kid was still in college, and Dente explained that the college market was big on both Quaaludes and Valium. He said I could buy either from him for $1.60 a pill, and my nephew could easily sell them for $2.00, or possibly as much as $3.00 each. But I said the kid wanted cocaine and had given me money to buy ten grams. It was actually $400 in marked money from the state. Dente was happy to accommodate me. We drove over to his house on Elm Street, and he sold me the ten grams. The entire transaction was captured on tape, and surveillance photos were taken of me going into the house and coming out. I ended up getting the state a bargain. I paid only $375 for the ten grams, and when I turned the dope over to Ed to be analyzed in the police lab, I was able to give him his change.

Over the next couple of months my "nephew" branched out into the pot business. This made sense to Dente, who thought he was selling to a college crowd. On March 9 I bought a pound of very high quality pot from him for $1,400. It had a street value, I was told, in excess of $5,000. In May we decided to make another cocaine buy from him. On May 24, in a recorded conversation, we agreed to a price. On May 31 I met with him to pick it up. I was in for a surprise.

With Billy and Ed rather frantically following, we got into Dente's car and started off for the Bronx. We drove around for almost an hour looking for "Julio," Dente's supplier, who was supposed to have a shipment for him. We finally found the guy in a club, only to be told that his shipment hadn't come in and that we were going to have to wait, perhaps a few weeks. Dente was pissed, but what could he say?

In early July he called me to say that my "package" was ready. I was to meet him at the Italian American Veterans Club on Clifford Avenue to pay for the drugs and to pick them up. When I arrived he wasn't there, but Freddie Stewart was, and he had the package. I had to think fast. I told Freddie I needed to talk with Dente personally about this buy and some subsequent ones, so he made a call, and the three of us met at the Howard Johnson's on Route 9. I paid Dente $6,000 in state money for what was to have been five ounces. Again, the whole transaction was on tape, and this gave us more than enough to get both him and Stewart on first-class felony drug-trafficking charges. I was actually a little relieved when Billy told me the state crime lab had found only 4.95 ounces in the package. They had short-weighted me. I don't know if Dente did it or if Freddie had removed a taste for his private use, but somehow knowing they had cheated me made me feel a little better about what I had done.

Just before Nicky and I left for our weekend trip to Vegas and our attempt to get Grayhound machines into Caesars Palace, Scoops and I drove down to Cherry Hill to meet with Cousin Anthony at Don Manno's office. The meeting was going to be a kind of briefing to bring Anthony up to date on what was going on in the north. Also, I had been contacted by a guy close to John Gotti who said that John was concerned by what he had been hearing about Philip Leonetti possibly testifying against him. Gotti wanted to talk with Anthony about Philip and, in the way of mob protocol, was reaching out to him through me. It was all a pain in the ass. Gotti should just have picked up the phone and called, and we should just have called Anthony with our report rather than drive a hundred miles to deliver it in person. But as always, Anthony was absolutely paranoid about phones. He assumed that every phone he talked on was bugged, so he held all meetings face-to-face, and usually in Manno's office.

On the way down it seemed all Scoops wanted to talk about was money. He had just found out that during the last major trial in Philadelphia in December 1987, the one in which the guys had been acquitted, Oscar Goodman and his wife had run up a $36,000 hotel bill at the Four Seasons. Oscar was defending Philip at the trial, with Nicky Sr. picking up the tab, and Scoops just couldn't get over it—a $36,000 hotel bill in addition to the several hundred thousand dollars Nicky had paid for his and Philip's legal fees.

But mainly he wanted to talk about the money that Nicky Jr. was going through. Basically Nicky was spending money, our money, like it was water. He was about to leave for Vegas with a broad and ten grand in gambling money. If he had that kind of money to gamble with, Scoops thought, he should be spending it on his own upkeep and stop taking money from us. "I'm trying to say we have to curb this," he said. "Pretty soon the Kid'll want a Mercedes, you know what I'm trying to say, George?"

I certainly did. I had gone shopping with the Kid the day before and watched him pay $450 for two pairs of slacks. I also knew that the week before Nicky had brought a bunch of his friends up from Atlantic City and spent about a grand in a night of eating and partying.

Scoops just shook his head and then offered the opinion that maybe I was lying; maybe the Kid really wasn't spending all that I said he was, and I was putting some money intended for him into my own pocket.

Scoops then tried to figure out how much the Kid had spent since he was with us and where the money was coming from.

"How much is he getting from that route?" he wanted to know.

"About twelve hundred a week," I replied.

"A week? He winds up with that a week?"

"Yeah," I said.

"Well, what about the other money he's getting?"

I said he was getting some here and some there, and of course the money I was giving him.

"That's about two G's a week in all," Scoops figured.

"Yeah," I agreed, "but he spends, he spends about fifteen hundred."

"He's got to tighten his belt. That's what I'm saying. He's got to tighten his belt. I mean, we're all here feeling sorry. But who the fuck makes twelve here, twelve there? He's got to be cut back."

All this was not to say that Nicky Jr. wasn't an entrepreneur at heart. In fact, I have never met anyone inside the mob, with the possible exception of Richie Martino, who had more ideas about how we could make a killing. Nicky's only problem was that while Richie made millions with his ideas, Nicky's never seemed to pan out.

His latest was a beauty. Tyrone DiNittis had met a couple of guys who were about to start marketing a drink product, a new thirst quencher like Gatorade only it was supposedly better tasting and better for you. At first they were going to call it "Sportsade," or something like that, and Nicky thought it was a great idea. He and Tyrone had formed a company with the clever name of the Tyrone Corporation, with Nicky owning seventy percent and Tyrone thirty percent. They then signed a contract with the two guys giving the Tyrone Corporation the sole distribution rights in eastern Pennsylvania and Delaware and a one-third share in the overall ownership of the company. The key was that through Tyrone they were going to get Sylvester Stallone involved, both as an investor and as the product's spokesman. If this happened, they were going to change the name of the drink to "Rocky Power Boost." It couldn't miss, said Nicky. According to him, they believed they could sell 220,000 cases a month nationally, and after a year, if they weren't doing at least 100,000 cases a month, they would fold the operation.

Nicky was sure this was going to make him a millionaire. To make matters even better, the two guys hadn't asked him for a dime. He got his distributorship and ownership position for free. The reasoning was so complicated, it almost made my head spin. These two guys told Nicky they needed a major "test market" to get the product rolling. They chose Philadelphia, and they were going to Nicky (and Tyrone) for three reasons, they said. The first was to make the connection with Stallone. Second, they wanted Nicky's help through family connections to get shelf space for this new product in supermarkets and convenience stores in the Philadelphia "test market." It was cheaper, they said, to offer this deal to Nicky than to pay for shelf space or to pay agents "commissions" to get the product into stores. Finally, they needed a $4 million loan to get the thing off the ground. Nicky said he thought he could get them the money through the Ricciardi brothers, Tommy and Joey, who were Lucchese family members with access to this kind of financing. But Nicky bragged that so far he had put out nothing.

As far as Scoops was concerned, it was a stupid idea, and he just laughed about what we called "the MGM deal." We called it that because Tyrone had learned that while Stallone might be a spokesman for the product if the money was right, the name "Rocky" was actually owned by MGM, which appeared to be less than interested in the deal.

"Tyrone is a swindler, Georgie," Scoops said that day on our way to Cherry Hill. "Everything Tyrone is connected to is a scam of some sort. This water thing is no different. Don't you put any of your money out. This Kid is just a big hole that sucks in money."

Actually I had another theory about the two guys who were pushing this water deal through Tyrone. I figured them for FBI agents. I always believed that Tyrone was an FBI informer, and I think this was some kind of operation that the FBI was running against Nicky, probably to see where he would get the financing and what kind of strong-arm tactics he would use to get the product into stores. They probably thought his father had put away millions more than what was in the safe they stole for Philip. Nicky was also talking about selling franchises to his uncle in Pittsburgh and to our friends in New England. If this was an FBI operation, that would also give them new access there.

The bottom line was that this was too good a deal to be true, and you know what they say about that kind of deal. It also never happened. It all just sort of went away. As I said, Nicky's great ideas never seemed to pan out, and if it was some kind of FBI sting operation, the Feds just let it drop when it started to fizzle.

But this was not a conversation I wanted to pursue too far with Scoops. I didn't care what the Kid spent as long as he was having fun, was happy, and was keeping the information coming. Scoops was bitching because he had to give the Kid a couple of hundred a week out of his own pocket. As always, he never minded spending money as long as he was spending it on himself. In short, he was having as much trouble putting out for Nicky as he had for Patty and for Ann and the kids when I was in jail. But in the case of the Kid, Scoops was being told he had to do it. If he didn't, there would be consequences, and he didn't want to face those.

After the weekend in Vegas with Nicky, I went directly back to Newark. But Nicky returned several days later, after detouring to Marion to see his father. When he flew into Newark from St. Louis on February 26, I was there to pick him up. He had brought back quite a bit of information from his father. That's exactly what we figured he would do, and Billy and Ed were following us in a van recording every word.

"My dad says that Bobby is getting Philip's three-oh-twos," Nicky told me, "and Philip's talking a lot about John Gotti and Paul Castellano."

Three-oh-two is the number for FBI interrogation forms. Whenever the Feds interrogate someone, the details are written up on a 302. Because it was considered likely that Philip would appear as a witness in Nicky Sr.'s subsequent trials, he was entitled under discovery to copies of the 302s the FBI was writing up on Philip. Bobby Simone was getting them and was talking with Nicky Sr. about them. Then too, according to the Kid, as a follow-up to John Gotti's request that he be kept informed about Philip—the request I had passed along to Cousin Anthony at the meeting in Cherry Hill earlier in the month—copies were also passed on to Gotti's people and to Gotti himself, in case they had not gotten a particular interview in their own discovery process.

"My dad had several meetings with Gotti and the Bull [Sammy Gravano], and Philip was there as underboss," Nicky Jr. said. "Dad says that even before they whacked Castellano, Gotti had told him it was coming and why, and that he had received the Commission's permission to make the hit. Philip has told all this to the FBI and will be a major witness against Gotti. Bobby is worried that because Dad had knowledge of the hit before it was committed, they may charge him as an accessory."

Nicky also told me that it was probable his father would be transferred back to Philadelphia for a sentencing and maybe for another trial, and he had been speculating if it might be possible to make a break while he was outside Marion.

Nicky detailed the plan: "We have this guard captain at Olmsberg [a state prison in Pennsylvania where Nicky could conceivably be housed if he came back]. When Philip was in there, this guy would bring him in whatever he wanted—food, booze, wine, books, anything. We paid him every week while Philip was there. He bragged all the time that he could let anyone simply walk out the front door for between two hundred thousand and four hundred thousand dollars. My father wants me to contact the guy to see if he was just running his mouth or if he was serious. If he's serious, maybe it's something we should consider. If we can get him out and into a car, we can put him on a boat for Sicily. This might be our only shot."

I thought about this possibility for a moment. Given that Nicky Sr. was in the most secure cellblock of the most secure prison in the federal system, I could not exactly picture the Feds leaving him in a situation where any one guy, no matter who he was, could simply walk him out. But stranger things than that have occurred. I imagined that Billy and Ed would certainly want to talk with the FBI about this bit of information.

Nicky then started talking about his own shooting. His father was still sure that Joey Merlino was behind it, but the more he thought about it, the more he believed that Stevie Vento was probably in it with him. For Stevie, it was an act of revenge.

Stevie was a young guy about twenty-five whose father, a big-time drug dealer, had been around Nicky. Nicky thought the guy was cheating him, but the guy was a big earner and Nicky didn't want to whack him, just send him a clear message. So he had his kid shot in the head. The kid survived, and the father fell into line. Now the kid, Stevie, was following in his father's footsteps dealing drugs and was starting to make big money. Nicky Sr. was sure Stevie was carrying a grudge and had probably helped Merlino, whom he was close to, pull the trigger on Nicky Jr. "We'll deal with him the same as we'll deal with Joey when the time comes," Nicky said. "Dad wants him taken care of, too."

Nicky had talked some more with his father about the video poker machines and was now surer than ever that that was where his future was. His father had told him to aggressively pursue getting machines placed in New England, in western Pennsylvania, and in Vegas. "We need to talk some more with Carmen about prices, George," Nicky said, ever eager to pursue the big bucks. "I'm going to want to get a lot of machines, and he had better come down on his prices if he wants our business."

In January, John Mavilla, the zoning commissioner, called to say he wanted to be indicted. He didn't actually ask to be indicted, but by calling me out of the blue, it had about the same effect.

Back in May 1988 I had collected $6,000 from Pat Giordano and Daniel Fasano at Giordano Waste Hauling to pay Mavilla to give them the zoning variance they needed for their new building. This transaction had preceded my working for the state. I had told Ed and his superiors about the payment, but there was nothing we could do about it because we had no evidence—that is, until Mavilla called me.

Actually, I had met John at a function back in October at the East Ward Democratic Club in Newark. At the time he reminded me that what he had gotten for Giordano was a two-year variance that would be coming up for renewal. For an additional fee, higher than the first, he said he could guarantee a five-year variance of a kind that was automatically renewed every five years thereafter unless some kind of formal protest was lodged.

It was only a passing conversation, which quite frankly I had all but forgotten. But Mavilla did not forget, and his January call to ask if I had talked to Giordano about its coming "problem and opportunity" caused us to target him. If Mavilla was going to push it, then we felt we had to react. So on January 26 I began to set the whole thing in motion by meeting and recording a conversation with Fasano at Giordano Waste Hauling. He expressed some annoyance about having to pay again, and especially a higher amount, but he would be willing to do so if it meant he wouldn't have to go through the variance process again soon. I next met with Mavilla on March 1 outside the Clifford Street Social Club.

"I don't know when this fucking guy is coming up," said Mavilla. "I know it's got to be up in May, and he's got to have his application in."

I told John that Giordano had talked to his lawyer who had said there should be no problem with getting the variance extended. I also told John I had explained to Giordano that he had said there would be problems in the extension because Conrail was already beefing.

"John, what do you want?" I asked.

"You know," he responded with annoyance, "you throw my fucking name around . . . I got fucking problems. Yeah, you can tell him Conrail, Conrail is investigating. What did we give him? What does he have now, two years?"

"Two years now, John, two years."

"What do you think you can hit him for if I guarantee you at least five years?"

"You tell me what you need."

"I need money so fucking bad. Frankie's on my back like you can't believe."

Frankie was Frank Spiro, a bookmaker who was around Joe Poliveccho, a tough Gambino captain. Mavilla was a gambler, and a losing one. He needed money because he had lost more than $20,000 during the past football season. He still owed Frankie and Joe Polo more than $9,000, and they were the kind of guys who pressed hard for their money.

We talked back and forth for a few minutes, and I again mentioned that Giordano was going to get a zoning lawyer. Mavilla said that was silly, that he could give us the money instead of paying a lawyer's fee. "He don't even have to hire him. Give us the fucking cash . . . because this is not going to be any problem."

We talked about how long a variance Mavilla could guarantee.

"I could almost guarantee you five. Five I could give him with no trouble," he said. "I could even go ten. Ten I might be able to get away with."

"Why can't it be a permanent right?" I asked.

"No, I can't do permanent."

"Can we do ten, though?"

"I may be able to. Why don't you work out a deal for five and for ten."

"Five thousand for five?"

"Yeah, five for five, ten for ten."

"Okay, yeah. I can guarantee you I can get the five from him," I said.

"I trust you, George. I trust you whatever you can do. . . . You work out the best fucking possible deal you can work out with him."

Bingo, we had him. Even if all this went no further, Billy and Ed said we had him for soliciting a bribe even if it was never actually paid. Giordano was happy to pay, especially if he could get ten years. The last time we had hit him for $6,000 for the original variance, kept $4,000, and gave Mavilla only $2,000. This time I didn't really care if we got anything. So $10,000 for a ten-year variance seemed a bargain to Giordano. But then we found out that Mavilla had jumped the gun on the whole thing and that the original variance was not due to expire until May 1991. So much to Mavilla's disappointment, the way everything was left was that Giordano would pay but not until after the first of the year. But actual payoff or not, we were convinced we had enough to get Mavilla for soliciting the bribe and both Pat Giordano and Danny Fasano for conspiracy to pay it.

One thing I learned from my own experience was that card games always took on a life of their own. Some games lasted years, with players showing up night after night. Our huge monte game in the Bronx had been like that. Other times games would seem to be going great guns, then suddenly someone would start a game somewhere else, your players would drift away, and your game would just dry up. That's what happened to the monte game we were running in Newark. For about three months it went great, then it started to peter out as the players found other games or left for winter stays in Florida. By early February we had shut it down.

That same month we were approached by the Colombos about going into a new baccarat game with them. I got a call from Dom Prosperi—a guy we called "Doode"—who was a gambler around "Jimmy Ran," Jimmy Randazzo, a made Colombo guy who ran his family's business in Jersey. They were going to hold the game in the huge back room of a deli owned by Doode in Newark.

I was all for getting into this new game. It would help make the game even larger, and it would allow me to get a whole new cast of characters on tape. The other guys were less sure because we were being offered what amounted to the short end of a complicated deal. It was going to be a Colombo game, and they were offering to let us and the Gambinos split twenty-five percent if we brought in guys to play and helped run things. Having to split only a quarter of the cut did not go down too well with our guys, especially Slicker, or with the Gambinos, especially Babe DeVino. But in the end we decided that something was better than nothing, so we agreed to go in.

Then suddenly the offer was withdrawn. That kind of thing didn't happen often, especially after we had what we thought was an agreement. Scoops, Slicker, and DeVino were angry, and they got a lot angrier when I found out that the twenty-five percent we had been offered was going to go to the Genoveses.

A meeting was called to discuss the matter. I told Scoops, Slicker, and Babe that I had learned that Guliermo, a Genovese guy who was around the "Chin," Vincente Gigante, would get the twenty-five percent cut because he was going to bring his whole crew down from Paterson to play in this new game. Guliermo was an Italian of the old school, as were most of his crew. They all still spoke Italian and clung to the old traditions. We called guys like this "greaseballs" or "greenhorns," and we didn't have much regard for them.

Slicker said that he had seen Doode talking with Blackie Luciano, the Gambino captain, the night before. "He came up to Blackie last night," Slicker told us, "but I don't know what he said."

"He's a two-faced motherfucker," DeVino said of Doode. "Did you speak to that greaseball? Were you at the game? I knew something was in the wind."

"He told me, 'Ah, Jimmy worked out a deal with them,' " I said. " 'George,' he says, 'I mean I offered it to you.' "

"Yeah," said DeVino. "I knew something was in the wind. He wouldn't talk to me about it. He wouldn't tell me what happened."

"And now he says no," Slicker said.

"Yeah," I replied. "Now he says no."

DeVino was defiant. "If we don't go, they ain't going to have nothing. Them greenhorns are coming looking to shoot at us. What do you think they're coming for?"

What happened was that the game started with Guliermo and went great guns for a while. From time to time I would drop in and play a bit or just stand around with Doode and the rest and talk. But the greaseballs found some other game they liked better, and gradually they stopped coming. By the end of April, Doode was talking with me and Blackie again about us coming back in.

By March my arrangement with the state police had become very much a full-time job. We had recorded almost two hundred tapes, and every day I spent hours listening to them and reading and correcting transcripts.

In a way this investigation was a constant blizzard of paperwork. These tapes would ultimately be used in a courtroom, so each and every one of them had to be handled just so. This was the way things worked. When a tape was recorded, it was first officially logged in and authenticated. It was then taken to headquarters where a copy was made and logged in, and the original placed in a safe. Then a rough transcription was made of the copy, and we went over it to determine what parts of the conversation we were interested in. At times, out of a several-hour-long tape, all that might be relevant was five or ten minutes. Once we selected those sections of importance, I usually sat down with the rough draft and the copy of the tape and made corrections. Quite often those early drafts contained many references to "IA" or "UM." IA meant "inaudible" and UM meant "unknown male." Since I had just lived through the conversation, I could usually identify who said what, and often I could make sense of what the transcriber initially could not.

Then, too, when wiseguys got together, we had a shorthand way of talking, almost a code. On first hearing a conversation, even Billy and Ed often missed what was the most important. Some conversations were an avalanche of numbers, for instance, when we were talking about the take from video poker machines. Those numbers were critically important for us to be able to prove a conspiracy, one of the main crimes these guys would end up charged with, and quite often I had to walk everyone back through a conversation, explaining what the numbers meant and who the many *he* and *hims* referred to.

It's one thing to bug a conversation and quite another to have a person who was actually in the conversation actively involved in interpreting it. The cops and the FBI do a lot of wiretapping, for instance, but often they don't have the slightest idea what they are hearing. Street names and nicknames are used, phrases such as "our friend in Queens" pop up constantly, and unless one of the parties to the conversation is there to interpret, the cops or the Feds are left to try guessing as to what is being said.

In early March we did a major assessment of just where the investigation was. Based on the transcripts we already had in hand, the Attorney General's Office thought it had enough to get indictments against most of the guys I dealt with in the Bruno-Scarfo family, including Cousin Anthony, Scoops, Nicky Jr., Slicker, Nicky Oliveri, Anthony Dente, and Gene Wilson. We had enough on the video poker business to shut down Grayhound and to indict and convict everyone connected to it. We had John Riggi, the boss of the DeCavalcante family. We had John Mavilla, the zoning official. What we needed now was more on guys from other families such as Michael Perna of the Luccheses and Blackie Luciano and Cabert of the Gambinos. So we made the decision to concentrate more on guys we didn't have enough on and to broaden what we had to link guys to additional crimes.

It was about this time that Ann and I took our first "vacation"— at least vacation was what I told Scoops, Nicky Jr., and the other guys. It was really a house-hunting trip. As I said, Ann was approaching this relocation thing in a very organized way, and by about the first of the year our house was starting to look like a travel agent's office. Ann had written to literally hundreds of chambers of commerce and had gathered material on many communities within the general areas where we thought we might want to go, places the state said were safe enough to consider.

We gradually narrowed the areas down to about a dozen, with kind of an "A" list and a "B" list. Each of these areas met our general criteria, and the officers from the state's relocation program said each seemed acceptable to them from a security perspective. But since we had never visited any of these places even on vacation, we were pretty much in the dark about what they were really like. We needed to see for ourselves what we were getting into.

When I agreed to work with the state, I hadn't given much thought to all the practical problems involved with suddenly relocating somewhere strange almost overnight with a new identity. For instance, how do you buy a house or even rent one? It's very difficult to walk into a bank to apply for a mortgage on a new home, and when they ask for references, you say you don't have any because you were effectively born yesterday. Renting is very difficult for the same reason. The landlord wants references, and you can't supply them.

Schools are another problem. Enroll your kid in a new school, even a public school, and they want to see the kid's previous transcripts. How do you explain the transcripts are in a different name? And last but not least, credit is a major hurdle. You might have perfect credit under your old name, but how do you apply for new credit cards under your new name with no credit history that you can give out?

I think that first house-hunting trip finally focused me on the many problems to be associated with this relocation thing. The state relocation experts kept assuring us that the state would help us overcome these hurdles. They had been through it all before and knew exactly what our problems were going to be. We could count on them, they said, and they would begin their work just as soon as we had decided where we wanted to go.

The itinerary of that first trip included the five stops on our "A" list. It made for a very complicated airline ticket, but Ann and I went from one to another, crisscrossing much of the country. Our plan was to narrow down choices on this trip and then in a subsequent trip or trips actually find a specific place we wanted. But that ended up not being necessary. One place turned out to be love at first sight for both of us. We got to what was our number one choice on paper, drove around, and within a matter of hours we knew this was the place. So we started house-hunting. This was a little tricky because we hadn't chosen our new name and couldn't very well tell a realtor our old name and then a few weeks later buy a house under a different name. But we got around it, and within our two-day stay we had found a perfect house that the owner didn't want to vacate until August. That was just right for us, so we made an offer conditional on financing. Then we returned to New Jersey and told the relocation guys it was time for them to get into gear.

11

PATTY RETURNS

May Day, 1990, was one of those days when it seemed as if I worked from dawn to dawn. In that twenty-four-hour period, Ed, Billy, and I ended up recording eight complete tapes because several things were occurring at the same time. First of all, I had been summoned to meet with Cousin Anthony in Cherry Hill. He said he needed to talk with Patty, who was still in Florida, and he wanted me to reach out for Patty and arrange the time and place for a phone call.

There were times I thought that living in the mob was much like living in the Old West, in the days of the Pony Express. Anthony wanted to talk with Patty, and in this day and age that should have meant picking up the phone, dialing a number, and the two of them talking seconds later. Instead, Anthony had sent word to Nicky Jr. to tell me to come all the way down to Cherry Hill. So I drove down, spent ten minutes getting a public phone number in Philly and setting a time for Patty to call, and then I drove back to Newark and called Patty to give him the time. Getting Israel and the PLO to the bargaining table was probably not as complicated.

Nicky Sr. had been brought back from Marion for a long sentencing hearing and was in a local Philadelphia lockup. This meant that for the first time in more than a year Nicky Jr. could visit his father and sit down with him face-to-face without the close observation that was always present at Marion. He could talk to his father privately. If need be, the two of them could whisper in each other's ears, and Nicky Sr. could give orders without using some kind of code.

Then, too, the issue of whether we and the Gambinos were going to go into the Colombos' new card game was coming to a head. As I had predicted, Guliermo and his crew of Genovese greaseballs had beat up on the game, taking out of it what they could, and had moved on to some other game. Now Doode had come crawling back to us to offer the same twenty-five percent that had originally been on the table. We probably should have told him to get screwed. His game was in trouble, and we knew it. But we had plans. Babe DeVino and I figured that we would play along for a while, but as soon as it became clear that a lot of the income in the game was coming from guys we were bringing in, we would demand a new 50–50 split under the threat of taking our players into a new game. We didn't really have the capital to start our own new game, but we figured the bluff would work, and at 50–50, the Colombo game could end up a very profitable enterprise for us.

On April 30 I had recorded my first conversation with Patty. For some reason Billy and Ed started putting some pressure on me about Patty. I guess they were under pressure from the top to get assurances that he was not back in Jersey. I told them he was in Florida with no intentions of returning. But just to be sure, they asked me to record a phone conversation with him. So I said okay.

During the call I told Patty that Nicky Jr. was down in Philly seeing his father and afterward was due to meet with Phil McFillin to pass onto him anything Nicky Sr. wanted to communicate to Cousin Anthony. He complained, as always, about the pain in his stomach. We talked a little about this and that, and then the conversation turned back to an old topic: Joey Sodano.

Joey was still crying poor and insisting he was just too broke to pay his tribute to Philadelphia. Nicky Jr. was going to speak to his father about it during their meeting in Philadelphia and find out if Nicky Sr. wanted to take "action." Patty figured that since Joey had been around him, the problem with Joey would become his problem.

"What's the Nodder doing?" Patty asked, using Sodano's nickname.

"Nobody knows," I answered.

"Well, I told Cheese he should go somewhere," Patty continued, using his pet name for Scoops. "Actually, I can't talk on these fucking phones 'cause there's a guy here selling watches, and I don't know—"

What Patty had started to say in mob speak was that Scoops should have tracked Joey Sodano down and brought him in for a good talking to.

"Cheese ain't going to do nothing," I said.

"I know he's not," Patty agreed.

"Cheese ain't nothing but a drinker and a talker."

"That's all he is," Patty agreed again. "Just showtime."

Patty became more concerned about the guy selling watches next to him and broke off the conversation. He said he would call me at 10:00 the next morning "at that phone," which was our code for a pay phone on Michigan Avenue in Kenilworth. In that conversation he was calling from a more isolated pay phone and was better able to talk. He repeated his anger that Scoops hadn't taken his role as captain seriously enough to have handled the problems with Joey Sodano. I told him I was due to see Nicky Jr. later in the day and hear what his father had to say in their meeting the day before. Patty told me he would call me back at the same phone at 7:30 that evening to get a report.

When I saw Nicky Jr., he reported that his father had quite a bit to say about Joey Sodano. "He says, first of all . . . if Joey Sodano starts crying more to have, ah, Scoops and Anthony go see Joe Butch, because I forget the name he says Joey Sodano's with, you know, doing business with the machines."

"Frankie Loc," I said, filling in the name he forgot.

"Okay, yeah. . . . He says go see Joe Butch and find out what business he's doing and tell them this guy's not helping us out. But first maybe we should reach out for Joey Sodano and tell him he has to do right and that this comes from my father."

Joe Butch was Joe Corrao, one of the most powerful of the Gambino captains. In fact, the talk on the street was that if John Gotti had to go to jail, Joe Butch would become the next Gambino boss. Our family was close to Joe Butch, and Patty and I had eaten many a dinner at his restaurant, Cafe Biondo, on Mulberry Street in Little Italy. Even though Frankie Loc was the Gambino consigliere, having moved down to that position after John Gotti made Sammy Gravano the underboss, Joe Butch had more power. But it was both embarrassing and risky to go to Joe Butch. Having to ask him what one of our own crew was doing made it clear that we had lost control of Joey Sodano. That would show us as weak and inept. Then, too, if

Joey was deeply involved with Frankie Loc, we could be putting both him and Joe Butch in a difficult position because maybe Frankie did not want outsiders knowing much about his business. I knew Patty would counsel against doing this when he heard about it. It didn't much matter to me personally—I would be long gone before any repercussions hit—but from my own experience in doing business with the Gambinos, it sounded like a lousy idea.

Nicky went on to tell me that his father had admitted that going to the Gambinos was a last resort and that we had to meet with Sodano directly first. "We need to see if he wants to help," Nicky said his father had told him. "We say we know your book's dead, but you're doing other business here. What are you supposed to do? You're supposed to help your friends. That's more or less the bottom line."

Nicky Sr. also had a second Joey on the brain: Joey Merlino. For both the Scarfos, senior and junior, whacking Merlino was topic number one. Joey was now in jail, and so both Scarfos were just marking time waiting for him to get out. But a new worry had emerged. Nicky Sr. had heard from some sources in South Philly that the Luccheses might be making a move on recruiting Joey in jail. He was not a made guy, so theoretically at least Joey could move over and join another family. This was generally frowned upon, but it did happen occasionally when a guy had a serious falling out with his own family and wanted to move along. Since both the Scarfos were counting the hours until they could kill Merlino, this could probably be considered a serious falling out. So the Luccheses could probably get away with recruiting Joey.

The rumors were that a Lucchese captain named "Vince" was in the same lockup as Joey and had taken a shine to him. Supposedly the guy had offered to take Joey in when they got out and had promised that if he went with the Luccheses, they would straighten him out immediately.

This would greatly complicate plans to kill Joey. As Patty always said, "Keep your friends close but your enemies even closer." If Joey became a made member of another family, then we would need that family's permission to whack him. If they didn't give it, it would mean either risking a war by whacking him anyhow or else having to go to the Commission to try to resolve the matter. Neither option was attractive.

"George," Nicky Jr. said, "my father wants you to reach out for Michael Perna. Find out who this Vince guy in the slam with Joey is. If he's a Lucchese, tell Michael that we would have a serious problem if this guy tries to take Joey. Tell him we would like for him to pass this along."

I did just that later in the month. Michael said he would look into it, and he got back to me a couple of days later. "The story is bullshit, George," he reported. "We don't have anybody in that joint. We don't even have a Vince in any joint. Besides, we wouldn't touch Merlino on any account. The rumor just isn't true."

I passed this along to Nicky Jr., who got the word to his father. The response from his father was one of relief.

"My dad says he's glad it's not a worry," Nicky Jr. told me. "He also reminded me that when Joey gets out, the two of us and our friends have to take him to dinner." There it was again: Nicky reminding me that I was still under orders from his father to kill Joey Merlino as soon as possible after he got out of jail.

The day got even busier after I left Nicky. I met Dente at Howard Johnson's for lunch. He was with another guy, and they wanted to talk about drugs. Dente was still having cocaine supply problems, and they wanted to know if I had heard about any additional sources. Billy and Ed were, of course, taping the meeting from the restaurant parking lot.

I left Dente, and our little traveling caravan headed for Slicker's house. We were trying to make a final decision about getting into the Colombo card game, and Nicky and Slicker's son Carlo were going to come over.

"Guliermo don't want to have anything to do with Don Doode," Slicker said.

"I know," I responded.

"The way they fucked us, we can fuck them," Slicker said, meaning we could get in the game and gradually ease the Colombos out. "Babe says they must have cut ninety to a hundred thousand out of that game."

In fact, that was what Babe DeVino was reporting. In less than two months the Colombos and Guliermo claimed they had made $100,000 in profits from the game. But I didn't believe it.

"What do you think we should do here?" Slicker asked. "Joe Rackets, he's jerking off. Said he would call. This guy never called. Did you talk to Babe about this?"

"I talked to him," I told Slicker. "I talked to him, and Babe said that Blackie don't want nothing to do with it."

"Yeah, all right, but now what?"

"Blackie don't want nothing to do with it," I repeated.

Actually, the question facing us was not whether to join the game or not. We had pretty much decided we would. The question was whether or not to take another branch of the Genoveses in with us. Word had just come down that they were interested, and Slicker was to meet later that night with Joe Z, Joseph Zarra, the Genovese capo in Jersey.

"What are you in favor of giving Joe Z?" Slicker asked.

I told him if the Genoveses came in, they would want at least half of our action.

"Why's he gonna get half?" Slicker protested. "What do we get, ten percent? . . . See, Dom Doode, he don't give a fuck about us. Right or wrong?"

I told Slicker he was right, Doode didn't give a damn about us. And as far as the Gambinos were concerned, they already owed us money, and if they wanted to come into the game, they could earn their way in.

"If Blackie don't want in, fine," I said. "Fuck Joe Rackets and fuck Cabert! Let them earn. They're on Roosevelt Avenue every day taking away from us with open craps. Do they send us any money? They don't send us five fucking cents. Why do we have to worry about them?"

Slicker agreed. "So I don't think we have to make it four ways," he said. "But what's Joe Rackets gonna do? I say give him a fucking piece for him and Bobby [Cabert] to earn. That's all."

It was good advice, but it left Slicker very nervous. If he was going to tell this to Joe Rackets, he wanted me there. I didn't give a damn.

I was at the pay phone at 7:30 to get Patty's call. We talked over what Nicky Jr. had relayed from his father. I told Patty that I had advised Slicker to let Joe Z and the Genoveses in the card game, and since Blackie wanted no part of the deal, to tell Joe Rackets he could work his way in for a share. Patty agreed that was the businesslike way of handling it.

Truthfully, I didn't know how Rackets would respond. I didn't figure that Cabert was all that interested in this. Telling Cabert no was different from telling Rackets no. But Cabert would have made his interest known directly. This was one of those situations that he would take if it was given to him, but he wouldn't ask for it. No, this looked as if it was just Rackets' play, and since he already owed us, we could afford to say no.

I picked up Slicker, and we went to the Cage Social Club. We told

Joe Rackets the way things were. He could work his way in, but we were going to bring in Joe Z. He was not happy, but since his boss had not made an issue of it, he couldn't either. Then Slicker met with Joe Z and said we would be happy to have them. I drove him home, went home myself, and fell into bed. It had been an exhausting day.

The next day the wiretap the state police had put on the phone of Nicky's cousin Johnny Parisi paid off. They recorded two long conversations between Nicky and his father that were almost funny.

One conversation was almost exclusively about Joey Merlino. Nicky Sr. was outraged that his son had to be hiding out in Newark. "His father wants him in Philly," he said, speaking of himself in the third person as he often did. "He belongs with his family."

"Right!" the Kid agreed.

"Number one, you understand?" Nicky told his son.

Then the conversation turned to this mythical Lucchese guy who was supposedly trying to recruit Merlino. "Before you start adopting people, find out who they are," warned Nicky Sr.

"Right!" said the Kid.

"He's a fucking liar."

"Right."

"A little drug-dealing motherfucker."

"Right."

"Suspected of shooting Scarfo's son."

"Yeah."

Later in the conversation Nicky Sr. reminded the Kid that it had to appear the Scarfos did not suspect Joey of being behind the botched hit on Nicky Jr. "Put him straight. Don't be promising this guy," Nicky Sr. said. "In fact, stay friendly with him in case you have to invite him out, in case you have to invite him to dinner."

He then reminded the Kid that even with Joey Merlino in jail, it was still too dangerous for him to be back in Philadelphia because we could not be sure who might be aligned with Merlino.

"They want to hurt me," Nicky Sr. said.

Nicky said he understood.

"You're all right, then. You're all right where you're at."

"Yes."

"You understand."

"Yes."

Then the conversation turned to me. Nicky Sr. wanted his son to make sure I understood that I would be straightened out sometime soon. "And tell Georgie again, I said have patience," Nicky Sr. told his son. "Tell him it'll work out. Just him. You think he understands?"

"Yeah, he does,"

"Tell him I'm praying for Patty to get out of that trouble."

"Me, too," said Nicky Jr.

"Is it a bad beef?" his father asked.

"Yeah, I think so," Nicky answered. "It should be a loan-sharking case, but they made it RICO."

"Well, tell Georgie to have patience. Tell him he'll go to dinner with them guys, too."

"Right, right," said Nicky Jr.

"You follow?" his father wanted to know.

"Right," the Kid replied.

"Okay, then, let's go slow."

I had been talking to Patty four or five times a week ever since he left for Florida the day after New Year's. At first everything was fine, but then he started to complain again about the pain in his stomach. I told him to go to the doctors down there, but he put it off, saying what could they tell him down there that the doctors in New York hadn't already told him. Finally I told him to stop complaining to me about his pain unless he went back. He promised he would. But after that he stopped complaining, and we stopped discussing his health. If I asked, he would simply say he felt "better" or "fine."

With everything that was going on, I didn't get a chance to go down to Florida to see him. In the back of my mind I figured maybe a week or so after I got back from the house-hunting trip I would grab a plane to Miami for a few days. But things got busy and suddenly it was May, and I thought I would simply wait for Patty to come north again. He planned to come up to New York City in early June for a few weeks and then take the train to Chicago to catch a plane back to Italy for the summer.

But suddenly those plans changed. His stomach pain was getting worse, so he went back to the Florida doctor who sent him to an oncologist. This doctor thought Patty might have cancer and wanted to put him in the hospital for a battery of tests. But Patty talked with John Praino, and they decided he would take the train up to New York and get the testing done at Sloan-Kettering.

I saw him the day he arrived. He looked terrible. He had spent the winter in Florida but was deathly pale. He went right into the hospital, and the doctors ran their battery of tests. They came back with a crushing diagnosis: liver cancer, in such an advanced stage that it was inoperable.

I was devastated. I think it was the worst piece of news I had heard in my lifetime. But Patty was surprisingly upbeat, and he tried to lift my spirits. "George, don't worry," he said. "I'm not going anyplace any time soon. The doctor told me the good news is that the kind of cancer I have is relatively slow spreading, so I should be here for a good long time."

I pressed him for more details about how they were going to treat him. Finally he shared the bad news. "The bad news is that this kind of cancer almost never responds to chemotherapy. They said the pain and the bother is simply not worth it. They said I could have a couple of years, but beyond making sure I'm comfortable, they can't do much."

I think I was more upset than Patty was. He knew that with the indictment hanging over his head, he could never come back to Jersey. He had no real idea why New Jersey wasn't searching for him more diligently, and I couldn't tell him. He believed he would have to spend the rest of his days looking over his shoulder. This was not very attractive to him, so the fact that he had only a couple of years left didn't seem to bother him.

Patty asked me to tell absolutely no one about the cancer. Many of the guys knew he had been ill. "Tell 'em I have an ulcer," he said. He had told Anna Marie, and John Praino knew. But beyond that, no one else should know, especially his wife Lee. For whatever reason, he was the most adamant about that. He virtually begged me not to tell her. I felt bad about it, but naturally I complied.

I did tell Billy and Ed. Patty was not going back to Florida, so I would be seeing him almost every day. And the way we were now working, it would be very difficult for me to sneak into New York every day or every night without them getting wise. So I told them the truth: Patty had come back to New York City and would be staying with John Praino. He had just been diagnosed with inoperable cancer and had a year or so at most, and I could continue to guarantee that he would not set foot in New Jersey. They thought a moment, then agreed that even with Patty next door in New York, they would continue their end of the bargain and not try to apprehend him. But they raised an interesting issue I had not even considered. I had been willing to record a single phone conversation with

Patty to prove he was in Florida. Now would I be willing to go the next step and record my meetings with Patty?

My instant reaction was "no way," but we talked it out and I reconsidered. Given his state of health, nothing that I recorded about Patty would ever be used against him. Patty had grown extremely worried about the condition of the family. I knew from talking with him in Florida that he had come around to Scoops's way of thinking that if Cousin Anthony didn't begin to assert some independent authority and if he didn't appoint a new underboss and some new captains, we would drift apart and would eventually be swallowed up by the New York families. With Patty back in New York it was likely he would begin to take on more involvement in day-to-day family activities. So I agreed to begin taping my conversations with Patty for them to be used as evidence against other guys. I felt uneasy about it, but I became more comfortable when it became clear that Patty's cancer was much more advanced than the doctor originally thought. He would probably be dead before any indictments were handed down because of what I was doing. Patty would probably never have to know.

On May 17 I picked up Cousin Anthony at his place on the shore at Toms River and drove him to Manhattan for a meeting with Patty. We got to Gino's, and he and Patty took a long walk around the block a couple of times while I waited at the bar. We then sat down for dinner and talked about nothing in particular. Anthony and Patty trusted me, but as long as I wasn't straightened out, Anthony was not going to discuss his business in front of me. Actually, it was a mark of his respect that Anthony even invited me to eat dinner with them. As we were leaving, Anthony asked me if I could bring him to New York to meet Patty again later in the month. I told him of course I could. We agreed on lunch, again at Gino's, at a date to be set later.

On the way back to Toms River, Anthony talked about a lot of things but very little about the family. He asked me how I thought Nicky Jr. was getting on, and I said fine. He said twice how much he and Nicky Sr. appreciated what I was doing for the Kid and how I could count on being rewarded. "Some changes are coming, George," Anthony said, "and don't worry, you will be involved."

I figured that Anthony and Patty had talked about Joey Sodano and that Anthony had probably passed the problem on to Patty. I met the next day with Patty at John Praino's, and the three of us went out to lunch. It was the first time one of my meetings with Patty was recorded.

As I suspected, part of the conversation Patty and Anthony had held during their walk was about Joey Sodano. But basically it was brief and consisted of Anthony asking Patty to reach out for Joey and tell him he should do what was right. The rest of their conversation concerned the family. Nicky had sent word through the Kid to Anthony that he should become a more active boss. And as a first step, Anthony had offered the underboss's job to Patty.

I have to admit I was surprised. When Nicky Sr. was about to go to jail, he had offered Patty the job of acting boss. He offered it to Anthony only after Patty had said no. So Nicky obviously had the highest regard for Patty. But with Patty on the lam, it meant that if he took the job, he would have to do it from New York and Florida. So I was surprised at the offer, but I told Patty I thought he should take the job.

He was not sure. "George, it's all right to take the job," he said, "but guys will start yakking. You know what I mean. 'Cause you know what will happen. Nobody knows me." He was concerned that the other guys would be jealous, particularly Scoops with his big mouth. I agreed that Scoops would probably make trouble. Then I told Patty I had asked around, and the chances were that Joey Sodano was still down in Florida.

"What else is new?" Patty said. "You just have to catch him when you can catch him. Maybe you shouldn't go. They might resent it, you not being straightened."

"Cheese should go," I said, meaning Scoops.

"Cheese ain't going to go," Patty said simply. "You know what I'm trying to say to you. He likes the title, but he don't want to back the title up. Maybe he shouldn't have the title much longer."

He didn't come right out and say it, but reading between the lines was easy. Both Patty and Anthony were getting tired of Scoops's inaction. I would guess they had talked about taking Scoops down.

The conversation then got back to whether Patty should take the job of underboss. "I don't want to be an absentee landlord, you know," he said. "I just want to see what happens with us. This is strictly, strictly between us. Don't tell Slicker. If I make this move, it's gonna be the way I want it."

Then he returned to the subject of Scoops. "Come on, he don't give a fuck. You think they don't know he's acting?" Patty said. "They're gonna watch him and what he's doing. It's good if he keeps doing what he's doing. In a little while they're gonna tell him step down. Anthony said, 'You and Georgie can do the running around, and in a little while you can push him out.' If it happens, I don't want you to be nasty to anyone. Use diplomacy."

Patty worried about whether to say yes or no to the job. We talked about it half a dozen times, and on May 23 I again went out to dinner with Patty and John at Gino's, and again our conversation was recorded. At dinner Patty said Nicky Sr. had sent word to Anthony that he had changed his mind, and it was okay to straighten out some new northern Jersey guys. He still didn't want any ceremonies in Philly, but we agreed that we needed more made guys in the north. "I told him [Anthony] that I was going to propose you and John [Praino], and I'll try to get Nicky O through, too," Patty said.

I told him I thought that was terrific. Because of protocol, for Nicky Oliveri to be straightened out, Michael Mandaglio, the guy he was directly around, would have to give his permission. That should not be a big problem, we agreed.

We then talked about the video poker machine business, and I told Patty that Nicky Jr. was making contacts in Connecticut to sell some machines up there. Pat was worried about police undercover agents and told me to approach a sale to any guy we didn't know well very carefully.

I then reminded him that he had promised to meet Anthony before the end of the month for lunch. I assumed Anthony wanted an answer about his job offer.

"Whenever, George," Patty said. "Whenever it's convenient with both of you. I don't care, you know."

I went down to Philly and met with Anthony in Manno's office. We agreed on May 30 for lunch with Patty. That morning I picked Anthony up at Toms River again, drove him to Manhattan, and we met Patty and John Praino outside Gino's a little before noon. Billy and Ed were there first and got some pictures of their meeting. As before, Anthony and Patty left John and me at the bar and took a walk. This time it was a long walk; they were gone a good half-hour. When they got back, again we had a long lunch saying little or nothing of any substance.

After lunch I drove Anthony back to Toms River, and he had less to say than on the last trip. We drove in silence much of the way, and by the time I dropped him off, I was almost bursting to find out what had been said. As soon as I could, I called Patty at John's. I knew he wouldn't talk on that phone, but I had to ask.

"Pat," I said, "just tell me: Did you say yes or no?"

"I said yes on my terms" was his somewhat cryptic reply. "We'll talk about it tomorrow."

The next day I met Patty at John's house, and he told me that Anthony had really pressured him to say yes to the underboss position. Then he said he had told Anthony he would take the position with the understanding that he would have to run things from New York or from Florida. Anthony agreed. He repeated that he had demanded John Praino, Turk, and I, and maybe Nicky Oliveri, be straightened out as soon as possible, and Anthony agreed. Finally, he had demanded that Scoops have no part in any of this.

"I'm going to put you up, George, and put up John," Patty said. "You're responsible for a guy if you put him up. If he goes wrong or goes bad, you got to kill him. I told him I would put you two up but not Nicky O. That's Mike Mandaglio's responsibility. Someone has to go talk with him, and I don't want Scoops going there."

"So that means you took the job, Pat?" I finally asked flat out.

"Yeah, I guess I did. I guess I'm the underboss."

Patty was absolutely disgusted with Scoops. Through me he had prodded him once again to do something about Joey Sodano. Scoops did nothing, of course. As a result, Patty wanted to have nothing to do with Scoops at all. He should have told Scoops he was now the underboss, but he just didn't want to deal with him in any way whatsoever. I thought I would do it Pat's way and keep the matter quiet, but then Nicky Jr. returned from a trip to Philly to say he had learned about it from Cousin Anthony. I knew he couldn't keep it quiet, so I told Pat he needed to make an announcement. We set up a dinner meeting.

On June 14 we met at the Lobster Box in Queens. There was Pat, me, and John Praino, and I had brought both Scoops and Slicker. Also present were Billy and Ed in their recording van in the back of a parking lot.

It was not a good night for Scoops. First Patty told him and Slicker that Anthony had made him underboss. Slicker seemed genuinely happy. He congratulated Pat and was clearly sincere. Scoops said all the right things—how pleased he was, how it was long overdue, how much he hoped that Patty's problems with the State of New Jersey could be resolved so he could come back to Newark.

Yeah, sure.

You could see it in his eyes and in what I guess they call his body language. Scoops was not pleased. He was a captain like Patty. He was Patty's equal. And since Patty was in exile, Scoops had the authority. Now here was Patty saying he was once again Scoops's superior, and worse, that he would be just across the river in New York and was going to be taking a much more active role in the day-to-day affairs of the family.

I got a little nervous hearing Pat say that because I knew Billy and Ed were in the van hearing it also. I was worried about how they would react, so later I explained to them that Patty had said that for effect because he wanted to throw a scare into Scoops. I repeated again that Patty had planned to go to Italy for the summer and now was planning to stay in New York only to be close to Sloan-Kettering. They said they would have to take a wait-and-see attitude.

Scoops received a second blow at that dinner when Pat told him and Slicker that Anthony was going to pressure Nicky Sr. to be allowed to begin straightening out guys and that John Praino, Turk, and I would be in the first group. Slicker again seemed genuinely happy for us. And again Scoops said all the right things, but he gave me a look I wish I could have preserved on film. He would have been happy to see me stay exactly where I was.

The rest of the dinner was spent socializing—neither Scoops nor Slicker had seen Pat in almost a year—and in bitching about the usual subject: money. We had been in the new card game now for three weeks, and we had yet to see a dime. The game was going good and they were cutting good money out of it, but so far Doode and Cabert, who was involved through Babe DeVino, were holding back and hadn't sent any dough our way. Scoops was getting angry, and now that Patty was back on the scene, he wanted the new underboss to do something about it.

Patty looked at me, and I sighed. God forbid that Scoops was owed a cent and someone didn't pay him instantly. But in a way he was right. Fair is fair. If they were cutting—and they were—the split should have been made. I said I would talk with Cabert. I wasn't feeling sorry for Scoops, I simply wanted the chance to get Cabert on tape again.

By now the end of June was fast approaching and the planned end of Operation Broadsword. All along we had figured that we would have more than enough on tape by June to indict and convict the entire circle of guys around me. That was, in fact, the case. The people at the Attorney General's Office had been carefully studying all the tapes and had concluded that they would be happy to go before a grand jury and ask for almost fifty indictments. They were already calling what we had done the deepest penetration of organized crime in New Jersey history. Yes, there were a few more things we could do. With Patty now the underboss and more involved in overall family matters, perhaps we could get some additional guys on tape. Then, too, the investigators also wanted more on tape involving some of the guys from other families who were now in this new card game. But we had done enough already to begin cutting back a bit and give Billy, Ed, Charley, and the other state troopers fewer sixteen- and eighteen-hour days. Besides, the overtime was killing the budget, or so they were being told.

We now planned to end Broadsword sometime in July to allow Ann and me and the kids time to get settled in our new home before the school year started around Labor Day. But there was yet another matter to finish up. My own criminal case was still moving forward, and it looked as if it would actually go to trial sometime in mid-August. When I made my deal with Ed Quirk to become his informant two years earlier, he had promised that as long as I cooperated, my case would be put on a back burner. But the operation had now stretched out well into the second year. They had been able to slow down the judicial process, but they couldn't slow it down much more without raising all kinds of suspicions. So while all this other stuff was going on, I was required to make various court appearances like the rest of my codefendants. I guess that I was in court nine or ten times during the year I had the transmitter on.

The state had seen to it that the case was assigned to Judge Felix Martino, who had a well-deserved reputation among New Jersey law-enforcement agencies as one of the slowest judges in the state. He was never in a hurry to get a case to trial and was more than willing to agree to almost any request for a continuance coming from either side.

At the same time the case was given to Deputy Attorney General Jim Clair to prosecute. He, too, had a reputation in the Attorney General's Office for not being the fastest and most gung-ho prosecutor around. They also made a decision, which I never agreed with, to keep Clair completely in the dark about my role as a state police agent. But rather than making him an active participant in the plan, which I thought was the best idea, they loaded him up with so much other work that he fell far behind on everything and had to seek continuances and postponements.

The strategy had worked well for a year and a half, but now the case was slowly edging forward to trial. Over the last few weeks I had been sitting with my codefendants for hours at a time during motions to suppress evidence, and the so-called driver hearings to authenticate the tapes that had been made from bugs and wiretaps that were to be used for my trial. Finally, all the pre-trial stuff was completed, and the judge and the lawyers were in final negotiations for a trial date. It looked as if it would be sometime between the third week in August and mid-September.

So the plan was to bring Broadsword to an end sometime in early to mid-July. But once Cousin Anthony and Patty started talking seriously about straightening me out, we began to entertain the possibility of my sticking around at least that long. At the backs of all our minds was the idea of recording the ceremony. That had happened only once for law enforcement, in Massachusetts, the year before. And it had happened by accident. The police had a mobster's house bugged, and that's where the ceremony was held. Never before had law enforcement learned about a ceremony before it happened and then bugged it. The Feds had never done it, and no local or state cops had ever been able to bring it off. We all felt it would be a fitting end to Broadsword.

The question was exactly how long that was going to be. There had been talk about straightening me out for at least three years, but something always came up. Now that it seemed pretty clear it was going to happen, the question was when. Patty said it would happen quickly, but "quickly" to these guys could well be December. We pretty much decided to play things by ear.

Over the next couple of weeks Ann and I developed a kind of routine. The kids were home for the summer, but we put them in various day camps so they could have some fun and wouldn't be around the house all day. In the morning I would either help Ann pack or be in court. Packing was actually rather difficult. We were taking only our clothing and personal things with us. We would walk away from everything else. We didn't know exactly when we were going to leave, but we assumed that it would be by July 20. So by mid-month we had to be ready. The plan was that when we decided to pull the plug, I would leave while indictments were drawn

up and arrests were made. Then at some point soon afterward, prosecutor Clair would be brought into the plan. I would come back, go
before Judge Martino, plead guilty to one count, and be given probation.

To make packing more difficult, the kids had no idea what was
going on. We figured there was no way they could keep this secret.
At first we told them we were just getting ready to have the house
painted. If any of my friends came into the house and saw the disar-
ray, we were going to use the same painting excuse. But as the
packing became more serious, the kids obviously knew something
was happening. So we told them we were going to move to a larger
house nearby, and they would all have their own rooms. That was
actually the truth if you used a rather elastic definition of "nearby."
But it kept them quiet, and they began to pitch in by getting their
stuff ready to move.

At this point about the last thing I needed was another complication. But Nicky Jr., my ever-present charge, was there to supply it.
The Kid was getting bored. The sports drink thing wasn't panning
out, and he was having trouble getting video poker machines into
western Pennsylvania through his uncle and into New England.
Most of all he wanted to get out of northern Jersey and back with
his friends in Atlantic City or with his family in South Philly. He
was still being told to lie low and wait, but waiting had lost its
appeal. And Nicky's solution to that problem was simple: start killing people.

He was his father's son. He figured that if he managed to kill some
of the people involved in the attempt to kill him, he would earn the
respect necessary to walk safely around the streets of Atlantic City
and Philadelphia. He had talked with his father about this, and
naturally Nicky Sr. had encouraged him. Initially the Kid wanted
to find a way to reach inside prison and whack Joey Merlino. It was
possible but complicated, so Nicky finally agreed that it would be
better to wait until Joey was out. But Stevie Vento was walking the
streets, along with some other guys who had been around his father
and who were likely suspects. That's where the Kid wanted to start.
Nicky Jr. decided he just had to whack Stevie Vento.

He spent a considerable time on the Fourth of July telling me all
this, and I figured I had better get Pat involved to head it off. An
intrafamily war was about the last thing we needed, and the state
police were not going to allow me to get involved in whacking Stevie
Vento.

On July 5 I picked Patty up at John Praino's and drove him to Sloan-Kettering for more cancer tests. We talked about a wide range of things on the way in, and our conversation was picked up clearly by the bugs in my car and transmitted to a tape recorder hidden in the fire wall in the trunk.

I brought up what Nicky Jr. had in mind. "He just wants to kill somebody to kill them, just for the sake of doing it," I said. "He's just like his father. He wants to impress the old man, he wants to show him. He figures if he can do some work, if he can make his bones, his father will straighten him out."

Patty received the news with a sigh. He clearly wasn't feeling very good, and about the last thing he needed to hear was that his first job as the new underboss would be to head off a family war. "Killing Joey Merlino is probably not a bad idea someday," he said, "but it can wait. This other stuff is not good. We don't even know if Vento was involved. I'll talk with Anthony and have him call the Kid off. But I'm afraid this is something that ain't gonna go away."

We continued talking about various other family problems that Patty was now getting involved in. In Down Neck, the Feast of Saint Michael was coming up, and Patty thought it would be a good idea if we got involved in the parish celebration again. A new wrinkle we were considering was installing video poker machines in some of the bars and clubs along the streets where the festival was held. If we could get hold of enough machines, we might be able to take in an additional $10,000 to $20,000 during the ten days of the festival.

I parked near the hospital on the Upper East Side and went in with Patty. Billy and Ed had a duplicate set of keys to my car, and while we were inside they opened the trunk, removed the tape from the recorder hidden in the fire wall, and put in a blank tape for the long drive back to the Bronx.

On the way home Patty was a little more talkative than he had been on the ride in. The doctor had given him a new pain medicine, and it seemed to kick in immediately. He started with some troubling news that I guess he hadn't wanted to spring on me earlier. "Scoops tells me the old man has sent word that he's a little leery of making new people now," he said.

I told him that Nicky Jr. had told me the same thing.

"What's the old man got in mind, do you think?" Patty asked.

"Well, the Kid told me his father wasn't leery, just that he wants to wait until he comes home. He thinks he's going to get out on an appeal bond. He says just be patient."

This clearly disturbed Patty. "Anthony wants to get this done. But I don't want to go up against the old man."

"Patty, he ain't never coming home," I said.

"George, I know it. But what do you want me to do? Do I tell Nicky ... you ain't never coming home?"

"What does Cousin Anthony say?" I asked.

"Anthony says he wants to do it," Patty replied.

"Then let's do it."

"Yeah, I want to, George."

The conversation then turned to Scoops, and I made the comment that it looked as though he was trying to keep the ceremony from happening. "He ain't looking for any of us to get there," I said.

Patty exploded. "Fuck! If it wasn't for me, he would never be there. He knows that. He should have no animosity. I went through hell to get him straightened out. He knows that. Why is he abusing you?"

Patty made it very clear that the first order of business was getting me straightened out. Then, he said, we would deal with Scoops.

Three times over the next week I came into New York to drive Patty to Sloan-Kettering. If anything, the pain in his stomach was getting worse. The doctors ran additional tests and now realized that Patty's cancer was far more advanced than they had thought. They were sure it had spread from his liver to his stomach and probably to other parts of his body as well. Their diagnosis was extremely glum. At the very outside Pat probably had a year. More likely he had only six months to live, and it was possible he might go very quickly. We could be talking a matter of weeks.

I went into a depression when Patty told me the news. He said he was telling only three of us: me, John, and Anna Marie. I begged him to tell his wife and kids, but he was even more adamant than before. They were not to know, Cousin Anthony was not to know, no one in the family was to know. If he had only weeks or months to live, he wanted to spend that time with Anna Marie.

But he ended up sort of hinting to Cousin Anthony, who reached out for him to talk again about what was becoming the Scarfos' favorite subject—Joey Sodano. Anthony wanted Pat to get Joey to agree to resume his tribute payments, and in the course of their conversation, Pat told Anthony that he would consider it a personal favor if the straightening out ceremony took place sooner rather than later. I guess Anthony read between the lines because when I saw Pat that night, he told me the ceremony was on for Sunday, July 22.

Then somewhat amazingly the Sodano problem was settled in a single phone call and one lunch. We found out that Joey was back in town, and when we contacted him, he instantly agreed to meet with Patty on the afternoon of July 17 at Emilias Restaurant in the Bronx. Patty wanted the meeting set up at the restaurant so Scoops wouldn't know where he was staying. His biggest fear was that Scoops would drop by unannounced, find Pat with Anna Marie (whom Scoops didn't like), and then tell his wife, who was a good friend of Patty's wife.

I picked up Patty and John Praino at John's house and drove them over to Emilias Restaurant. About half an hour after we got there, Scoops and Joey Sodano came in. Patty was angry that they were late. Joey just gave Scoops a dirty look. It was obvious who was at fault.

The business part of the lunch was over in about two minutes. Patty just said, "I hear you haven't been doing the right thing, Joey." Joey then began to explain how he hadn't been doing so well lately. Pat held up his hand and said, "Joey, I understand, but you have to do something."

Joey just nodded; they didn't call him the "Nodder" for nothing. "Okay, Pat. For you I'll make it right." That's how simple it was. Joey agreed to pay at least $1,000 a month starting in August.

What surprised me about this lunch was that Patty said absolutely nothing to Scoops or Joey about John and me and the other guys being straightened out, and it was supposed to happen the following Sunday. As we were driving back to John's house, I asked Patty why.

"I don't want him there, period," he replied in a tight voice. "This is not his thing," he said, talking about Scoops. "I've been talking with Anthony. Things are going to be happening in this family, and Scoops will be my problem to take care of. In the meantime, this thing will be just between us."

As soon as the date was set, Billy, Ed, and the state police started making plans for the ceremony. I agreed to wear a body recorder in addition to the transmitter so we could be sure of getting everything. Patty had decided the ceremony would take place at John's apartment in the Bronx rather than his house. Everything was a go, and suddenly I got a call that it was canceled.

I don't know who was more upset about the cancellation, me, Patty, or the state police. Patty said he had gotten the word from

Philadelphia, but he had not talked with Anthony himself. Then we got further word that Anthony wanted to meet with me at Donald Manno's office the following Tuesday.

When he arrived at Manno's conference room that day, Anthony could not have been more apologetic. He told me that the previous week he had had a visit from a couple of FBI agents trying to throw a scare into him. That kind of thing happened often enough that he didn't even give it much of a second thought. But he was worried that the Feds might have a tail on him, so he thought it best not to come to New York until he could figure out exactly what was going on. He was now pretty sure he wasn't under surveillance.

"We could do it anytime at all, George," Anthony said.

"Want to make it this coming Sunday?" I asked.

"This Sunday?"

"Yeah, this Sunday."

"Sure, George, Sunday's fine."

I then told him why I thought it had to be done very quickly. Patty was dying. "He didn't want me to tell you this," I said, "but you'll see when you see him. He's turning a little yellow."

"Oh, Jesus, don't tell me."

"He's been going to doctors and hospitals, and they know it's cancer."

"Oh, for Christ's sake!"

"Tony, I'm not supposed to be telling you this—"

"You didn't say nothing."

Our conversation then ranged over a number of other areas. I told Anthony we had straightened out the problem with Joey Sodano, and he would start paying tribute again starting the first of the month. I could tell Anthony was relieved. It was not so much the money as the lack of respect that Joey had been showing. Anthony knew if it lasted much longer, Nicky Sr. would order Joey whacked, and that would have been a shame, to say nothing of the potential problems it might have caused with the Gambinos.

I think we all felt strange that we were going to have this ceremony and Nicky Jr. was not being straightened out. But apparently his father had sent back word through Bobby Manna that if the ceremony was going ahead, it should only be for me and the guys from the north around Patty. It should not be for anyone from Philly and absolutely should not include Nicky.

That got the conversation around to the Kid's spending habits. "He's running me straight to the poorhouse," I told Anthony.

"Yeah, I know."

"I told him, Anthony, I told him, 'Nick, we have to tighten our belts.' "

"This I have to see," said Anthony, laughing.

I had another problem. The money that was going to start coming in again from Joey Sodano was supposed to go directly to the Kid, but I was afraid the way he went through money, he would blow it without putting anything away. "Anthony," I said, "he don't know that Joey is paying again. Why don't I just hold the money for him so he don't blow it."

Anthony agreed with me. "Yeah, George, that's good. That's using your head. If the money problem with him gets worse, I'll speak to him."

So that day I drove back to Newark on top of the world. Five more days and I would finally be a made member of the Bruno-Scarfo family. Then this whole thing would end, and Ann, the kids, and I would be on our way to our new life.

It almost didn't happen. That night I went to New York to have dinner with Patty and report on my meeting with Cousin Anthony. Patty looked terrible, and we ate in because he didn't have enough strength to leave the house. He seemed very relieved that Anthony had agreed to the following Sunday. "The quicker the better," he said. He also repeated what he had said earlier: "Don't tell Scoops anything about Sunday, and tell the rest of them not to say anything to him, either."

I told Pat that Scoops had left for a week at the shore, and not telling him would probably not be a problem.

I left John's a little after ten and headed for the card game. I thought I would just make an appearance for appearance's sake and then head home. Actually, I had another motive: I was owed quite a bit of money from the game as well as from some of the guys who were playing there. I figured I would be leaving shortly, and if I got some of this cash, I could take it with me to buy a second car and other extras the state wouldn't be paying for. In other words, I would see if I could do a little debt collecting.

I was standing at the game when Ralph Perna, Michael's brother, came up to me. "Someone close to Patty Specs has screwed and is working for the state," he said.

I was shocked to the core. Hoping it was sufficiently dark that he didn't see how pale I had turned, I asked him what he meant. He said the mole they had in the Attorney General's Office had heard that the state police were mounting some kind of major operation and that it was built around somebody in the Bruno-Scarfo family who was around Patty.

"Who?" I asked.

"Don't know," Perna replied. "But our guy will keep looking, and I'll let you know as soon as I hear."

I thanked him and got out of there as quickly as I could. I then did something I rarely did: I got Ed Quirk out of bed.

He was as shocked as I had been. They thought they had neutralized this mole, and Ed thought it was impossible for the guy to have found out about me. He promised to get right on the phone and said he would call me in the morning.

To say I did not have a very restful night would be quite an understatement. Ann woke up once during the night to find me wide awake. I told her I couldn't sleep because of the excitement of leaving the next week, and the ceremony and everything. I did not say it looked as if I had been found out and that tomorrow I might just get a bullet in the brain. I didn't say it, but I thought it. I had sort of grown complacent. I guess we all had. Going to all these meetings wearing a wire had just become commonplace. I really didn't think about the danger anymore. It had always been there. But as success followed success, the danger had receded. Now all of a sudden it was back, and it could not have come at a worse time. We were so near the end, but we still had to get over that last hurdle.

The next day Ed called a major meeting with me, the operational guys, and his superiors at the safe house apartment. They had spent most of the night doing it, but they had finally figured how this guy had found out about my existence and what I was doing. "George, we don't think he has learned your name," Ed said, "but we can't be absolutely certain." That being the case, Ed said he believed we should just pull the plug then and there and not take any more chances. Dave Brody said they could rush through a grand jury presentation if it was necessary.

I objected. I asked Ed if it was reasonable to believe they didn't know my name. He said it was. I said I had come this far and wanted to see it through. But then Billy or one of the other guys brought up a chilling thought: Considering how long it had been since the Bruno-Scarfo family had straightened anyone out, was it possible that what was going to happen was not my making but my unmaking, so to speak? Was it possible that I was going to get hit on Sunday and not straightened out?

I rejected that idea out of hand. For me to believe it was a setup, I would have had to believe that Patty was at the center of the plot. That I simply refused to consider. Nevertheless, Ed and Billy agreed they would have to be prepared for any eventuality on Sunday. They would be ready to get me out of John's apartment if anything went wrong.

12

THE CEREMONY

Ask most happily married men the most important day in their lives, and the reply will be their wedding day or the birth of a child. Ask a priest, and he will almost always say the day he was ordained. Ask a made guy, and he will usually say the day he got straightened out. Later on you might make captain or underboss, or you might make some terrific scores, but the day you always remember is the day you were officially accepted into the family. If I was still the wiseguy I had grown up dreaming of being, this would have been the most important day in my life. Instead, it was the most hectic.

It wasn't supposed to be so confusing. The plan was to pick up Cousin Anthony at Penn Station in Newark and then drive to John Praino's apartment in the Bronx. After the ceremony we would have a few drinks, and I would drive Anthony back to the train, then go home to finish packing and maybe go out that night to hang with a couple of the guys.

What is it they say about best-laid plans? We had carefully back-timed everything. I had to be at the station to pick up Anthony at 10:00 A.M. That meant I had to pick up Beeps and Slicker about 9:30 in order to make it. So it was planned that I would meet Billy, Ed, and the technicians to get wired at about 8:00 A.M. I was up early and spent about an hour helping to pack stuff. If our plans held, and Ann insisted they would, we were all going to be on a plane the following Wednesday morning. She still had a lot to do. I left the house about seven and headed for a motel where Billy and Ed had taken a room.

"George, I still don't know if we should be doing this," Ed said as the technician was taping the small recorder to the inside of my thigh in my groin area. "You've been through so much already, risked so much, and we're so close to the end. Maybe you should just go through this without any recorder. We'll get what we can with the transmitter. I just don't want you to get burned now."

At the same time he was also talking himself into allowing me to go into the ceremony wired. One second he would say how dangerous it was, the next how careful the planning had been, how much backup there would be if anything went wrong, and how it would all go without a hitch.

I knew he was just nervous, but so was I, and he wasn't helping me all that much. What I needed that morning was a lot of optimism, not what amounted to a pro-and-con discussion of what I was about to do. So I tried to tune him out as they got me ready and gave me a final briefing on all the backup that was available and what I should do if everything suddenly fell apart.

"We can be inside within a minute or two with a lot of firepower if things go wrong," Ed said. "So just keep your head and stall if something bad starts to go down. We'll hear you, and we'll be there. Don't worry."

On that happy note I set off to pick up Cousin Anthony. My first stop was the club where I was picking up Slicker and Beeps. And just as I went inside to get them, my pager went off. The phone number was John Praino's house. I called immediately.

Suddenly it was panic time. John said that Patty had weakened during the night and really couldn't travel to the apartment for the ceremony. He had decided to go ahead and hold the ceremony at his house so that Patty wouldn't have to move. Norma, John's wife, was going shopping about noon, and we could hold the ceremony while she was out. John wanted my help in getting hold of everyone and telling them of the change. That was all simple enough if you didn't have to factor in dozens of New Jersey and New York police who were already beginning to stake out John's apartment, now a location about five miles from where the ceremony was actually going to be.

I told Beeps and Slicker to use the clubhouse phone to try to reach some of the guys while I went out to the public phone to call some of the others. Actually, I was frantic. Suddenly I could picture the ceremony taking place with the nearest cop—to say nothing of the recorder—five miles away. If this is the way it was going to go down, I was thinking, then this damn recorder in my crotch had better work. I reached the pay phone and desperately tried to call Billy and Ed, but as I feared, they had already left for the Bronx. I tried them on their car phone but couldn't get through. My last hope was that someone would be at the safe house. There was. I told him of the change, and he got Billy and Ed on their radio. They said they would shift everyone, but it would take some time. "Stall, George. Give us some time" was the message they relayed to me.

If I wasn't nervous enough already, this was the capper. Now I was worried that they wouldn't be in position by the time the ceremony started or that so many people moving into a residential area on a Sunday morning would attract too much attention. As it was, John's wife, Norma, was already suspicious that their house might be under surveillance because Patty was there. On Friday she had told John about seeing a car in the neighborhood with Jersey plates and two guys sitting in it. John went out to see, but it was gone. When he told me about it, I called Ed because I thought it might have been a state car. He assured me that it wasn't. Apparently it had been a couple of guys from Jersey just passing through. But it had really spooked Norma, and I was afraid she would take notice of the small army descending on the area.

Slicker, Beeps, and I finally got hold of everyone and told them of the change. Then we got in the car and raced to the station to pick up Cousin Anthony. His train was on time, and he was in a very happy mood. All the way over to John's he was talking about what a great day this was for me, what a great future I had, and how much he was counting on me. "George, this is the most important day in your life," he said. "Today you become one of us. It's long overdue. I'm happy I can do this for you."

I was not so happy. I was still apprehensive, and John's opening line to me when we walked in his front door really did nothing to help set my mind at ease. After he greeted us and got a cup of coffee for Anthony, he took me aside. "You ride the mirror coming over?" he asked, meaning had I been careful that I wasn't followed. I told him that I had been careful and was sure no one had followed us over from Jersey. "Good, George, that's good," he said. "We can't be too careful on a day like this. Think what it would mean if the cops took us down."

Norma was still there, so we spent some time socializing, waiting for the stores to open and for her to leave to do her shopping. Once she did, things began to move quickly because we had to be finished by the time she returned. We got some folding chairs and set them in a semicircle in the living room. Then the ceremony began.

Patty was so weak that no one wanted to burden him by putting him through the full traditional ceremony. Normally each of us would have been brought into a room to go through the whole ceremony one at a time. The same speech would have been given five times, the same ritual performed—the gun and the knife put into our hands as each of us repeated the oaths. But in deference to Patty, most things except the actual oaths were done jointly, and because John was afraid that somehow his wife would come back early, the gun and the knife were kept in a paper bag on the table in front of us.

All told, it took about an hour for all five of us with the blood, the knife, the gun, and the oath. It was a very solemn occasion. And at the end of the ceremony Cousin Anthony turned even more serious. He put his hand on Pat's shoulder and said to us: "This here, he'll be like your father. You have problems, you come to him. He can solve them." Then he looked directly at me and said, "In the event he's not here, he'll designate someone else. Whoever is designated would be the same as him or I; whoever it may be. And that's the way it will be."

That was it. The ceremony was over, and Patty clearly appreciated that. I know I did. The heat, the weight of the recorder, and just the stress were getting to me. It was like having a Walkman stuck in your underwear except that a self-contained Nagra recorder is quite a bit heavier. I couldn't wait to get it off. I still had the fear that something would go wrong and the damn thing would slide down my leg or fall out of my pants or make some kind of obvious noise. I just wanted to be rid of it.

The opportunity presented itself almost at once. During the ceremony Patty's doctor had called. We waited until it was over to call back, and the doctor said he was phoning a local drugstore to leave a new pain prescription. Patty was to take it immediately, and if he had no relief by evening, there was general agreement that he would check himself into the hospital where stronger drugs could be given intravenously. Someone had to go to the drugstore to pick up the new prescription, and I quickly volunteered. I assumed that Billy, Ed, and the rest of the crew were in place outside the house and would hear over the transmitter that I was about to leave. So when I walked out to my car and pulled away, a small caravan tailed me to the local drugstore. Ed followed me into the drugstore. Those still watching the house had radioed that no one else had left to follow me. He was clearly very excited. "George, we got it. You were right," he half-whispered. "We got every word. It's unbelievable. We recorded the ceremony from start to finish."

There was no place to remove the recorder in the drugstore, so we went across the parking lot into a McDonald's. It had one of those tiny four-by-four, one-stall bathrooms, and more than a few people seemed to notice and smirk when the two of us went in and locked the door. But they must have thought we were pretty speedy because it took only about thirty seconds to drop my slacks and rip off the tape holding the recorder.

I was proud of the slacks I was wearing that day. They represented one of my major victories over the New Jersey State Police bureaucracy. When Billy and Ed told me they wanted me to wear a recorder into the ceremony in addition to my normal transmitter, they explained that in order to rig the microphones so they could pick up what was being said, they would have to cut out both pockets of my pants to run the mike wires from the recorder in my groin area to the microphones on the insides of the pockets. I told them there was no way I was going to let them cut up a pair of my good pants. "You guys want me to do this, then let's go shopping," I said. "You guys can buy me a pair of pants to get cut up."

That caused a tremendous fuss. Jake Hahn was in charge of the unit's budget, and it seemed that his main mission in life was to save money for the New Jersey State Police. Whenever he had to pay for anything, it was as though it came directly out of his pocket. Success or failure of the mission was not as important to him as following all the correct accounting procedures. He was the bane of all of us, and he tried to convince me I could wear an older pair of my own pants. When I insisted that I was not going to wear old clothes to my straightening out and I was not going to ruin my good clothes, he reluctantly agreed I could get a new pair of slacks on the state. When we got to the store, I was immediately herded toward the cheap section. I walked right on by, and even Billy and Ed blanched when I picked out a nice $195 pair of slacks. For me it was like I was buying the mob equivalent of my confirmation suit. So they plunked down a state credit card, and then I gave my brand-new, very expensive slacks to a technician to have the pockets cut out.

After Ed and I left McDonald's we crossed to the back of the lot where the van was parked half out of sight. The guys were all congratulating themselves and speculating about how jealous the Feds and other law enforcement agencies would be when they heard of our coup. They quickly played part of the tape that was in the recorder, and the technician was amazed. The quality of the recorded tape was even better than the reception they had gotten through the transmitter. So we had the entire ceremony on two tapes. I thought that was quite an achievement.

But I had to get back. We might be near the end of Broadsword, but the way I looked at it, there were still things to be done. Given the number of guys present at John's house and the fact that Cousin Anthony was there, all sorts of stuff might come up. I was especially interested in getting Cousin Anthony on tape. We didn't have all that much on him, and this was our chance to really tie him up so that a later charge of "leader of organized crime" could be easily sustained against him.

I guess somehow it was inevitable, after recording almost four hundred conversations—more than six hundred hours of tape—that possibly the most important conversation I ever had in the mob went unrecorded. Back in John's house, the afternoon finally wound down. We ate some burgers and hotdogs, drank some beer, and generally did what a bunch of guys do during a summer backyard barbecue. But some things in that backyard were a little different. As usual, when mob guys got together, the major topic of conversation was money. Nicky Sr. had sent word from jail that he was pissed at a guy for holding back a share of some money he thought should have gone to him. Cousin Anthony wanted us to do the collecting.

"I mean this guy—I tell you, I get so fucking mad sometimes," Anthony complained.

Then he turned to a problem Nicky Jr. was having. When he was arrested, a guy who was around us named George Borgesi had signed for the Kid's $10,000 bond, and Nicky later paid him the ten grand. Now that the case was over and the bond returned, Nicky wanted his ten thousand. Borgesi had gotten it back from the state in cash —the way he had put it up—but he gave it to his aunt, who was the wife of another guy who was around us, Joe Ligambi. George had given it to her to give to Joe, who would in turn would pass it on to Nicky Jr. But she, bless her heart, misunderstood why Borgesi was giving her the money. She thought he owed it to her husband, so she used it real quick to pay a lot of bills. Now the Kid wanted his money back, but he was unsure if he should get it from Borgesi or from Ligambi. Cousin Anthony asked me to straighten the whole thing out.

"Now listen," Cousin Anthony said to me, "you're going to have a lot more voice now, George. I'm going to depend on you to keep this Kid straight. You've got to hammer it into him, he don't understand. No, he thinks everything comes on trees. That ain't the way, George. You know it ain't the way."

While we visited and ate and drank, Cousin Anthony and Patty spent most of the afternoon alone in quiet conversation. We weren't sure what they were talking about, but later I found out they were discussing the future of the family. Anthony knew that Nicky Sr. was still resisting turning over real power even though we all knew he was never coming back from Marion. Then, too, we had never begun to really rebuild after so many other guys had been either killed or, like Nicky Sr., hauled off to jail. The two of them, Anthony and Patty, had been around long enough to know that a major rebuilding effort had to be undertaken or else the Bruno-Scarfo family would simply wither away. Anthony believed that in allowing this ceremony Nicky had given him the word to begin the rebuilding effort. Now Anthony was asking Patty for his recommendations on what to do next in New Jersey.

At one point Slicker and I brought some food or a beer over to Cousin Anthony. He saw us coming and kind of changed the subject. We chatted for a minute, and then Anthony turned to Patty and asked, "What do you want me to tell Cheese about this afternoon?" (Again, Cheese was the other name we had for Scoops.)

"Yeah, what do we tell him about why he wasn't here?" Slicker chimed in. "I don't want him coming to me complaining and beefing. I told the guys to say that George called us on Sunday morning and not on Saturday night—called us Sunday morning about eight o'clock."

"Duke," Patty said, using another nickname for Slicker, "why do you fear him? If you want, I'll take him down if you don't want him there."

"No," Slicker responded. "I didn't say that. It's not fear, it's just that he asks too many questions."

"You know what you should do," Patty said. "Tell him that Cousin Anthony says if you keep questioning people, he's going to look to take you down. Just say you're giving a little warning."

I could see Slicker almost pale at the thought of being the one to tell Scoops to effectively mind his own business or be taken down as captain. So I interjected something about our not being the ones to tell him something like that. Patty just said disgustedly, "I don't care. Tell him whatever the fuck you want."

Finally the afternoon just wound down. Patty got very tired, excused himself, and went back to his bedroom. A number of the guys were anxious to get home to their families for Sunday night dinner. Anthony wanted to get back to Philadelphia. As a sign of respect, Turk would join Slicker, Beeps, and me to take him back to the train station in Newark. As they got ready to leave, I went back into the bedroom to say good-bye to Patty.

"Georgie," Pat said in a very weak voice, "I'm not going to be around much longer. Today was the start of something big for you. They all like you—Anthony, Nicky, all of them, other fellas, other families. Cousin Anthony is going to talk to you. Listen to him real close. Take it a little slow now, George. Listen and don't talk. Don't be a hothead. Someday, maybe someday real soon, you might be going to run this crew. You'll do good, I know."

Then he kind of slumped down as if the day's effort had all been too much. "We'll talk some more tomorrow, George. Now I'm tired."

"Yeah, sure," I said in a kidding voice. "Yeah, sure I'm going to be some boss. You're going to be here quite a while, Pat. Let's not worry. I got to get Anthony to the train. I'll see you tomorrow."

I thought it had been the painkillers talking, but I soon learned otherwise when we got to the station. Anthony said his good-byes to the other guys and then turned to me. "Walk me to the train, George. We need to talk."

As we walked through the station, Anthony came right to the point: "George, you know the family is having its problems with so many guys gone. We need new blood, new leaders. Pat and I have talked it out. Pat considers you the best, considers you to be like his own son. I want you to see him tomorrow, let him talk with you. I want you to know if anything happens to him, I'm going to give you a position. I have no problem giving you that position or any position. You and guys like you are our new family."

I was honestly speechless. I guess I stammered a bit, and all I could answer was "Whatever you want, Tony Buck. I'm not going to disobey you."

"Sure, George, I know. I know you'll do well. Go see Pat in the morning. He'll give you some news."

I walked back to the car half in a daze, trying to sort out what I had just heard. I wasn't exactly sure what Pat was going to tell me the next day, but what Cousin Anthony had just told me seemed clear: When Pat died, I would become the underboss.

I guess I felt both confused and elated. Things could not have been going much better. I had recorded my own initiation, and now I had been told that in the near future I would become the number two man in the entire family. But not for a minute did I think that this was what I had been hoping for, working for, ever since I was a kid. That ambition had evaporated long ago. My only thought was that Broadsword could continue and possibly reach heights that none of us had ever even dreamed. And for that to happen, I would have to keep working for the state. But Ann and the kids were packed and ready to go. She had made up her mind that this was the end, and I knew she wouldn't wait. I was torn, and as I got back in the car, I honestly didn't know what I was going to do.

After I dropped off Slicker, Beeps, and Turk, I met Billy, Ed, and a couple of other troopers at the same motel where we had met that morning. I was elated. I was flying. I felt I had accomplished the impossible. "What do you think of what Anthony said at the train?" was the first thing out of my mouth when I saw Billy.

His face sort of dropped. "What did he say?" he asked. "We stopped recording after you left the drugstore. We felt it was just too risky, what with John's wife coming back and all. It was your safety we were thinking about."

Now my mouth dropped open. "You didn't get it? You didn't get the stuff at the train?"

"No, George. We followed you, but the recording van had gone back because we felt we had all we were going to get for the day. Besides, Jake was worried those guys would go on overtime."

There went Jake again, trying to save the State of New Jersey a few dollars, and we had lost what might become a critical conversation. "Hey, don't worry," I told Billy sarcastically. "All we didn't get was Anthony telling me that when Patty dies I'm going to be the underboss."

Now it was Billy's turn to be open-mouthed. He asked me to repeat exactly what Anthony had said. I repeated the conversation word for word as best I could remember, and Billy wasn't so sure my interpretation was completely right. "Position" could mean many different things, he said.

"No, Billy," I insisted. "If you had been recording, you would have heard the way he said it. It was pretty clear. When Patty's gone, I'm going to get his job. I'm going to be the underboss."

We both kind of looked at each other. If I was right, we both knew what that would mean. But neither of us wanted to start talking about it just yet. That was a conversation for later.

My elation over what we had accomplished that day, and what we still might accomplish, withered with the first look Ann gave me when I told her what had happened. She was not at all happy about the prospect of my staying even one day longer than we had planned. She hated this life, she hated my living this life, and just the thought of my becoming underboss filled her with both fear and anger.

"George, we agreed. It's over," she said. "We're leaving in three days, and the kids and I are not coming back. If you have to take a couple of weeks to finish things up here, that's okay, that's what we agreed. But no longer. The kids are going to start school the day after Labor Day. I want you there. I want this thing and this life to be finished."

In almost everything, once Ann made up her mind, it stayed made up. And more than any other subject, my staying in this life was now closed. I knew it was fruitless to argue, and besides, a part of me said she was right, it was time to go. But a part of me was still contemplating what Billy, Ed, and I might be able to accomplish with me as underboss: the places I could go, the people I would be dealing with—me and my transmitter. The opportunities would be just about limitless. We already had enough evidence to bring down one boss. Give me six or eight months as the Bruno-Scarfo underboss, and there was no telling who we could catch in our dragnet. But I knew I would have an awfully hard time selling Ann on the idea, and now certainly was not the time to start.

About ten that night I got a hurried call from John Praino. The day had been too much for Patty, and the new medicine was not helping. John said he was much weaker, and when he called the doctor, it was decided that Patty should be admitted to the hospital. An ambulance had been called to take him to Westchester Square Hospital. John said there was no sense in my coming over now. With stronger drugs perhaps Patty could sleep through the night. So I told John I would be there first thing in the morning.

Nicky Oliveri and I got to the hospital a little after nine. Patty was sitting up in bed looking very old and very weak. They had given him several IVs and the pain had been reduced, but he was still very uncomfortable.

We exchanged small talk for a few minutes, and then the doctor came in and we left the room. When we saw the doctor leave, we went back in, and Patty asked me to help him to the john. After he got back in bed, he asked Nicky O to take a walk because he needed to talk with me. Once Nicky left, he became very serious. I asked him what the doctor had told him, but he brushed that off.

"George, my time is ending, and your time is now starting," he said. "Cousin Anthony and I have talked, and he has talked with Nicky through the Kid. You kept the Kid safe. Nicky appreciates that. When Joey Merlino gets out, you'll kill him. Nicky knows that. Starting today, you are capo. The other four new guys are now yours. But you don't have to take this position if you don't want to. You can tell Cousin Anthony no. If you take it, you assume the responsibility. If you take it and you make a mistake, there are consequences. Guys can start to build a case against you, and you could get killed. I want you to do this. I want you to come out on top. But it's your decision."

Then Patty turned the conversation around to Scoops. "Anthony is not happy with Scoops. He'll have to work that out. You will probably get some of his guys. I don't know how that will work. Don't talk to Scoops or anyone about this yet. Get introduced to him as the new captain but only mention the new guys. Anthony is going to call him down to Philadelphia to talk with him. Depending on how he answers, he might or might not be taken down. That's not your business. You are now captain, and you can assume the position within the family. But don't tell anyone outside the family until Cousin Anthony talks with Scoops. That might take a couple of weeks, so be patient."

That little speech seemed to take all Patty's strength. He said he was tired and wanted to go to sleep. I told him I would come back that night. Patty said no. Anna Marie was coming over. "I'll see you tomorrow, George."

After I left the hospital, I dropped Nicky O off and then headed to a meeting with Billy and Ed so we could begin sorting out what was happening. I had been made a captain on the same day I was straightened out. As best I could remember, that had never happened before in the Bruno-Scarfo family. The only thing comparable was when the Gambinos straightened out John Gotti years ago. So I guess that I was in pretty good company.

Billy and Ed were more than a little interested in what Patty told me, and when I informed them that I was now capo and the other four guys straightened out yesterday were to be my crew, they broke into smiles. Those smiles broadened when I told them that Patty had confirmed what Cousin Anthony had said at the train. I was to become the underboss when Patty was gone, and judging from the way he looked that morning, we were talking weeks or a few months at most.

Then Billy, Ed, and I started to talk about what was on all our minds. Did what was happening change things, and if so, how? Obviously, with me as captain and possibly taking over for Patty as underboss, it was very enticing to contemplate running Broadsword for another year. There was no question that Ann and the kids were going to leave that week. We thought maybe we could invent some kind of scenario that would explain Ann and the kids leaving and my staying behind. "Divorce, that's it," I said. "These guys almost never see Ann anyway. I'll explain that we have separated, and she's filing for divorce. That way I can stay here alone, and they'll never question why they don't see Ann."

So we kicked that idea around for a while. We figured that, at most, it would take a year to achieve all we could, and I guessed I could talk Ann into staying with the kids in our new location without me that long. I could fly there every few weeks, maybe staying a week every five or six. We would survive.

There was just one problem: Cousin Anthony was from the old school. He had the old Calabrian belief in marriage and family. He did not believe in divorce, and if I announced a divorce, maybe he wouldn't make me the underboss. Stranger things than that happened all the time. I would have to talk with him, and if he objected, maybe I could say Ann and I had just separated and were trying to work things out. If he really objected to guys divorcing, that story wouldn't hold him forever, but it might hold him long enough. The more we talked, the more it seemed like a divorce-separation story would provide the framework for a workable way for me to continue working for the state while Ann and the kids started over in safety.

But then Ed entered a sobering note into the conversation: "George, I don't know how much longer we can keep this operation and your identity secret. The initiation yesterday brought a whole bunch of new guys into this. They didn't know if we had bugged the house or had some guy wearing a wire, and if it was a wire, who was wearing it. But pretty soon people are going to start putting two and two together."

This brought the conversation back to the mole who had almost learned my identity and to other leaks that existed within the various parts of the New Jersey State government.

"George, we believe the guy never learned your real name," Ed said. "But he found out you existed, and if we hadn't identified him as quickly as we did, it's possible he could have learned enough about Broadsword and about you to make a very educated guess as to who you were. He's isolated now, and he's out of the game. I don't think there are any others in anywhere near the position this guy was, but to be honest, the longer we keep this up, the greater the chance that you'll be found out. And we can't have that happen."

So nothing was decided in that conversation. We agreed to let things rest awhile, maybe even for the couple of weeks of my "vacation." Billy and Ed would go back and talk with their bosses. I would talk with Ann and see exactly how negative she was to the idea. We didn't have to make a decision right away.

That night I went Down Neck and hung around the Belmont Tavern, a restaurant we used to go to on Bloomfield Avenue. My initiation ceremony was supposed to be a secret, but it seemed as if everyone knew. All kinds of guys came up and congratulated me. Later in the evening both Michael Perna and Bobby Cabert came in. Since I had been straightened out, before I could talk with either of them, I had to be formally introduced by another made member of our family. That assignment fell to Slicker, who was eating with me. I was formally introduced to them both, and they warmly congratulated me.

Scoops had not been invited to the ceremony for the simple reason that Patty did not want him there. And I knew Scoops was not going to be happy about that. He was the captain, after all, second only to Patty in our crew. It had been a significant measure of disrespect not to invite him, and I knew Scoops well enough to know he was going to be both hurt and very angry over the slight.

Scoops had been down at the shore and got back on Tuesday morning. But I couldn't just go over and see him. Even with Scoops, mob protocol was now involved. Before I could talk with him, I had to be formally introduced, and like the night before, that assignment fell to Slicker. So Slicker, Nicky O, and I went over to see Scoops at a coffee shop next door to a clubhouse we had. The four of us ducked into the entranceway leading up to an apartment over the coffee shop. First Slicker introduced Nicky to Scoops. Then he introduced me.

"Scoops, this is George, *amico nostro*," Slicker said. Scoops started to smile, but Slicker went on. "George is the captain over the new guys." Patty had told Slicker the previous night that I had been made captain.

I could see something flash in Scoops's eyes when he heard that. The smile sort of died on his face. Suddenly I was not only straightened out, but I was equal to him as a captain. I knew instantly that this was going to be more than simply difficult.

But Scoops didn't say much. He begged off quickly, saying he had to get over to the used car lot he owned, and I had to get back to Ann and help her finish packing. So I left first, and within the hour I had a call from Slicker. He said Scoops had been beefing about not being at the ceremony and about my being made captain without him being consulted. I thought I had better have this out with him face-to-face.

I went over to Scoops's car lot in Irvington, and I honestly tried to be as conciliatory as possible. I told him the simple truth, that Patty had not wanted him at the ceremony.

"Jesus, what am I, a piece of shit?" he demanded to know. "Jesus, didn't he trust me? It's about the broad, isn't it, George?" he fumed. "For Chrisssake, I've known about the redhead forever. I should have been there, George. I'm the captain. I should have been there."

I told him we hadn't wanted to bother him down at the shore, making him come all the way back up; and I told him how things had been put together at the last minute. But I could see he was still fuming.

I also noticed a subtle difference in our conversation. Ever since I got out of jail, Scoops had been the made guy and I was not. So I always had to watch not only what I said to him but how I said it. Then he became captain, and although I was with Patty directly, he had been on the run, so I had to deal with Scoops. Now, however, for the first time, I was speaking to Scoops as a complete equal. Not only was I straightened out, but I was also a captain. Our relationship was changed forever; he knew it and I knew it. I still tried to be deferential to pacify him, and he knew I was going out of my way to be polite. The bottom line was that we both knew from that point on I didn't have to be deferential to him ever again. But from his tone and his manner, it was apparent that Scoops was not ready to accept me as an equal.

My final words to him were "Scoops, I had no say in whether you were at the ceremony or not. It wasn't my call. Take it up with Cousin Anthony. You know I'm going on vacation. I'll be back in two weeks. We can straighten all this out then."

After I left Scoops, I went back to the hospital for an hour. Patty was very weak. He seemed only mildly interested in my conversation with Scoops. "Don't worry about him, he ain't worth it," Patty said. "When I get out of here and get my strength back, I'll deal with him."

I reminded Patty once again that I was going on vacation, and again I offered to stay if he didn't want me to leave. But he insisted he would be fine with a little rest, and he told me to have a good time.

From the hospital I went back to the club to hang awhile. A bunch of guys came by to congratulate me. Then Nicky Jr. came in. He said he had been talking with his father, and his father had sent along his congratulations, not only about being straightened out but about becoming a captain.

"I talked with my father, George, and we agree," Nicky Jr. said. "I'm going to be with you, and so will a bunch of the other guys." What he was saying was that it wasn't just going to be the new guys I would be in charge of. He was going to become a member of my crew, and so were some of the others, most of them now reporting to Scoops. This was more trouble, I thought.

That night Billy and the relocation experts came over to the apartment to talk with Ann and me. We were leaving the next day, but I had been so busy I hadn't really thought about it. And then with all this new stuff coming up in the last few days, my mind was still swirling with the possibilities. In any event, I would be returning for at least a while. But Ann would likely be leaving New Jersey for good, and I could tell she was both excited and apprehensive.

We talked about others who had successfully relocated and how they and the state would always be there to help us if we needed it. They talked a lot about practical stuff—money, school transcripts, furniture movers. Several state troopers were going with us, both for security reasons and to help the kids get into their new schools. They would stay with us the entire two weeks.

Very early the next morning we left for the airport and the start of our "vacation." If someone had noticed, he might have wondered

about the amount of stuff we were taking for just two weeks. Ann
and the kids went in a van with the luggage. Billy and I had a bit of
unfinished business we decided might be accomplished in the final
hour before the plane left. With Billy watching me from a safe distance, I went to see a guy who worked in the Essex County sheriff's
office and was close to the same judge who in 1983 had given me
immediate work release instead of jail time on my gambling conviction. We had been trying for months to figure a way into the judge,
to find something that we could use to try to bribe him for. It had
finally come to us.

Actually, the story I ended up telling this guy was mostly the
truth. I told him Patty was back in the country and dying of cancer,
and that he wanted to live out his last days with his family in New
Jersey. Because he was still under indictment, the only way that
could happen was for him to give himself up and then for a judge to
grant him bail. But since he had previously fled, no judge I knew
was likely to give him bail. So what I wanted was for the judge to
grant bail immediately to Patty, and I told the go-between that I
was ready to pay dearly for the favor. I assured him there was no
way Patty was going to flee, he was too sick; and I assured him that
no way was Patty ever going to live long enough to stand trial. It
was simply a well-paid favor for a dying man, a man the judge had
known and liked for years.

Actually, I believe the judge would have been happy to do this for
Patty for no money. But we wanted to get him for accepting a bribe,
so that was the way I had put it to the go-between. It was hoped that
on this morning he would name his price and maybe even take the
payoff.

It was not to be. So I told the go-between I would see him when I
got back from a vacation I was leaving on.

Billy and I got to the airport just in time to make the flight, one of
several connections we made that day to eliminate any attempt to
trace where we were going. The kids were so excited about flying,
they could hardly sit still. And I don't think Ann and I could believe
this was finally really happening—a new name, a new town, a new
life.

13

SAYING GOOD-BYE

One of my all-time favorite movies is *My Blue Heaven* with Steve Martin. Martin plays a typical eastern wiseguy who has been sucked up off the streets of New York into the federal Witness Protection Program and overnight finds himself dropped into some faceless suburbia. The movie is meant to be a broad farce, so I'm sure that neither Martin nor the movie's writers realized how very close to the truth some of the scenes are. For instance, there is one scene in which Martin, in a nice three-piece sharkskin suit, is out mowing his new lawn—which was something he had never seen before.

The same thing happened to me. On the Saturday morning after we arrived, I was standing outside our new house contemplating our new front lawn. I was a city boy. I had lived my whole life in apartments and two-family flats in and around Newark. Given the air quality, grass probably can't even grow there. So here I was looking at this seemingly endless patch of green, thinking, What do I know about lawn care? I did know that you don't wear a coat and tie to mow a lawn, but not much more. A stranger in a strange land, was I going to hire a lawn service or get in the car and drive to Sears to buy a mower?

We had arrived at our new location on Wednesday and had gone to a hotel to stay for what we thought would be about two weeks. In that time we had to buy furniture for the new house and have it delivered, buy a car and get it licensed, and enroll the kids in school. Then, Ann and I had decided, I would end my "vacation" and go back to Newark to continue the work as long as it was doing us good. I told Ann it would take a month or two at the outside, but I knew I was going to be pressured to stay perhaps six months to see who else we could pick up in our ever-expanding net. I felt I would just have to play things out and see where they would lead.

So there I was talking myself into hiring a lawn service because I couldn't bring myself even to contemplate mowing a lawn when my satellite beeper went off. I looked down and saw it was a 201 area code number I didn't recognize. The call turned out to be the worst possible news. It was from Nicky Oliveri, and the return number was a pay phone at Clara Maas Hospital in Bloomfield, where Pat had been transferred the day before to be near his family. Pat was dead.

I had last talked with him two days earlier. Nicky O had paged me, and I called him back at a pay phone right outside Pat's room at Westchester Square Hospital. "Our friend ain't doing so good, and he wants to talk with you," Nicky had said. So I called Patty back immediately on his room phone. I now realize that he knew he was dying and wanted to say good-bye. But at the time he only seemed to want to bust my chops.

"You having a good time on that vacation?" he inquired rather sarcastically. "You know you're never going to see me again."

"What do you mean?" I said.

"I'm not going to be here when you return. I know it. It's my time."

I said I would fly back immediately, but then Patty switched the tone in his voice and laughed it off. "Nah, nah, don't bother yourself. . . . I'll see you when you get back."

I begged him to allow Nicky O to tell his wife, Lee, where he was and what shape he was in, so she and his kids could come and be with him. But he said no. If they came, that would mean Anna Marie couldn't, and he didn't want that. I told him it just wasn't right, but he could be stubborn. "Say a prayer that I'll still be here when you get back in two weeks," Patty said. "But George, if I'm not here when you get back, just remember I love you." It was the last thing he said to me before he hung up.

I should have gone. I should have been on the next plane. I knew Pat was very sick, but it was less than three months since he had first been diagnosed with cancer, and who dies that quickly? Even though I thought he was only being melodramatic, if I had really been on vacation, I would have flown back. But I had only two weeks to attend to a thousand details. In a way, they were among the most important two weeks of my life, and I felt I couldn't leave Ann in the lurch.

Still, I should have been at Patty's side. If I didn't know it after my talk with him on Thursday, I sure should have known it after I got another page from Nicky O on Friday morning. He told me that Patty was slipping in and out of a coma and was sinking. He said we had to tell Lee and that we should move him to a hospital in New Jersey so he would be near his family. I agreed, and Nicky said he would take care of moving him to Clara Maas.

When I hung up, it was clear how bleak the picture was. I started to think that maybe I could get a plane to Jersey on Sunday or Monday, which I thought would be time enough. I was still sure that as tough as he was, Pat would last at least another week or so.

But the next morning, as I stood in my new living room surrounded by unpacked boxes, listening to Nicky O tell me Patty was gone, all I could feel was numb. It made little difference that Nicky said Patty had never come out of the coma and wouldn't have known if I was there or not. I should have been there. I belonged there. I loved Patty. He had been the most important man in my life.

I knew I had to call Anna Marie. No one else would. I wasn't sure if she even knew that Patty had gone into the hospital. I reached her at the beauty shop where she was working and knew instantly from the tone of her voice when she answered the phone that she didn't know. "He's gone" was all I could think to say. She was devastated by the news. She had loved Patty and had stayed by him for years. Now she was going to be alone.

Rushing back for the wake and funeral was not a simple matter. As far as Nicky Jr., Nicky O, and the rest of the guys were concerned, I was on vacation with the family in Virginia Beach. Given that I was not in Virginia, the logistics were complicated—and almost immediately became a lot more complicated. As I was talking with Billy about how I could get back, my pager went off again. It was Nicky Jr., who wanted to express his and his father's condolences and insisted, absolutely insisted, out of respect for Pat and for me, that he personally pick me up at the airport. My saying no would have been a sign of tremendous disrespect. But how could I let him pick me up? After all, I was supposed to be coming in from Virginia. How to explain I was arriving on a flight from somewhere else?

I thought about telling him just to meet me at the curb, but with

Nicky, and a lot of these guys, meeting someone at the airport meant going all the way to the gate. I couldn't let him do that, obviously, nor could I let him take me home, because while my old furniture was still there, the apartment was in shambles. All the family clothing, our kids' toys, our personal stuff, and even the pictures on the walls were gone. Saying that we were getting ready to repaint just wouldn't cut it anymore. So I had to find some way of dissuading Nicky from meeting me at the airport. In the end I did quite a song and dance about having to fly standby in order to get back quickly. I told him I didn't know exactly what flight I could catch, and maybe I would even have to backtrack and make a connection through Atlanta or somewhere. In the end he bought it, thank goodness, and accepted my promise to call and go to see him the minute I got in.

When I arrived, I took a cab from the airport to my sister-in-law's house where there was a set of keys for my car and house. I called Slicker as soon as I got home, and he told me I should come over right away because there was a problem with Patty's family. I stopped by Nicky Oliveri's and picked him up and then headed over to Slicker's. Nicky Jr. was there, as were Scoops and Turk. The first thing Slicker said to me was that Lee and Patty's son Frankie were livid and very bitter because they hadn't known he was dying. They didn't even know he was back in town from Florida. Slicker said the family was blaming me, and Frankie didn't want me to come to the wake or the funeral. He had always been very jealous of me. I think Frankie thought his father should have been grooming him to come into the business, not me. I knew that it had really angered him when he and his mother had to take money from me while Patty was in Italy. I knew it made Frankie even angrier that I knew where his father was and he didn't. But that was the way Patty wanted it. I had nothing against Frankie. He was Patty's son, and I respected him. But he was not the kind of kid who would have been a success at our thing. Patty knew that, and I respected his judgment. So Frankie grew up hating me.

Slicker went over to see the family and got the problem smoothed over. We helped Lee and Frankie with the funeral arrangements, which actually were made as much to accommodate our family as Patty's. The wake had to be at least two full days because when a high-level mob member dies, his funeral becomes an important social—and even business—occasion. He must be waked long enough so that members of other families can come and pay their respects, not only to the widow and his actual family but also to our family. It was a ritual that was closely observed, and for certain people, not to come would have been considered a major affront to the Bruno-Scarfo family—in fact, almost a blood insult. So Pat had to be waked both Monday and Tuesday, and we had to choose a funeral home that would understand our special needs. Out of respect to Pat and his status as underboss, it had to be a place that was properly impressive. It also had to have enough space, including some private rooms, so that not only could respects be paid but a little business could be conducted quietly between men who perhaps didn't see one another all that often.

But even as we were trying to make the arrangements and Slicker was smoothing over the problem I was having with Frankie, Scoops picked up right where he left off with me the previous Tuesday. He was all over me. It was obvious he was still angry that they had held the initiation ceremony without first telling him. It was also clear, reading between the lines, that he was even angrier that Cousin Anthony and Pat had made me a captain and thus equal to him. He asked me a couple of times if I thought Cousin Anthony and Nicky Sr. would make him the new underboss. Even though he had been sitting there all day with Nicky Jr., he was afraid to ask the Kid if he had talked with his father about it. So he wanted me to ask Nicky Jr. if he had called his father. Had I talked with Tony Buck about the situation, he demanded to know. Didn't I think he should be the underboss? Would it happen quickly? Would I act as his capo?

Over and over he kept coming back to the point he had made on Tuesday, that Pat should not have held the ceremony without his being there. It was an insult, he said, it made him angry. "It wasn't right, me not being there," he whined. "At least Pat should have called and told me, or you should have told me before." Then he went on about Cousin Anthony making me a captain immediately and putting the other guys who had been made with me under my control. "Cousin Anthony should have let me know. Patty should have let me know. This just isn't right."

But most of all he was all over me about Cousin Anthony not circulating a "list." One of the major rules of protocol within the five New York families was that whenever one family was about to make a guy, his name was circulated among the other families to see if any of them had a beef with the guy. Once a guy was a made member of a family, it became a really big deal if another family had a problem with him. There was really no easy way to deal with that kind of situation, so it was better to make sure before it happened, before a guy was made, that none of the other families had a beef with him. And since most initiations were of more than one guy at a time, it was usually necessary to circulate several names at once. That was what Scoops meant by circulating a list.

The fact was that even though we operated in northern Jersey, the Bruno-Scarfo family was not a New York family, and we were under no obligation to circulate a list before a ceremony. In the past, as a courtesy—especially if the guy was very active with New York family members in business—we would circulate his name. But we were not obligated to. I guess technically, given what I was doing and who I was doing it with, my name probably should have been circulated. But there had not been enough time. We had to hold the ceremony before Patty's death. Pat and Cousin Anthony had talked about it, and Anthony had said it was no problem. And it wasn't; but to hear Scoops talk, you would have thought the breach in protocol had been immense. He kept saying, "Don't worry, George. We can get it made right. We'll circulate your name now, and I'm sure no guy has any problem with you."

Even though there had been no breach of protocol, circulating a list after a ceremony was asking for trouble. If anyone got it in his mind that the ceremony hadn't been right, now you were talking about a major breach. And if a list circulated with my name on it and some made guy in another family raised an objection, maybe because I had beat him out of some money in a card game, then the breach would have been huge. I could not simply be unmade. Once you're made, you can be unmade only one way; by being put into the ground. They would have had to kill me, and do it very quickly. So what Scoops was playing with was nothing less than a potential death warrant with my name on it.

When Scoops and I talked on that Sunday night at Slicker's, I kind of gave him the benefit of the doubt. Actually, I was thinking about Pat, how much I missed him already and how difficult the next few days was going to be. I wasn't thinking clearly. I thought that Scoops was hurt and only being a little stupid, so I just told him to cool it, that we would get the whole thing straightened out after the funeral.

But a conversation I had with Nicky O later that evening changed my thinking abruptly. "Scoops is making a problem for us," he said, getting my attention instantly. "He reached out for Cousin Anthony while you were in Virginia to bitch about you being made captain without him being told, and to complain about not being told about the ceremony. Since then he's been telling everyone about there being no list and what a problem it is."

That was all it took to bring me out of my fog. With absolute clarity I realized I was in big trouble. My first thought was whether Beeps, Turk, or Slicker told Scoops that Cousin Anthony had said I would take over as underboss when Patty died. And, for that matter, if Scoops and Cousin Anthony did speak, did Anthony himself tell him? I thought the answer was no on both counts, but I couldn't be sure. Anthony had said to keep it quiet, and certainly Beeps and Turk would not have risked angering him. Slicker might be upset that I was possibly going to be elevated over him also, but there was nothing in what he was saying or the way he was acting to make me believe he had given it a thought. And I couldn't believe that Anthony would tell us to keep it quiet and then say something to Scoops while Pat was still alive. No, my best estimate was that Scoops was guessing he was going to be pushed out. I knew Scoops was sure that Cousin Anthony didn't like him, and there was certainly some truth to that. Likewise, it was very clear that Anthony liked me a lot— witness his making me a captain immediately after the ceremony. So without actually knowing that Anthony had come out and said it, what Scoops was becoming increasingly paranoid about was the possibility that I would jump over him by taking Patty's position as underboss.

I arrived at Dooley's Funeral Home in Cranford the next afternoon, feeling as odd as I ever had at any point in my life. We were burying a man who might as well have been my own father. I was absolutely heartbroken that he was gone and so angry at myself for not having been there when he died. But at the same time I felt a certain amount of relief that he died never knowing that I had been acting as a government agent and that my work was going to bring down everyone around him. If he had known, he would have hated me and would not have hesitated to have me killed. It would have been a matter of honor. His dying had worked out for the best.

If all that was not enough, here was Scoops, a man I had known since I was seven years old and who now saw me as a rival and an enemy. He was out to either kill me himself or get me iced by one of the other families. Then, to top it all off, I had to be careful since I was again wired, with Billy and Ed in the van on a nearby street, because who knew what might be said in my presence with this many mobsters gathered in one place at the same time?

Even as I was paying my respects to Patty and then enduring an icy reception from Patty's family, I began to hear what was going on. First thing, Slicker came over to me to tell me that Scoops had been buzzing in John Riggi's ear that there was some problem in the way I had been made but he was taking care of it. Then Scoops himself came to tell me all about it. "He's beefing," he said, referring to Riggi. "He says, 'You know about the list. . . . I don't see no list. I want you to get ahold of Tony Buck, and I wanna know who okayed it in New York. I'm not putting you on the spot. You tell Tony Buck to make a meet, and I'll meet him.' And I think that's why he didn't want to meet youse, George. I couldn't do it."

As a newly made member of my crew, I had to be formally introduced to members of other crews, even if I had known them for years. The funeral was the first time after the ceremony that I saw a lot of these guys, so it was to be expected that I would be formally introduced as a made member to dozens of them, including John.

But Scoops went on to tell me not to worry, that Riggi's main beef was with Turk because he drank too much and had a loud mouth, and because he got into a fight with a guy from Riggi's crew. "But don't tell this to the Bird," Scoops warned me, using our nickname for Turk.

Then Scoops said that Riggi had warned him not to introduce any of us yet. "He says, 'Now Joe, I don't wanna meet him. I didn't see no list. And do yourself a favor, don't introduce me to anyone. I'm telling you as a friend.' He says don't introduce him to anybody until we straighten this out. So let's keep it quiet until we get to the bottom of it. . . . What could I say to him, George?"

I told Scoops that so far Slicker had introduced me to one of the Colombo crew, Jimmy Randazzo. Then Scoops said he would introduce me the next night to various people but that tonight we would have to cool it. Not knowing if John Riggi really felt that way, I had to go along with what Scoops was saying.

After we left the funeral home we all went to Tardes Restaurant in Kenilworth for an early dinner because we had to be back at the funeral home by 7:00 P.M. At dinner Scoops started in again about the lack of a list.

I was getting fed up, so I told him what Patty had told me when Scoops first brought up the list business the week before: "I asked Patty about that, and he said, 'George, I've been in this business a long time.' He said don't worry about it. 'If I had to show a list,' he said, 'I would have had a hard time getting Scoops straightened out.'"

Scoops reacted angrily. "My list went in. They all saw my list. I'm telling you, with you guys they didn't see no list, and New York didn't see no list. . . . I just found out New York closed their book after all them guys got straightened out a few months ago. There was nothing that was supposed to have been done."

That remark added yet another dimension to the whole affair. Now Scoops was alleging that the Commission had closed everybody's books on new members, and our ceremony had violated that order. I thought that was simply bullshit, and so did Nicky Oliveri, who had as much at stake in this as I did. "Who was hollering down there, Joe?" Nicky O asked Scoops rather sharply.

It was suspicious that he was rather vague in his response, so again I repeated what Patty had said after I told him Scoops was making a stink about no list. "He says to me, 'George, this is our thing. You don't have to worry about New York.' He says we do what we want. We're Philadelphia. We do what we want."

By the next day I had talked with some people, and it became clear to me that if John Riggi had any problem with the ceremony, it was only because Scoops had raised the issue. So when I arrived at the funeral home, again wearing a wire, I was primed for a showdown with him. But before I could say anything, he rushed over, grabbed me, and said to "come meet some important guys from the Gambino crew."

It was weird. For a moment I thought Scoops had lost his mind. He was acting as if he was doing me a big favor introducing me to these guys, most of whom I had known for years. Standing in the group were both Blackie Luciano and Joe Rackets. Then, considering all the bullshit that had been going down over this list business, I was shocked when Scoops said, "I want you to meet George Fresolone, *amico nostro.*" Okay, I thought, he was coming to his senses and beginning to introduce me around formally. But then as I listened in growing disbelief, Scoops said to these guys something as extraordinary as anything I had ever heard in the mob.

"We are acknowledging George, but you guys don't have to acknowledge him or any of our new members if you do not want to," Scoops told them. "We have a few problems. But we'll make it right, don't worry."

Then even more amazingly, Scoops turned to me and said in front of these Gambino guys, "I talked with John Riggi, and you know how much he likes you. He says he'll talk with John Gotti, and they'll pass a list around to the other families and they'll take care of it."

We made small talk with these guys for a few minutes, but they were passing one another some strange looks, not knowing quite how to respond to what Scoops had told them. So as soon as I could properly walk away, I grabbed Scoops and all but shoved him out of the room. We went outside the funeral home, him and me and Slicker and Nicky Oliveri. I was now a made member, and like Scoops, I was a captain. I was his mob equal. Up until then I always had to bite my tongue when I talked with him. Now for the first time in a very long time I could talk to him as an equal, and a lot of what I had been holding back came rushing out.

"Joey, have you got a problem with me?" I yelled at him, the anger clear in my voice. "You have got to stop this crap about any list. If I could, I would pull Pat from that box for thirty seconds, and he would set you straight. He would tell you we don't need no list. He would tell you that Tony Buck said that, and he would tell you that if we had needed to circulate lists, you would never have been made because I know that Joe Bayonne had a beef against you when you were made."

Scoops was a little shocked that I knew at the time he was made some in the other families thought that he was a snitch. Pat had told me the whole story. He kind of stammered and then tried to look hurt. "No, no, you don't understand, George. I'm just trying to do you a favor, to get this thing resolved."

"There's nothing to resolve," I shouted. "Stop talking about this crap. The way you're running your mouth could get all five of us killed."

But he didn't stop. That night and then the following morning at the funeral, several guys from different crews mentioned that Scoops had said one thing or another to them or that they had heard about it from someone else in their crew. Most wanted to know what was going on. I laughed it off, but I knew it was no laughing matter. Scoops had been around for a long time. He was far from stupid. He knew exactly what he was doing. My lifelong friend had turned on me. He had become my blood enemy. Quite simply, Scoops was building a case against me. He was setting me up to be killed. And if things kept going the way they were, he was going to succeed.

It was ironic. I had spent a year wearing a wire. On any one day, one slip and I would have been dead. Here I was near the end of the whole thing—Ann and the kids were already safe, and we were just going to wind up some loose ends, maybe get John Gotti and a few others—but now I was more scared than I had ever been. I was not going to be killed because I had become a government agent. Rather, I was going to be killed for the oldest reason in the mob: because some wiseguy saw me as a threat to his power, and there was only one way in the mob to deal with such a threat. So as I watched Patty being lowered into the ground, I was absolutely sure I would be joining him very soon unless I did something about it—and did it very quickly.

I was worried; in fact, I was scared stiff. But Ed and Bill—hell, the whole New Jersey State Police and Attorney General's Office—were positively ecstatic at what had happened over the past two weeks. They had this vision: the underboss of the Bruno-Scarfo family, who was actually their agent, wearing a radio transmitter as he went about on his daily rounds. It would be as high a penetration of organized crime as had ever happened. Think of it—I'm sure they were saying to one another—we can bring down half the major wiseguys in the two-state area. The Feds will kill to get their hands on our tapes. We'll be owed so many IOUs by so many law enforcement agencies that we'll be golden for years. They didn't say all this out loud, of course, but it was clearly in their eyes when we met the morning after Patty's funeral.

It was assumed that I would return to "Virginia Beach" to resume my "vacation." Then, as planned, once Ann and the kids were settled in the new house, I would return for another month or two to see how much more could be accomplished. But this thing with Scoops made that plan virtually impossible. There was no way I was going to let Scoops run around like a loose cannon while I was out of town. If I had done that, it wasn't impossible that the first thing I would see on my return was a bullet. Scoops seemed to be a man on a crusade.

Some of the state police's top brass, and some on the Attorney General's staff, thought maybe I could get Cousin Anthony to talk to Scoops and call him off. But I knew better, and so did Billy and Ed. They were beginning to hear from their other sources that Scoops was having a problem with someone and that someone was likely going to be whacked. The problem was not the way the ceremony had been conducted or whether or not a list had been properly circulated. The problem was that I was now a threat to Scoops, and he knew or at least suspected that unless he acted quickly, he would end up seeing me as the underboss and be reporting to me.

Cousin Anthony could not convince him I wasn't a threat because Anthony, I'm sure, wanted to play me off against Scoops. And since

I was supposed to be the young mobster on the make, there was no way I would go to Cousin Anthony and ask him to make peace between us. If this played out the way it seemed, I would be expected to go to Anthony not to ask him to make peace but for permission to whack Scoops. To do otherwise would be to lose too much stature in his eyes. I knew this, and so did those on the team who knew how the mob really worked. There was no simple solution to this problem.

There were only two ways it could be dealt with: We would have to end Broadsword and I would drop out of sight, or else I would have to arrange for Scoops to be killed. There are certain situations in mob life where you are given only the option to kill or be killed. It was clear to me that this was one of those situations. As I saw it, killing Scoops or waiting to be killed were the only options he was giving me. And at that point I hated him enough for what he had done to my family, to Pat and Pat's family, to kill him.

But I have to admit I was of two minds. On the one hand, I was really tired of all this. The strain of wearing a wire day after day knowing one mistake would be my last, or that at any time the mole who was somewhere in the investigatory network would learn my identity, was beginning to wear on me. I wanted to put an end to it all and get started with my new life. But on the other hand, at that moment I never hated these guys or the life more. Patty's funeral had turned into one of the mob events of the year. Hundreds of wiseguys showed up. And there were all sorts of crocodile tears from guys in our own crew. It made me furious. I remembered vividly the days when Patty was on the lam in South America and Italy, and the only support he and his wife and kids got was what I could earn. None of these guys had been willing to fork over a dime or lift a finger to help. Now here they were making a big public show about how much they mourned his passing. It made me want more than ever to take every one of them down.

Early on the day Patty was buried, I told Billy and Ed to inform the brass from the state police and the Attorney General's Office point-blank that I was ready to continue. But before I could consider spending even a week more doing this, I had to resolve the situation with Scoops. "Either you let me take care of my problem," I said very bluntly, "or we pull the plug and I never return from my vacation."

Deep down I knew I wasn't really giving them a choice. Just as they would have been unable to stand by and watch me kill Joey Merlino, they couldn't sanction my killing Scoops. Whatever the possible good it might eventually bring, the New Jersey State Police could not condone premeditated murder. But I left the choice up to them. If they wanted me to continue, they would have to let me handle Scoops. I would talk with Cousin Anthony and deal with it. I would then continue my work with the state for some period. But if they were unwilling to sanction my killing Scoops, then I would stay permanently on vacation.

After the burial, Scoops and I took what must have been fifty or sixty guys over to Michelangelo's Restaurant for a long boozy lunch that ended up costing us $1,500 each. About an hour into the lunch I got beeped. It was Ed. He and Billy were down the block in a supermarket. I excused myself and met them there. I gave them my transmitter. If I returned from my vacation to continue working with them, I would get it back again. But even though the final decision had not been made from on high, I think the three of us knew this was the end.

After the lunch, which ended about dinner time, Dente, Beeps, Turk, and I went over to the Holiday Inn in Elizabeth, where I was going to spend the night before going back to "Virginia." We started to drink, and for the first time in more than a year, I almost drank myself unconscious. When I said good-bye to the three of them, it was with more than a little sadness and emotion, which I tried not to show. I actually started to cry, and I guess they thought it was because I was drunk and had just buried Patty. But I knew I would likely never see the three of them again and that they would all probably be arrested before the week was out. I was leaving for a new life, and they would be leaving for jail. For just a minute I had some doubts and some regrets. But I chalked that up to all the martinis. I can't remember being as hung over as I was the next morning when I dragged myself onto that airplane.

When I arrived at my destination, as I expected, the call came from Ed almost at once. The brass had talked it over and had come to the conclusion that I was right. If I was to continue, and they wanted me to, I would have to deal with Scoops. But there was no way they could sanction that. They could not simply turn a blind eye. So there was really only one answer—my vacation would become permanent. Operation Broadsword was officially ended.

I felt good, really good, about what I had accomplished. I remembered that Toms River motel room a year earlier when I had told Billy and Ed what I planned. I had done exactly what I said I would do, and much more. I had recorded a ceremony, I had gotten not one but two bosses, and I had gathered more than enough information to shut down Grayhound, Scoops, and all the rest of the guys who had left Patty and my family high and dry when we needed help. I knew Billy, Ed, and Charley had believed in me from the start. I also knew everyone above them had believed at least initially that I was just some putz looking to make a deal. But I had delivered. I was leaving with my head high. If there was precious little honor left in organized crime, I felt that over the past year I had regained mine.

EPILOGUE

A NEW LIFE

Almost immediately after telling me they were pulling the plug on Broadsword, Ed, Bill and their bosses in both the state police and the Attorney General's Office began to worry. They knew that my "vacation" story wouldn't hold up for very long. Within a couple of weeks, if I wasn't back, I would surely be missed. Their worry was that once this happened, Scoops, Cousin Anthony, and the rest might start putting two and two together, figure out that I had flipped, then panic and run. So the Attorney General moved immediately to get what amounted to temporary indictments so that arrest warrants could be obtained for all those who would likely be indicted based on my tapes.

On Tuesday, August 21, 1990, not quite three weeks after Patty was buried and I left saying I was resuming my holiday, a hundred and fifty state police officers along with fifteen investigators from the Attorney General's Office fanned out across central and northern New Jersey and began making arrests.

By the time Attorney General Robert Del Tufo and State Police Superintendent Justin Dintino met with reporters in Trenton late on the morning of the 21st, thirty-one individuals had been arrested and brought before Superior Court Judge Michael Degnan for arraignment. Eight others could not be found that morning and were arrested later. Another two were not arrested but given summonses because the charges against them were not class one felonies.

Among those arrested in the initial sweep were Scoops, Nicky Jr., John Riggi, Cousin Anthony, Slicker, Dente, John Mavilla, Nicky O, Beepsie, John Praino (who was arrested in New York), Joey Sodano, Gene Wilson, Bobby Spags, Michael and Ralph Perna, Jimmy Randazzo, Dom Prosperi, Carmen Ricci and the others at Grayhound,

Brian Petaccio and Alan Cifelli. Besides Bruno-Scarfo guys, those arrested included members of the Gambino, Genovese, Colombo, Lucchese, and DeCavalcante families.

When Del Tufo and Dintino met the press they were ecstatic. "I believe this represents the final nail in the coffin of the Nicodemo Scarfo crime family," Dintino said. "Operation Broadsword is the deepest penetration of organized crime in New Jersey history," Del Tufo said. In a separate press conference Captain Joseph O'Connor, head of the Philadelphia Police Department's Intelligence Division, called the arrests "a dream come true." Who, he asked, "could ever have believed that such a thing would happen?"

The story made the front pages of *The New York Times, The Philadelphia Inquirer,* and every paper in New Jersey. At first the state only gave out sketchy information about my role in Broadsword. I was identified as a "career gambler who had spent a term in prison," and as a "close associate" of "mob boss Pasquale 'Patty Specs' Martirano," but little more was said about me. So in the days that followed there was some intense speculation about who I was, what I had done, and why I had done it. As bit by bit the state revealed how Broadsword had come about and the unique part I had played in it, I became the subject of dozens of newspaper and television profiles.

Without doubt my personal favorite was written by George Anastasia of *The Philadelphia Inquirer,* who for my money is the best organized-crime reporter in the country today. The headline was "Little League Coach at Night, Mobster by Day." I had for several seasons coached my son's Little League team and the story went on to include quotes from many of the parents of other boys on the team about what a "regular guy" I had been, and what a good coach. I guess I liked that story so much because it made me seem human, not some being from outer space, the way most stories portray anyone in the mob.

When my former colleagues learned what I had done, they reacted in ways both comical and sinister.

Late in 1992, the Somerset County Police raided a clubhouse at Chestnut and Adams Streets in Newark, where a new monte game was taking place. To their surprise, they found on the wall a beautifully engraved plaque that read as follows:

GEORGE FRESOLONE
THE BIGGEST MOTHER-FUCKING RAT
IN NEW JERSEY HISTORY AND
THE OTHER 49 STATES

They removed the plaque as "evidence" and turned it over to Billy and Ed. When they are done with it, they are going to give it to me as a souvenir. I can't exactly hang it in the family room, but I'll find someplace private where I can put it up.

That was amusing, but other reactions were not funny at all. Within weeks of the word getting out that I was the cause of all these indictments, intelligence units of the state police, several local police forces in Jersey, New York City, Philadelphia, as well as the FBI, learned I was the target of at least three different contracts. There was now a substantial price on my head.

Predictably, the first came out of Marion and was issued by Nicky Sr. According to what the Feds, the Philadelphia police, and the New Jersey State Police all learned independently, Nicky was way beyond angry. Maybe it was because I had gotten so close to his son, and that Nicky Jr. had also been arrested. Or maybe it was because he had given permission for me to be straightened out and immediately be made a captain and put in line to become underboss when Patty died. My flipping made him look like a fool. More important, in the mob world it made him look weak. If he had any hope of holding on to the family and continuing to run it out of his cell, or even of having a say in who the permanent new boss was to be, it would pretty much go by the boards once it became known what I had done.

Probably Nicky's only hope of regaining some measure of respect was to have me killed quickly. Now if there was one thing Nicky was notorious for, it was being cheap. In the bad old days, he used to put out $5,000 and $10,000 contracts on guys, and he had numerous takers. But now he was said to be offering $100,000 to anyone who could find me and kill me quickly. That's how badly he wanted me. And for that kind of money, I was sure a lot of guys were out looking.

The second contract was reportedly put out by John Riggi, the boss of the DeCavalcante family. I heard that John had really been stunned when he learned it was me who had flipped. After all, he had known me since I was a kid. At the time we rolled up Broadsword, John was already in deep trouble with the Feds. From what I heard, their case against him was weak, and so he had some hope of making a deal with them—perhaps even getting away with no jail time, just probation. But the Broadsword indictment killed that chance. The Feds could now roll up the New Jersey indictment into their own, or use it at sentencing. John was going to go away for a long time and he was furious. So he put out a contract on me for a substantial amount.

The third contract was probably the most serious. It came out of New York City, and was issued by the Gambinos. Reportedly, John Gotti was pissed that a number of his guys had been indicted as a result of what I had done, and was also very angry at the number of mob guys who were starting to inform or to work with the cops. He supposedly wanted to set me up as an example of what happens to snitches.

This contract was taken so seriously by both New Jersey officials and the Feds, that New Jersey Deputy Attorney General John R. Corson filed an affidavit stating that "La Cosa Nostra has targeted Mr. Fresolone for murder because of his cooperation and pending testimony." Corson did so because in a related case a defense attorney was demanding that the state present me to be deposed and then cross-examined. The State of New Jersey refused, saying that it was simply too dangerous for me to appear in court at that time under any circumstances.

Since that day I have been back in New Jersey maybe a dozen times to appear before investigative committees, grand juries, to prepare to testify, or to be ready to go into court. As one of my bodyguards noted one time, when I am in the state, I am accorded about the same level of protection Vice President Gore might be given when he visits. I arrive by different modes of transportation, sometimes planes, sometimes trains, and once by bus. I never arrive and leave the same way. I am driven in an unmarked state police car, with at least a half dozen bodyguards in flanking cars. I stay in safehouses guarded around the clock, and I am transported to the court or grand jury in bulletproof cars with a dozen or more guards. So far nothing has happened, knock on wood.

I knew that my life would be at risk from the moment I agreed to work on Broadsword. I accepted that risk and I still do. Despite the low regard I held most of those guys in, it did not occur to me that they would try to go after my family. But as the FBI has learned, that was almost what happened.

Recently the Feds turned Tommy Ricciardi, and he was debriefed by Dennis Marchalonis, the special agent in charge of the organized crime unit in the Newark FBI Office. Tommy told Marchalonis that in October 1990, about two months after we shut down Broadsword, he had been approached by Michael Perna to kill my brother. Ricciardi said that Perna told him, "I and Scoops are going to whack Fresolone's brother. We have to teach rats that they can't leave their families behind."

Tommy told Marchalonis that Perna wanted him to take part in the hit, but instead he met with Perna and Scoops and talked them out of it, because my brother not only had never done anything to hurt any of those guys, but he was not even involved with the Bruno-Scarfo family in any way. I'm glad Tommy recognized that even today you shouldn't kill civilians no matter what. And I am thankful to him that he apparently persuaded Scoops and Perna. I'm also thankful that I never got him on tape, so there was no evidence to indict him in Broadsword. If I had, maybe he would not have been so quick to go to my brother's defense. I owe him one, and I hope that someday I can do something to pay him back.

Through the years I have seen guys do incredibly stupid things, but nothing comes even close to equaling what happened on the night of February 3, 1992.

Patty had one of the largest funerals I can remember. For two and a half days, hundreds of people passed his open coffin. Admittedly he had died of cancer, and certainly did not look his best—or how I would like to remember him—but it had to be absolutely clear to anyone who knew him that it was Patty in the coffin. Even so, about eighteen months after we ended Broadsword, and just as the first trials of various defendants were about to begin, rumors started to circulate around Jersey that Patty was still alive, that he had flipped, and was going to testify against guys.

Unbelievably, some guys apparently decided to find out for themselves. On the night of February 3, they entered Ocean County Memorial Park and broke into the mausoleum containing Patty's crypt. Then they broke through an outside marble door and an inside door sealed with silicone and fastened with a kind of bolt system that needs a special wrench to open.

They pulled Patty's coffin down from a twelve-foot-high level, and then started to drag it across the cemetery. But something must have happened. Either the coffin was too heavy, or something spooked them. In any event, they left the coffin on its side, with Patty's remains half hanging out. Missing from the body was the lower jaw. Apparently, they took that to compare to Patty's dental records.

When I heard the news I was sick at heart. They couldn't even let Patty rest in peace.

As things turned out, I was at least indirectly responsible for the most vicious mob war to break out in the U.S. since Nicky Sr. went on his killing spree in the early 1980s.

My flipping put the final nail in Nicky Sr.'s coffin, at least as far as the Commission was concerned. Before he was arrested and indicted for crimes he committed during Broadsword, Nicky had at least a glimmer of hope that he would some day emerge from his cell at Marion. And as long as it was possible that he would return, the Commission allowed him to continue running things through Cousin Anthony. But the fact that he committed his Broadsword crimes from that jail cell ended all hope that he would ever see the light of day. Nicky was in for life, and his error of judgment in trusting me —and Nicky Jr.'s also—meant that neither would ever head the family. So for the third time since Angelo Bruno was whacked in 1980, the leadership in the family was up for grabs and, as they had the last two times, the Gambinos stepped in.

Once again John Gotti dictated who the new boss of the Bruno-Scarfo family would be. This time they reached down into the family in Philadelphia and effectively picked one of their own—John Stanfa.

Stanfa had been born in Italy in the same village as Carlo Gambino, and he was initiated into the Mafia back in the old country. He had fled to this country to a place with the Gambinos in Brooklyn, before moving to live with a cousin in Philly. He had been admitted to our family at the request of the Gambinos, and for that reason— and the fact he was driving Bruno the night he was whacked—he was never really trusted by many of the old-time guys. After the Bruno killing, Stanfa had dropped out of sight for some time; rumor had him hiding in Brooklyn. Then he had served a short bid in jail for lying to a federal grand jury investigating Angelo's murder. And then he had gone back to Sicily to let things cool down before coming back to Philly. When he was suddenly presented as the new boss of the Bruno-Scarfo family, the old distrust and resentment boiled over.

Two different groups were angered by the Gambinos putting Stanfa in charge. One group was what remained of the old-timers, the guys who had stood with Angelo Bruno. The other was what the press came to call "the young turks," mostly the sons of guys who had been around Angelo. Many of their fathers had been killed by Nicky Sr. in the early 1980s, and now they thought it was their time to take over.

Stanfa was no dummy. To his credit, he tried to make peace within the family by reaching out to both groups. To reach the old guard, he chose Felix Bocchino, who was seventy-three. Felix was an interesting guy. He had been around Angelo, but was reportedly angered by Angelo's letting the New York families into Atlantic City. I know he was also close to Tony Bananas, and many in the family believed that Felix was involved in the hit on Angelo. Once Nicky Sr. took over, Felix sort of disappeared into the background. He still controlled the streets in parts of South Philly, but he kept such a low profile that he was all but forgotten.

On the morning of January 29, 1992, Felix got into his 1977 Buick about half a block from the apartment he shared with his daughter. Just as he started the car, someone walked up to the driver's side and pumped six shots through the window, killing him instantly.

Immediately after the hit, I talked with a number of guys who were or had been in the family and with whom I was still in touch. They were almost evenly divided over who had done it. Some believed that Felix had a falling out with Stanfa, who wanted a major share of the street tax Felix had long been collecting from drug dealers and bookies in South Philly. Felix, they believed, had been whacked for resisting Stanfa. Others, however, believed that Felix had reached a deal with Stanfa and so he was killed by the younger guys who were opposing the new boss. Pick your theory—either could be valid. But whoever whacked Felix, the killing did have the effect of quieting things down for almost a year.

Stanfa tried to make peace with the young guys through Joey Ciancaglini, Chickie Ciancaglini's son. Chickie was serving a 45-year bid after being found guilty in 1988, and it was he, from prison, who had tried to insist, after Nicky Sr. fell from grace, that it was time for the younger guys, especially his sons. At first both Joey and his brother Michael, as well as his other brother John, who was also in jail, opposed Stanfa. But Stanfa reached out to Joey and made him his underboss. As a result, both Joey and Michael came to terms with Stanfa.

This almost got Michael killed. In March of 1992, two guys wielding shotguns tried to gun him down as he reached his front door after a night on the town. He apparently heard a noise behind him and just managed to dive through the open door ahead of the pellets that ripped into the door and the front of the house. After this try on Michael, cooler heads prevailed, and Joey Ciancaglini was reportedly able to keep the lid on the younger guys by arguing that Stanfa deserved a chance to show what he was going to do for them and for the family.

But the attempt on Michael showed Stanfa he really couldn't much trust anyone in the family, old or young. So he started to import young guys directly from Sicily to restock the family. He figured he would turn to those whose loyalty he knew would be absolute— greaseballs from the old country who would be totally dependent on him for anything. It got to be a joke around Philly that if you went into a pizza joint in South Philly, or in parts of South Jersey, and your waiter couldn't speak much English, he was probably one of Stanfa's new guys.

After quietly consolidating his hold on the family, Stanfa began to assert himself on the streets. First a guy named Rod Colombo, a small-time drug courier who ran cocaine from the West Coast to Philly, was found shot to death. It well could have been the result of a drug deal gone bad, but word on the street was that Colombo had been holding out.

It was more clear why Gee Gee Cappello was whacked a couple of weeks later. A pretty good sized bookie in South Philly, Gee Gee was reportedly resisting paying a new street tax that had been imposed by Stanfa.

Then to show how tough he was, Stanfa moved to try to head off anyone else becoming a snitch. If he could have reached me, I assume he would have moved heaven and earth to have me killed. But I was not available, and stupid old Mario Riccobene was.

Mario had been released from jail in 1984, and because he had turned government witness in exchange for a light sentence, he was placed in the federal Witness Protection Program. He stayed safely in it for eight years, but then he simply got tired of living away from the life he had always known in South Philly. Believing that most of the guys he had ratted on were either dead or in jail, and that the family structure had changed so much, he figured the heat was off and he returned to live with his aging mother in a rural New Jersey county.

But South Philly lured him back. He starting meeting with guys in the hopes he could persuade them to let bygones be bygones. He was not successful. On January 28, 1993, he showed up at a Jersey diner apparently to pick up a guy to go to a meeting. Waiting instead were a couple of shooters. All his life Mario had been a gambler, but that night his luck ran out. According to several eyewitnesses, he was gunned down at 7:11 P.M.

Already the younger guys had apparently had it with Stanfa's new loyal troops from the old country. Around New Year's Day, 1993, someone had tried to kill a guy named Biaggio Adornetto, who worked as a pizza maker in a South Philly restaurant called La Veranda. He was reportedly one of the Sicilian "new guard." According to what I heard, a guy in a mask waving a shotgun approached Adornetto and pulled the trigger point blank. But the gun misfired, and the guy had to flee the scene.

But in early March, the gun worked fine when a masked guy put five slugs into Joey Ciancaglini as he ate lunch in a small luncheonette he owned across the street from Stanfa's food importing business, the place that had become the family's headquarters. This luncheonette, by the way, was the first place of employment for Biaggio Adornetto after he arrived from Sicily.

Amazingly, Joey survived with five bullets in his body, including three in the head. He survived, but not in good shape. Reportedly he has long-term physical and mental problems as a result of the head wounds.

As best I can piece things together, after Joey was shot, things began to get a little crazy in the family. Apparently Stanfa took the Ciancaglini shooting to mean that he was correct in not trusting anyone from the former Bruno-Scarfo family. So he turned almost completely to his new Sicilian imports, and this turned Chickie Ciancaglini against him. As I understand it, Chickie from jail threw his weight behind Joey Merlino, who had become the leader of the younger guys who were opposing Stanfa. Michael Ciancaglini followed his father Chickie's lead and threw in with Skinny Joey, as the younger Merlino was known. Stanfa struck back quickly.

On August 5, Michael Ciancaglini and Skinny Joey Merlino were walking down the street when a bunch of guys jumped out of a car and opened up on them. Michael was killed, but Joey was only wounded. Now the war was really on.

On August 31, Stanfa was being driven down the busy Schuylkill Expressway in his Caddy during morning rush hour when a van pulled up next to it, the side door was flung open, and two guys opened up with automatic weapons. Again, amazingly, no one was killed. The gunmen shot up the car pretty bad, but missed Stanfa completely. They did hit his son Joey, 23, and he was rushed to the hospital in guarded condition. He survived.

Stanfa had moved against Joey Merlino by trying to take over his street tax business in South Philly. Guys representing Stanfa had told the bookies and the drug dealers that from now on they would pay Stanfa and not Skinny Joey. On September 16, two of Stanfa's guys who were shaking down Merlino's "customers"—Yonnie Lanzilotta and Michael Forte—were attacked by Merlino's guys. Lanzilotta was critically wounded and Forte escaped. Actually it was beginning to look like a typical Bruno-Scarfo family war in that neither side could shoot very well.

Two days later the Stanfa guys showed they were the better shots. Frank Baldino, a guy who had sided with Skinny Joey and who I hear was involved in the attempt on Stanfa on the Schuylkill, was gunned down in his car at a major South Philly intersection. The bodies were starting to pile up, and the city fathers decided they had had enough. They announced they were going to roust on sight anyone connected with either side. Several guys who were found carrying weapons were arrested. Then too, any time Stanfa or a half dozen of his key guys ventured outside, they were openly followed by a massive number of cops. That did the trick, and the war came to a quick end.

I wish I could say that I am happy with the way everything turned out, but that wouldn't be true. In the three years following the ending of Broadsword, I spent countless days and weeks poring over tapes and transcripts, getting ready for trials. Ed, Billy, and the others in the state police worked just as hard. I only wish the prosecutors had done the same.

With a few notable exceptions—and here I single out Assistant Attorneys General Charlie Buckley and Dave Brody, who prosecuted Scoops, Cousin Anthony, and the rest of the guys close to Patty—most of the prosecutors who have worked on the various cases have been downright lazy. With the evidence on the tapes, most of the cases we handed them were absolute slam dunks going in. There was almost no way these defendants would risk going to trial. The prosecutors knew this so they just sat back and waited to accept plea bargains. And I must say that most of the deals they ended up accepting were pretty lousy.

This ineptitude and laziness was the most apparent in the way they handled Grayhound and the prosecution of Carmen Ricci. In January of 1991, under incredibly tight security, I traveled back to Jersey to testify before the State Commission on Investigations about the video gambling machine industry. To protect my identity, I testified via a video camera set-up from behind a darkened screen. I told all I knew about how the industry was dominated by organized crime, how the placement of machines and the collection of money worked, and I told at length the story of Grayhound, Carmen Ricci, and the Bruno-Scarfo family.

Partially as a result of my testimony, and mainly on the strength of the extensive recordings I had made involving Grayhound, Attorney General Del Tufo announced a first for the State of New Jersey —a civil forfeiture action was being filed against a publicly owned company. Because of its criminal activities, the state was going to force the liquidation of Grayhound and take control of its sizable assets. In addition, the New Jersey Casino Control Commission barred any casino in the state from doing business with the company.

I wish I could say that is what ended up happening, but the state blew the Grayhound prosecution almost completely. It all started when the prosecution team assigned to the case made a basic judgment: my evidence against Ricci, Alan Cifelli, and Brian Petaccio was so overwhelming that the defendants could not possibly risk going to trial. The prosecutors believed the three would have to plea-bargain, so all the state had to do was wait and accept the best deal possible.

So the prosecutors spent about zero time preparing for trial. Instead they made an "offer" to Ricci. They wanted him to plead guilty to a third-degree felony that carried with it a four-year term—which would mean that he would serve about two years behind bars—and a fine of $2 million. In addition, Ricci would have to agree not to contest the civil forfeiture suit.

Ricci and his defense team thought about it for a while, and came back with a counteroffer. Carmen would agree to plead guilty, pay a $1.5 million fine, and agree not to contest the forfeiture of the company if he could get probation and no jail time.

No deal, said the prosecutors. The only offer that was on the table, they said, was the original—four years and $2 million. So a game of nerves began. Ricci stuck to his counteroffer, and the prosecutors continued to believe there was no way he would risk a trial and possibly ten to twenty years in jail. But while playing this game of bluff and counter-bluff, the prosecutors still made no real attempt to get ready for trial. Suddenly as the trial date approached, it dawned on them that Ricci was in fact going to trial, and they were not in any way prepared. It was starting to look as if they had screwed up so badly that Carmen might actually win.

They panicked. They quickly informed the defense that they were willing to accept Carmen's offer of $1.5 million and no jail time. But the defense knew what it was doing and said it was prepared to go to trial. So the prosecutors caved in completely. They agreed to a plea bargain where Carmen got three years probation, no jail time, and agreed to pay only a half million dollars. Cifelli and Petaccio got 18 months probation and no fines. Effectively, everyone walked.

Actually the Grayhound deal was even worse for the state. Ricci agreed to pay his half-million-dollar fine in two $250,000 payments six months apart. He made the initial payment, but I am told by the state police he has never made the second payment. Then in a further bargain, the State agreed to drop its forfeiture suit if Ricci agreed to withdraw from the company and forfeit his interest in it. The state police do not believe he has kept this bargain. He claims adamantly that he is no longer connected with the company. But the state police believe and are trying to prove otherwise. They also believe the company may still be making and distributing gambling devices. Simply put, after all I did, little appears to have changed with Grayhound.

In the end—at least as this is written—not a single case has actually gone to trial. Everyone has plea-bargained; a number of guys agreed to some pretty long time. Scoops held out to the bitter end, hoping to get some kind of good deal. But he finally caved in and agreed to fourteen years, and a half-million-dollar fine, as long as he could serve his state time concurrently with a federal bid he also got. It looks as though he will serve four years in federal custody and then will be released to New Jersey to serve an additional three, a total of seven years.

John Riggi also had the book thrown at him. He agreed to twelve years state time, which to him didn't make a lot of difference since he was assured of virtually a life sentence from the Feds. My work was instrumental in the latter situation; recordings we made of Riggi were played at his federal sentencing. I hear also that because of the long jail term Riggi is now retired. John Gotti, before he was convicted, had his friend Jack D'Amico made boss of the DeCavalcantes.

Among the others: Because of the serious drug charges against him, Anthony Dente agreed to thirteen years, the same bid that Frederick Stewart agreed to. Joey Sodano agreed to accept ten years and a $100,000 fine. Both Nicky Jr. and Turk Cifelli got seven years. Nicky Oliveri, Beeps Centorino, and John Praino got four years. I still feel bad for John.

Joe Zarra and Bobby Cabert Bisaccia each agreed to five years and Jimmy Randazzo to four years. "Jimmy Ran" served his time and then got himself whacked last year. Cabert's sentence is really meaningless, because he had previously been sentenced to forty years by the Feds. But our tapes helped persuade the judge to throw the book at Cabert, who because of health problems will likely never see the outside again.

Michael Perna got five years, while his brother Ralph walked away almost unscathed with only six months. This same short sentence, six months, is what the prosecutors agreed to for Blackie Luciano, Joseph Rackets Casiere, Ron Catrambone, Dom Prosperi, Robert Spagnola, and Philip DeNoia. Stevie Franks, who actually ran the bookmaking operation on a day-to-day basis, drew even less, three months. Then he died of a heart attack. What annoys me is that all of them could have drawn six years. When I went to jail in the mid-1980s for what were lesser gambling offenses, I had ended up with a two-year term.

Most everybody else got probation including Babe DeVino, Tommy Ferriero, Joey Laurence, Guglielmo ("Guliermo") Piccariello, Rocco Petrozza, and Gene Wilson. The same was true for the guys at Giordano Waste Haulers. Patrick Giordano and his partner Daniel Fasano both got probation after agreeing to testify against John Mavilla, while the corporation itself was fined $10,000. John Mavilla decided to hang tough, and for more than two years refused to accept a deal. Finally facing a trial date, in June 1994 he pleaded guilty to official misconduct of a public official.

The state decided to drop the charges against Nicky Sr., since he was now assured of spending the rest of his days in Marion. I was disappointed that they also decided to drop the charges against the two Gambino guys, Richie Martino and Zeff Mustaffa, because the

only crimes they could be charged with in New Jersey were misde-
meanors that were deemed not worth prosecuting.

The only other case still hanging around is against Cousin Anthony. Given his age and his health, almost any jail time at all is a
death sentence for him. He decided he had nothing to lose and refused all deals. Now he is also under federal indictment. As this is
written, he has been given an October trial date. I don't know if it
will ever happen.

Now it looks as though the Scarfo family has been dealt another
death blow. In March 1994, FBI agents fanned out across Philadelphia and southern Jersey and arrested twenty-four guys in the biggest mob sweep in years. Stanfa had simply gotten too big for his
britches.

In an attempt to end the bloodshed in the family, Stanfa had
made Frank Martines, who had been against Nicky and with Harry
Riccobene in the days of the Riccobene war, the acting underboss.
Then he went to two old guys, Shotsie Sparacio and Vincent "Al
Pajamas" Pagano, and made them capos. Then he took one of the
younger guys, John Veasey, and made him a captain also. Cousin
Anthony he made his consigliere. But most of these guys were fig-
ureheads. Stanfa relied on his new greaseball imports.

Stanfa also relied on his lawyer, Sal Avena, one of the top criminal
lawyers in the area. According to the FBI, just as Cousin Anthony
had used Donald Manno's office to hold meetings in because he
thought no law enforcement agency could bug a lawyer's office,
Stanfa allegedly used Avena's office. There was one major difference.
Manno's office was clean, but apparently the FBI had Avena's office
bugged for almost two years after getting permission from a three-
judge federal panel.

There was also another big difference. Manno had very carefully
avoided ever being present when Cousin Anthony was discussing
business, but Avena is accused of crossing the line from lawyer to
participant, as is Nicky's lawyer Bobby Simone, according to the
grand jury, which returned a multi-count indictment against Avena.

Simone was eventually indicted for his role in the attempted
shakedown of developer Willard Rouse, and he was convicted in 1992
of racketeering and conspiracy and sentenced to four years.

Stanfa has been indicted for ordering the hits on both Michael
Ciancaglini and Frank Baladino, and also for ordering the failed hit

on Skinny Joey Merlino and at least two other guys around him. Virtually everyone else who is anyone in the revamped Stanfa organization has also now been indicted. It looks like three strikes and you're out for the Bruno-Scarfo family.

One day you and your family are living in Jersey, in an apartment, the next day you're someplace where Jersey is as unknown as darkest Africa, and you're trying to explain to the kids why they suddenly have a new name and why they have to forget the old one ever existed.

Ann loves it. We left a cramped apartment and now have all kinds of room. The kids have their own rooms, we have a family room, we have a yard with grass that needs cutting. She is happiest that I'm not in the mob anymore. To her, it's as if we have been given back our lives, and I guess I agree.

But our new place has its drawbacks. I'm Italian. Bread is important in my life, the kind of bread you pick up each morning at the bakery around the corner. Where I live now, bread—at least they call it bread—is something that comes in plastic bags at the supermarket. I don't even want to describe what passes for Italian restaurants and Italian food.

But that's the least of our worries. I really believe that quite a few of the guys would like to see me dead. I imagine that some of the bosses, besides Nicky Sr., would like to make an example of me. So we are constantly looking over our shoulders, wondering if someone we don't recognize might be looking at us kind of funny. We have a neighbor who keeps insisting that I must be a mob guy on the lam, because he knows we are from Jersey, and he thinks that everyone in Jersey is in the mob. It's kind of funny most of the time, but occasionally it isn't.

Most of all I keep worrying that I am going to make some kind of mistake. Use my old name, tell someone something I shouldn't. I worry that the kids will say something. I worry about that a lot. But all in all, I like this new life much better than my old one.

If I had it to do all over again, would I have done things much differently? I ask myself that question an awful lot. The answer on one level is yes, I would do everything differently. But on another level the answer is probably no. Or perhaps to be perfectly honest with myself, if I had not been arrested in 1983 but had been straightened out then, made a captain by the mid-1980s, and then underboss by the end of the decade, I might have been able to run my portion of the family in a way that would have worked for me, and I could have gone on to be that rich wiseguy of my early dreams. But I now recognize that was a dream and never reality. I also know that I could be in jail—or dead.

At times I wish I had been born somewhere in Middle America and had never seen organized crime except in the movies or on television. But given where I was born and the atmosphere I was brought up in, going into the family seemed inevitable. I gave it my best shot. I tried to be a stand-up, honorable guy, but I was in the wrong business. Despite what these guys themselves might think, organized crime is not a thing of honor. And I certainly do not regret what I did with Ed Quirk, Billy Newsome, and the State of New Jersey. Scoops and Slicker and Turk and the rest had made a mockery of everything I had believed in, and they deserved to be brought down.

The other night Ann and I went to a party. It had a country and western theme and we danced the electric slide. Me, George Fresolone, wiseguy from Down Neck, line dancing and enjoying it. When her house landed with a thud in Oz, Dorothy was pretty sure she wasn't in Kansas anymore. Dancing the electric slide, I was absolutely certain I wasn't in New Jersey.

ACKNOWLEDGMENTS

I owe a deep debt of gratitude to a number of people who made this book possible:

First and foremost to my wife, who put up with me through all the bad years and now has put up with my writing this book. I know she believes that once it is out of my system, my old life will finally be behind us. I hope she is right.

To Ed Quirk and Billy Newsome, two police officers with great integrity, who changed my life around forever.

To Charley Crescenz, another police oficer who proved to be a quality human being, for among other things suggesting that I should write a book.

To Mike Hoey of the State Commission on Investigations for his encouragement and help in gathering material for the book.

From talking with others who have written books, I have come to realize how rare it is to find an editor who really cares deeply about a book. I was lucky to find such an editor in Fred Hills, and I owe him, his colleague Burton Beals, and their associate Laureen Connelly my deepest thanks for their initial faith in the project and for their untiring efforts to make the manuscript the best it could be.

To the best literary agent in the world, Mike Hamilburg. Without his faith in my story from the start, none of this would have been possible.

Then, to all the men and women of the Organized Crime Bureau and the Intelligence Division of the New Jersey State Police, I thank you for keeping me alive during the time we were running Operation Broadsword, and since. I am grateful to all of you for your support.

Lastly, to my co-author. You know how much I value your skill and your dedication to this project. And to your wife and family, my deep thanks for sharing you with me for these many months.